Youth
at Work

*The Unionized Fast-food
and Grocery Workplace*

STUART TANNOCK

TEMPLE UNIVERSITY PRESS
Philadelphia

Temple University Press, Philadelphia 19122
Copyright © 2001 by Temple University
Published 2001
Printed in the United States of America

⊗ The paper used in this publication meets the requirements of the
American National Standard for Information Sciences—Permanence
of Paper for Printed Library Materials, ANSI Z39.48-1984

Library of Congress Cataloging-in-Publication Data

Tannock, Stuart, 1969–
   Youth at work : the unionized fast-food and grocery workplace /
   Stuart Tannock.
       p.   cm.
   Includes bibliographical references and index.
   ISBN 1-56639-853-3 (cloth : alk. paper) — ISBN 1-56639-854-1
   (pbk. : alk. paper)
       1. Youth—Employment—North America. 2. Labor union
   members—North America. 3. Fast food restaurants—North
   America. 4. Grocery trade—North America. I. Title.

   HD6276.N68.T363 2001
   331.3'8164795'0973–dc21   00-060755

Contents

Preface

MY INTEREST in youth work and youth workers developed in a roundabout way. In the early 1990s, I went to graduate school at Stanford University interested in the study of language in social interaction. Research that I did in my first couple of years at Stanford with the anthropologist Shirley Brice Heath drew my attention to the topic of literacy and to the education and skills debates that have raged in the United States (in their latest incarnation, at least) since the early 1980s. A later opportunity to participate—in the role of discourse analyst—in Shirley's multiyear study of youth organizations in the United States further drew my attention to the practices, competencies, and identities of teenagers who, though they often enjoyed limited success at school, became productive and engaged workers in the context of projects and programs that were run by neighborhood-based youth groups. I began to wonder what happened to these youths when they moved from the education-focused environments of schools and youth groups into the profit-focused environment of the youth workplace. I wanted to know, too, how the dominant focus in the United States on promoting education and skills as the keys to individual success obscured what was really going on as these and other youths first entered the world of wage labor.

It was only once I had actually begun this study and started talking with young fast-food and grocery workers that memories of my own service-sector work experiences really began coming back to me. My family background was different from that of the vast majority of the young workers I was interviewing: I come from an upper-middle-class family in Canada, the son of a doctor and a hospital-based research scientist. Nevertheless, like many youths in North America—whether they come from poor, working-class, or middle- or upper-middle-class backgrounds—I worked through much of my youth (more than eight years in total) in a series of summer, part-time and full-time jobs in local restaurants, delis, and coffee houses. Indeed, at the age of thirty and after seven years of graduate school at Stanford University, I have still worked longer in the restaurant industry than in any other industry sector.

As I talked with young fast-food and grocery workers in the two cities that I call "Glenwood" and "Box Hill" in this study, I found that many of the work stories I was hearing were similar to my own. Restaurants can be miserable places to work. Managers micro-manage, ride high on tinpot power trips, and act as if they have no clue about what life is really like on the restaurant floor. How many times has the hackneyed phrase "If there's time to lean, there's time to clean" really been uttered by North America's ever-creative food-service management? Restaurant customers, for their part, constitute an ever-present source of possible aggression, hostility, and condescension in the workplace. And restaurant time seems to career endlessly from panicked rush to deadened emptiness, so that if you're not having to handle the stress of a fast-paced workday, you're having to figure out how on earth you're going to get through the monotony of a seemingly never-ending six-hour shift.

As for work stability in the food-service environment, you can generally forget about it. Workers constantly come and go, and in an at-will work environment, managers can fire staff whenever and wherever they desire. I remember working around the clock for days on end because a restaurant manager had fired a couple of workers in a fit of anger without having any replacements in line, leaving the rest of our crew horribly understaffed in the middle of a busy holiday season. On the other hand, when business is slow in the restaurant industry, shifts are frequently shortened or cut altogether at the last minute. Although I always loved having unexpected extra free time away from my work, the smaller paychecks that resulted could make it hard when I was trying to pay my own rent. It was, after all, my personal income that my employers were saving on when they tried to cut down on their "non-fixed costs."

No matter how bad it got, though, restaurant work was also a lot of fun a lot of the time. I met a wider, more diverse group of people through my restaurant work than I ever did in school—and in high school, I remember thinking how cool it was that I had work friends who were older than me and who knew about going clubbing or playing in a band or even just living out on their own. Many of my closest friends have been those I made through low-end restaurant work. Even in my worst jobs, I often looked forward to going to work to catch up on the latest gossip; to see what kinds of jokes, stories, and pranks we would all get into in the course of the night; or to throw in a tape and jam through a fast-paced shift: Being able to make money while listening to your favorite music never seemed too bad a deal. For all the asshole managers and pinhead customers I had in my restaurant career, I also had some awesome managers and many favorite customers—some of whom I considered, like my co-workers, to be my friends.

Like the young fast-food and grocery workers I talked to for this research study in Glenwood and Box Hill, I felt, when working during my youth, strongly invested in but, at the same time, disinvested and disconnected from my various service-sector jobs. No matter what job I've had in my life—from my youth service-sector jobs to my grad-school teaching jobs—I've thrown myself in and given my best effort. When I took a year off from college and worked as a busboy for a huge corporate chain restaurant and watering hole called The Chicago Pizza Pie Factory, I worked to be the best damn busboy that restaurant had at the time. There was a payoff to my efforts: My tipouts from the waitresses were often higher than the other busboys'. But my best friend at the restaurant—a struggling playwright named Larry Barrows—thought I was nuts. For Larry, busboy work was "just a job," and he wasn't about to do any more work at that restaurant than he absolutely had to. I can recall nights with Larry trailing me around the restaurant floor, talking nonstop about the play he was working on, utterly oblivious to the dirty plates and silverware that were piling up everywhere, while I happily did the work of two busboys for the both of us.

Despite my ingrained work ethic, however, I, like Larry, also viewed restaurant jobs as what we used to call "Joe Jobs"—not real jobs, not jobs that meant anything. Putting up with these kinds of jobs always made me feel licensed to take a little back from the local and corporate owners, who, I knew, were making a bundle off my own hard work and really didn't care whether it was me or somebody else working in their restaurants and cafés to make them their tidy profits. Sometimes "taking a little back" meant simply drawing the line on what I was and was not willing to do at work. The Chicago Pizza Pie Factory had a tradition that I hated of having the entire staff sing "Happy Birthday" to customers on their birthdays. As soon as I heard that birthday bell start to ring, I would make a beeline off the floor and hide out in the loading bay at the back of the restaurant until the singing was over. The Factory also made all of its staff wear name tags. But as busboys, who weren't directly responsible for customers, we hated having customers—who were often drunk or well on their way—bothering us and calling out our names. We quickly figured out that if we switched name tags with one another at the start of our shifts, customers could call out our names until they were blue in the face, and we'd have little idea they were actually talking to us.

"Taking a little back" from my Joe Job employers has also always had a literal meaning. For no matter where I've worked, the staff has considered low-level pilferage to be one of the few excellent perks of working in the restaurant trade. We'd help ourselves to food and drinks and give out freebies and discounts to friends and favorite customers. At the end of the day, we'd load up on leftovers to take home—some of which was completely legitimate activity, but some of which had to be helped along by changing the dates on food items so they looked as if they had expired when they really hadn't. I was actually fired from an early-morning job I once had at a fresh-fruit-juice and ice-cream stand called The Express after I was caught giving a friend a free milkshake. At the time, I was living in a one-bedroom apartment with four other guys, and I'd kept the whole lot of us well supplied with shakes, fruit, milk, and juice for the better part of two months. My employers, as it turned out, were not all that shocked by my thieving: They were paying most of us under the table, in envelopes stuffed with cash, to save on government charges and taxes. The day after I was fired, I got a call from The Express to come back and start working again, because they needed somebody to cover the 5 A.M. shift. So goes life in the low-end—which is also, quite frequently, the low-trust—service sector.

This study is an attempt to tell not my own story but, rather, that of two groups of young grocery and fast-food workers in the United States and Canada. Although our experiences frequently overlapped, there were also many differences. Most of the young workers I interviewed were from working- or middle-class backgrounds, and although many were either already in college or expecting to attend college in the future, few had any intention—in the way that I had had for a long time—to continue on to graduate school. I rarely worked for large, corporate employers such as those that dominate the fast-food and grocery industries. Thus, unlike the young workers in Box Hill and Glenwood, I never had to deal with "personality tests" when I was hired for my different restaurant jobs, with "mystery shoppers" coming in to spy on my work performance, or with "incentive programs" or "team competitions" that encouraged me to compete with fellow workers to see who could clean or sell or smile the most.

Most different of all is the fact that the young service-sector workers whom I studied were represented in their workplaces by trade unions. When I was working in the low-end service sector, it never occurred to me that I could belong to a trade union. As far as I knew, unions were primarily for adult workers in manufacturing and the trades. My grandfather, who had worked in the aircraft industry in England, had belonged to a union; he had been a shop steward and, later, a union staff representative. My parents were professionals and belonged to professional employees' associations. But as a youth worker in Canada during the 1980s, the only time I'd ever come across a union was when I had turned down—out of a vague and inherited notion that scabbing was a bad thing to do—a promised and rare opportunity for quick money from a group of school friends who were driving downtown to try to scab for Canada Post during a postal workers' strike. As was all too often the case in North America at that time, youths and unions seemed to be worlds apart. In this study, I explore what can happen when youths and unions are together in the same workplaces; when youth service-sector workers belong to unions; and when unions try— or, at least, are supposed to try—to represent the interests of youth service-sector workers.

Although this study is not an attempt to tell my own past work story, as I conducted my research in Box Hill and Glenwood—and later, as I analyzed the various data I had collected during my fieldwork—I realized that my own work past, and in particular my own failure to think much about my work past as constituting a central part of my personal history, was actually highly relevant to the story of youth work in North America that I begin to tell here. For youth work in North America is characterized precisely by its being largely invisible: It is so natural, so normal, and so inevitable that people often think little about it. No matter what background they come from, and no matter what future they arrive into, youths on this continent work, and they all tend to work largely in the same set of low-end service- and retail-sector "youth" jobs. Youth jobs don't mark out any particular past or future for the young workers who hold them; they are simply what you do when you're young. When I tell adults in the United States and Canada about my research, their response is often a version of: "So what? I did that, too, when I was young. What's the big deal? They're just kids!"

In North America, we become concerned when youths from disadvantaged class and race backgrounds get stuck in youth jobs—when they are still working in youth jobs in their mid- to late twenties, with no sign of being able to move on to anything better. The story of "getting stuck" is, indeed, a critically important story to be told, and it has been told many times elsewhere. But the story of "getting stuck," in the end, is not really a story about youth workers. If one thinks about it carefully, it is really a story about adult workers. The story of youth workers that I begin to tell here is not about "getting stuck." It is, rather, about youth work as constituting a phase in one's life—a phase that is often (although not always) disconnected from what comes before and what comes after in one's life, a phase that I call in this book the stage of "stopgap work." The "big deal" about stopgap youth work in North America is that, despite its invisibility—despite the fact that it is accepted by so many young workers (such as myself) as a normal and humdrum part of what being young is all about—there is nothing natural, inevitable, or, alternatively, accidental about it. As I will argue, the reasons youths work in the low-end service and retail sectors in North America have a lot to do with government, employer, and trade-union policies and actions that, when they don't simply abandon youth workers in the labor market, actively discriminate against them.

Acknowledgments

THIS STUDY was possible only because of the willingness of a number of young grocery and fast-food workers in the cities I call Glenwood and Box Hill to reflect on and talk to me about their work and union experiences. The workers who are the subject of this study must, out of concern for their individual privacy, remain nameless, but I thank them all for the generosity of time and spirit they showed in sharing a small piece of their lives. My hope is that I have done these young workers justice by adequately representing at least some of their diverse workplace experiences, concerns, and demands.

I also thank the leaders, staff, and stewards—who must also remain nameless—of the two union locals where I conducted my study for welcoming me into their union halls and for going out of their way to help me with my research. Union leaders and staff always made time to explain what they were doing and trying to do in their work with members, and they were instrumental in putting me in contact with young workers in the restaurants and grocery stores that they represented. Although I am occasionally critical of the work of these unions in this book, my critique is intended as an honest and serious attempt to give something back to these unions' staffs and memberships for the time and energy that they invested in me.

This book was written originally as a doctoral dissertation at Stanford University. Penelope Eckert and Glynda Hull worked as co-advisers on my dissertation committee, reading each chapter draft as I wrote it. Their criticisms at early stages of my writing led me to rethink and rework my initial analyses substantially. I thank them for the invaluable and, at times, decisive input they have had in this project. Carol Stack, who was also on my dissertation committee, has been wonderfully supportive of my work since the day we first met and has been very helpful in shepherding my manuscript from dissertation to book form. Michael Ames, my editor at Temple University Press, was willing to take on an unrevised dissertation and work with me through the subsequent revising and editing process. I am grateful to him for his enthusiasm and his swift and thoughtful responses in all of our interactions.

Many others have helped shape the production of this book. Rogers Hall and David Stern and the graduate students of UC Berkeley's Center for Research on Education and Work (CREW) provided a stimulating environment for the discussion of work and education issues when I was working on my dissertation write-up. Harley Shaiken and the "Transforming Work" class, also at UC Berkeley, helped me develop my thinking about work in the service sector as I revised my dissertation into book form. For helping me at various stages of my academic training, fieldwork, analysis, and writing, I thank Ingrid Baur, Sue Carter, Brad Davidson, Nato Green, Shirley Brice Heath, Kelley Hishon, Miyako Inoue, Robin Leidner, Tony Mirabelli, Tony Sarmiento, Jennifer Snyder, and Elizabeth Traugott. I thank Stanford University for providing the funding for my dissertation writing and research.

In more ways than one, this book has been a family project. My brother Steve let me sleep on his living-room couch on and off for most of a year while I did my fieldwork in Canada, for little more than a few washed dishes here and there. At my U.S. field site, my sister, Lisa, and her husband, Andrew, provided Sunday dinners and a welcome break from my research schedule of interviews and observations. My parents, Ian and Rosemary, have been a constant source of love, encouragement, and emotional and financial support. And throughout this project, my partner, Keli, has been a reader, an editor, and a sounding board. But more important, she has been a great friend and companion.

In the fall of 1999, my great-aunt—who was known to my family as "Aunty Margaret," and often simply as "Aunty"—died at the age of eighty-seven. Aunty Margaret left to each of the members of my family a small amount of money, which I was able to use to support myself while I worked full-time on revising this study for publication. Aunty herself worked in the service sector when she was in her teens and early twenties—as an operator in the telephone exchange back when the job involved connecting callers by pulling and putting in plugs in a mechanical switchboard. Years later, Aunty would complain about the "silliness" of the rules at the exchange—about how the young operators were forbidden to leave their desks without permission, even to go to the bathroom. But she also could recall the small pleasures and subversions: listening in on callers' calls and using the monitor line to chat with other operators down the row. I would like to think that, were she still alive, my great-aunt would have recognized a long-ago part of herself in the stories of the young workers that I tell here.

Youth at Work

The Unionized Fast-food and Grocery Workplace

Introduction

IN HIS 1999 State of the Union address, President Bill Clinton proposed raising the federal minimum wage in the United States. Clinton's proposal resurrected an old and familiar set of debates, claims, and counterclaims, as progressives once again lined up in favor of a minimum-wage hike and conservatives positioned themselves generally against. In these debates, a key question has long been: Who are the nation's minimum-wage earners, teenagers or adults? A large portion of minimum-wage earners are "non-poor teenagers," argue conservative think tanks such as The Heritage Foundation (Wilson 1998). Not so, say progressive analysts, who insist that adults—not teenagers—constitute the bulk of minimum-wage earners in the United States. "An increase in the minimum wage," trumpets a mid-1990s report by the liberal Economic Policy Institute, "primarily benefit[s] not affluent teenagers but full-time, *adult* women workers in low-income and middle-class families" (Mishel, Bernstein, and Rasell 1995; emphasis added).

Not so hidden in these debates over who really benefits from increases in the minimum wage lies a deep-seated, widely shared, and almost completely unquestioned age-based prejudice against youth (teenage) workers in America. For despite their many differences, both the progressive and conservative adversaries in the minimum-wage debates imply or directly assert that the greater the number of teenagers in the pool of minimum-wage earners, the less argument there is for raising the minimum wage. Progressives and conservatives challenge one another not so much in their depictions of teenage workers or the rights or interests of these workers to demand a raise in the minimum wage as in their claims of whether teen workers make up the bulk of the minimum-wage workforce. Conservatives, arguing that the largest group of minimum-wage earners are teens, insist that the minimum wage should, therefore, not be raised; progressives, on the other side, in claiming that most minimum-wage earners are adults, argue that the minimum wage should be raised.

1

When it comes to the issues of wages, health-care benefits, and over-all working conditions, youth workers are generally considered to be largely undeserving: they simply are not seen as meriting the same attention as adult workers. In a nation that frequently professes concern over the school-to-work transitions and the future social and economic well-being of its younger generations, there is a striking level of indifference to the plight of young workers and an amazingly open and unconcealed age-based prejudice against the young (Males 1996, 1999). Statements that would cause a national outcry if they were made about other disempowered groups in the workforce (e.g., women or minorities) raise not even a stir when they are made about youth workers. In the U.S. workplace, as Neil Howe and Bill Strauss (1993: 111) write, "bias against youth is so blatant that no one bothers mentioning it." It is telling, after all, that we live in a country in which it is illegal to discriminate against somebody in the workplace because he or she is old (older than forty), but it is perfectly legal to discriminate against somebody because he or she is young.[1]

Many concerns can be raised about the way teenagers are spoken of in the minimum-wage debates; here, I focus on one. In these debates, one of the principal arguments for why the presence of large numbers of teenagers among minimum-wage earners should be a sufficient reason for not raising the base level of pay in the United States focuses on the issue of teenage "need." Teenagers are typically presented in the debates as being largely "affluent"—as a group that can be contrasted with the adult (and deserving) poor. Teenage minimum-wage earners, so the argument goes, are most often the children of middle-class parents and work purely for discretionary income to spend on luxury purchases. In other words, teenagers don't really "need" the money they already earn, let alone the increased amount of money that a hike in the minimum wage would bring.

The ideological work that goes into constructing teens as wealthy and adults as poor in the minimum-wage debates is remarkable. First, as Katherine Newman (1999) points out in her study of young, minimum-wage fast-food workers in Harlem, the stereotype of the affluent, middle-class teenage worker obscures the fact that, in the United States, there is a sizable group of teenage workers from working-class and poor family backgrounds whose minimum wage earnings constitute critical financial supplements to the well-being of their parental families and households. Some of these teenage workers, moreover, are even having to support families of their own on what are often only minimum-wage paychecks—as should be widely recognized from the national hue and cry in a separate set of debates over "teenage mothers."

Second, calling teenage workers from middle-class backgrounds "affluent" obscures the fact that wealth in middle-class families belongs to adults, not to youths. "Youngsters," as Esther Reiter (1991: 17) notes, "generally have minimal say in how family income is divided, so even teenagers from well-off families [may] need to earn money." The level of access to financial (as well as emotional and personal) support that a youth has within a family is simply not visible to economists' measurements of overall household wealth. Abusive family situations may push some middle-class youths out of their homes, even as biased minimum-wage policies undermine their ability to achieve financial independence. Even in close-knit middle-class families, of course, teenage workers' ability to use their paychecks to cover at least personal expenses can be of invaluable assistance in easing pressures on what these days are frequently overburdened middle-class-family budgets.

Perhaps the most remarkable aspect of the affluent and undeserving teen stereotype, though, is that claims of teenage workers' affluence are being made at a time when the gap between average teenage and adult earnings is wider than it has been in more than thirty years (Howe and Strauss 1993; Males 1999). As Anton Allahar and James Côté (1994) have argued, North America is in the midst of a decades-long redistribution of wealth that has seen teenage—and more generally, youth—workers grow poorer and adult workers grow wealthier relative to each other. Teenagers today, as a whole, earn less in both absolute and relative terms than teenagers did thirty years ago. Thus, adults who now make casual assertions about teenagers' affluence were themselves considerably better off than today's teen workers when they worked during their own youth. The propagation of the affluent-teen-worker stereotype plays a central role in obscuring the critical fact of a declining overall level of youth earnings in the United States and an increasing dependence of youth workers on the financial support of adults.

Nowhere is the incongruity and hypocrisy of claims that teenagers do not "need" increased wealth more striking than in the changing relationship in the United States between the federal minimum wage and the average cost of college tuition. In the past decade, college tuitions have skyrocketed, and student borrowing has risen even faster (Flint 1998; Staples 1998; Zernicke 1998). More and more students are graduating from college buried under mountains of debt. Yet at the same time, the real value of the minimum wage in the United States has declined considerably since the late 1960s. In the mid-1960s, a college student would have had to work full time at the prevailing minimum wage for about six and a half weeks to pay for a full year's university tuition; by the mid-1990s, that period had almost tripled, to a little less than nineteen weeks (Males 1999: 315). Although the nation's leaders argue that it is more imperative than ever for youths to receive a college education, the country's minimum-wage policies are making it more difficult than ever for working youths to help pay for such an education. And as teenagers' ability to pay for college has declined, a multibillion-dollar-a-year, private-sector student-loan industry has exploded. This (adult-owned and -operated) industry takes full advantage of increased youth poverty to rake in handsome interest-based profits (Babcock 1997).

STOPGAP YOUTH WORKERS

This study focuses on the contemporary work conditions and experiences of youth workers (workers in their teens to mid-twenties) in North America—in Canada and the United States.[2] I begin with a discussion of the place teenagers hold in recent minimum-wage debates in the United States (debates that are not unlike those that take place in Canada), because having a sense of the extent and embeddedness of the prejudice against youth workers is critical to understanding, first, the current conditions of youth work in North America, and second, the reason North American youth workers' interests and experiences are so consistently overlooked and ignored. The minimum-wage debates illustrate how common and unmarked, how natural and easy, it is to dismiss youth (and especially teenage) workers as not being "real" workers and to pass over their interests as being unworthy of concern and of government and other forms of workplace intervention.

Youths in the United States and Canada today typically work in the lowest-paying, lowest-status jobs on the continent—in "dead-end jobs" or "McJobs" in the retail and food and entertainment service sectors. As a group, young workers have lower wages, fewer benefits, and less job security than any other age group in the workforce. Employers of young workers, by contrast, frequently rank among the continent's largest and most powerful. Enormous national and multinational corporations—such as McDonald's, Pepsico/Tricon (owner of Taco Bell, KFC, and Pizza Hut), and Walmart—have grown profitable and wealthy in small or large part on the backs of low-wage youth labor. Indeed, for industries such as fast food, the "indispensable ingredient" for growth and success has been less the widely touted routinization of their labor process or the enthusiastic embracing of franchising expansion schemes than the "systematic exploitation" of large pools of cheap (minimum-wage) teenage and youth workers (Gabriel 1988: 127).

Not only do today's youth jobs provide little in the way of support for college tuitions; they also tend to be disconnected from the kinds of jobs that most youths will eventually move into in adulthood. For most young workers in the United States and Canada, low-end service and retail jobs constitute what Valerie Oppenheimer and Matthijs Kalmijn (1995) call "life cycle stopgap jobs" (see also Jacobs 1993; Myles, Picot, and Wannell 1993). These jobs generally do not lead anywhere in terms of career opportunities; nor do most young workers expect these jobs to become sites of career employment. They are temporary way stations, more or less discontinuous with individual career paths. Future doctors, real-estate brokers, truck drivers, and waitresses may all work for a spell during their youth in one of the continent's hundreds of thousands of low-wage service and retail jobs. Some young workers take on stopgap jobs during or between periods of schooling; some take these jobs between finishing schooling and entering career-type employment. But whatever their particular trajectory may be, young workers take stopgap jobs primarily because they are young. Better jobs are not readily available for the young in North America. Low-wage, low-status service and retail jobs are the jobs that youths can expect, and are expected, to find.

Working in the low-wage, low-status service and retail sector has become almost a rite of passage for the youth of North America. Between entering high school and entering career employment, most youths now work in a series of stopgap service and retail jobs. McDonald's alone claims to have employed, at one time or another, one of every fifteen adults currently working in the United States. The time a young worker spends in any single service or retail job is usually not very long—a couple of months here, a few years there. But the time a youth spends in stopgap employment overall can add up to five or ten years, or even more. There are indications, moreover, that as economic conditions worsen for young adults in both the United States and Canada, young workers' transitions to higher-status, higher-wage, career-type employment are on average taking longer than they previously did (Bernhardt et al. 1998).

Most youths in the United States and Canada do eventually move up and out of stopgap service and retail jobs into higher-wage, more stable employment. Certain groups of youths who are disadvantaged by their race or class backgrounds are at greater risk of being unable to make this transition. But regardless of whether a transition to higher-wage, more stable employment is eventually made, individuals across North America are spending considerable amounts of time during their youth and early adulthood in marginalized and often exploitive conditions of employment. Even those who do make a successful transition out of stopgap youth work may spend as much as a fifth of their working lives in jobs that contribute minimally to their own futures; that involve mundane, repetitive, and often meaningless tasks; and that confer only meager salaries and low-level status—jobs whose most clearcut significance is the enormous amount of wealth they generate for those employers who have eagerly positioned themselves in the continent's low-wage youth-labor market.[3]

Despite their economic marginalization and their importance to North America's service economy, young workers are commonly overlooked or ignored by policymakers, researchers, workplace activists, and trade unions. Their erasure from North American public discourse as a coherent and distinct group within the labor force that has legitimate and pressing concerns about poor working conditions takes place in one of two ways. First, many commentators still fail to recognize the existence of stopgap youth work as a structural and substantive part of North American society and economy. To this day, one can find mainstream discussions of youth, work, and education that talk of normative "school-to-work transitions," as if youths in the United States and Canada moved directly from schooling to adult, career employment, and as if the intervening period of stopgap work did not even exist. When workplace observers find that large numbers of youths "flounder" in the low-end service sector between school and career, they often react with surprise and attempt to explain the "anomaly" by pointing fingers at the failings of the North American school system or at deficits in the skills or work attitudes of contemporary North American youths. Yet why should anyone be surprised at the existence of stopgap youth labor when North America's society and economy are structurally and centrally organized around having access to and using large pools of low-paid and transient youth labor? Entire industries are based fundamentally on access to cheap youth workers, and as consumers, we all benefit from the low-price goods that low-wage (minimum-wage) youth labor helps make possible.

The difficulty that many North Americans have in recognizing the structural existence of stopgap youth work derives in part from the simple fact that we don't really know how to talk about youth as workers, nor do we know yet how to talk about work as a temporary, short-term and disjunctive lifecycle experience. Youths are thought of in our society not primarily as workers but as consumers—in particular, as consumers of music, fashion, television, and other media forms (Griffin 1993). Pick up any teenage or youth studies reader and chances are that it will say little, if anything, about the fact that youths work and a whole lot about various subcultural youth "styles" that are consumed and produced outside the workplace. Even though the overwhelming majority of North American youths work at some point during their teenage years—often for considerable amounts of time—youths on this continent are generally thought of within the contexts of the school, the neighborhood, and the street, but not the workplace.

Meanwhile, work in North America is generally thought of and studied within a long-term perspective and within frameworks of class formation and class reproduction, social stratification and mobility, individual careers, and so forth. All of these frameworks, however, are of limited use in capturing the social position of stopgap youth labor. Stopgap youth work is fundamentally anti-careerist in nature, and it is generally more or less discontinuous with prior and future individual work and educational paths. Stopgap youth work in the low-end service sector, moreover, involves youths who come from, and will later end up in, both the middle and working classes.

Because age—unlike the other dimensions of workforce stratification that are commonly given recognition (race, gender, class)—has only the temporary membership of individuals, stopgap youth workers in the service sector can hardly be spoken of as a long-term "class" in their own right. Identification as a stopgap youth worker is ephemeral. We do, of course, know how to talk, and worry, about youths who get "stuck" in entry-level service-sector jobs well into adulthood, and about people who suffer long-term effects from difficulties they experience during their youth in the labor market. But once we start talking about such concerns, we have really stopped thinking about youth workers per se and moved on to the more familiar issues of class formation and reproduction and to the ways in which youth work experiences affect the later well-being of adult, rather than youth, workers.

The second way in which the interests and demands of stopgap youth workers are placed under erasure in public discourse recognizes the existence of stopgap youth work, but employs one or another variant of the undeserving youth worker stereotype (seen in the minimum-wage debates cited earlier) to deflect attention from the voices and concerns of young stopgap workers. Some workplace observers do acknowledge that most youths in North America work for a time in the low-wage, low-status service sector, but they argue that there is no need (or, alternatively, no way) to "fix" or change this system of stopgap work because there is allegedly a functional match between low-end service-sector jobs and the youth (teenage) workers who fill them.

Thus, on the one hand, we have the familiar image of the "happy teen worker," whom we met earlier in the minimum-wage debates. The prototype of the happy teen worker is the middle-class teenage worker who is still in high school. For this worker, low wages are not a problem because he or she is working only for extra spending money; part-time and irregular hours are not a problem, because he or she is not having to support himself or herself and needs only to be able to fit work around high-school classes; and low-status and monotonous work tasks aren't a problem, because he or she is able to learn from and appreciate the experience of simply having a job for the first time. The happy teen worker learns what it is to have real-world responsibilities, how to find ways to manage time and money effectively, and how to work cooperatively with co-workers, employers, and customers. What are bad jobs for adults, some workplace commentators claim, are perfectly good jobs for teenagers or youths.

The flip side of the happy teen worker variant of the undeserving youth worker stereotype is the equally widespread image of the "alienated youth worker." The prototype is the high-school-graduate youth worker who comes from either the working class or the middle class (as in the figure of the "slacker"). Just out of school, the alienated youth worker drifts through an endless series of empty, meaningless, dead-end jobs; drops in and out of the workforce almost at random; enjoys no real sense of connection with his or her work, workplace, customers, or employers; and finds the real focus of life after high school to lie outside the workplace in a fast-paced and occasionally high-risk social life that is shared with his or her same-age peers.

It may, at first glance, seem as if the image of the alienated youth worker lends credence to the concerns and complaints of young stopgap workers. But this is generally not how the image functions. The alienated-youth-worker image typically borrows on conventional "storm and stress" models of adolescence—models in which adolescence is considered a difficult and stressful period in the natural maturation process that sets youths apart from, and puts them in conflict with, the stable, responsible, and adult worlds of work and family (Griffin 1993). The alienated-youth-worker image often presents stopgap work as a natural epiphenomenon of adolescence—that is, if youths are alienated in the workplace, this is because alienation (from work, from life, from adults) is the natural state of adolescence. When youths are genuinely ready to settle down into a life of career work and adult responsibility, they will quite naturally move up and out of the youth labor market.

Some observers, in fact, see low-end service-sector work as providing a reasonably functional fit with storm-and-stress adolescents, because it allegedly matches their need to have little in the way of real commitment, responsibility, or investment. These jobs are designed on the assumption that the people holding them will not care much about the work they are doing and will not remain in their jobs for long periods of time. Because youth workers in the alienated-youth-worker image are seen as not really caring about work, there is little point seen in talking with them about ways to improve the youth workplace. Workplace reforms that involve the interests and voices of workers are worthwhile to consider only once youth workers have moved on into adult, career occupations in which they can and often do feel a real sense of commitment, connection, and investment. Adolescence is a difficult time inside the workplace and out, according to this argument, so the best we can do as socially concerned observers is hope that youths will eventually grow up and learn to behave as adults.

To begin to understand and engage with the experiences and interests of youth workers in the low-end service sector in the United States and Canada—to undo the erasure of the voices of youth workers—it is necessary to move beyond these and other such familiar stereotypes of work, youth, and youth workers. Thus, we need to: 1) acknowledge the structural existence of stopgap youth work; and 2) recognize that the social and economic environments of our continent's workplaces and labor markets have produced a distinctive workforce identity (or social position)—that of the stopgap youth worker. As will be described in detail in this study, somewhere between the naturalized and silencing twin stereotypes of the happy teen worker and the alienated youth worker lie the actual voices, experiences, interests, and agencies of contemporary stopgap youth workers.

As stopgap workers, young workers themselves do often accept that low-end service work is a natural and even appropriate step to take on their pathways up into the adult world of career work. Many young workers consequently embrace, engage, and identify with their stopgap youth jobs in ways that simply are not acknowledged by the alienated-youth-worker image. At the same time, young workers, as stopgap workers, also critique and distance themselves from their low-end service jobs in ways that are not acknowledged by the happy-teen-worker image. Indeed, many young service-sector workers position themselves as stopgap workers in the first place precisely because working conditions in North America's low-end service sector are so fundamentally impoverished—that is, precisely because they consider low-end service-sector jobs, in one way or another, to be bad jobs.

YOUTH AND UNIONIZATION

In this study, I am concerned not only with describing the contemporary work conditions and experiences of stopgap youth workers in North America, but also with moving beyond the passivity and fatalism that characterize the majority of discussions of youth work in the United States and Canada. The process that leads to the erasure of the stopgap youth worker as a distinctive and recognizable subject position in North American public discourse also frequently leads to the stance that interventions to improve working conditions in the contemporary youth workplace are unnecessary, unfeasible, or undesirable. To this end, I examine, from the point of view of stopgap youth workers, the significance that unionization can have in improving work conditions in the youth workplace. I explore such questions as: How do unions work with young workers in stopgap service jobs? How do unions in the low-end service sector reduce and transform—or, alternatively, reinforce—youths' workplace marginalization? What difference can unionization make in the work lives of young stopgap service-sector workers?

One of the most striking features of stopgap youth labor in the low-end service sector—particularly when considering the disempowerment of youth workers in North America—is, in fact, its extremely low level of unionization. In both the United States and Canada, young workers are less likely to belong to trade unions than any other age group in the workforce. This virtual absence of unionization among young workers means that one of the most vulnerable groups of workers on the continent—workers with little work experience, limited employment alternatives, low employment status, temporary work orientations, and no protection from anti-discrimination legislation—must typically confront some of North America's largest, most powerful corporations on an individual basis, without the benefit or support of collective action and representation. Under such conditions, quitting a job understandably becomes a young worker's signature final solution when faced with employer intransigence in response to his or her workplace demands.

The low level of unionization in the youth labor market is not incidental to the existence of this market. As government minimum-wage policies and the absence of antidiscrimination protection for young workers in the workplace have helped to foster a low-wage, low-status, stopgap pool of youth labor, so, too, has the labor movement's widespread abandonment of youth workers in North America over the past half-century. Unions historically have frequently tended to act in the interests of their adult members and to work against youths in the labor market, whom they see as a threat to adults' jobs and wages. Seniority rules and restrictions on apprenticeship openings are but two common strategies unions have used to exclude youths from stable, well-paid jobs and to relegate young workers to a secondary labor market.

Since the end of the 1970s, union abandonment of youth interests in the workplace has quickened. Between 1983 and 1991, the number of workers in the United States age thirty-five and older who were union members actually rose by 1 percent, while the number of workers younger than twenty-five who were union members fell by 23 percent (Howe and Strauss 1993: 112). Youth workers who remained trade-union members in this period were not necessarily all that better off than their non-union counterparts. "Nothing exemplifies [the] age-graded inequality" in the labor movement during the 1980s, write Howe and Strauss (ibid.), "more than the two-tier wage ladder" that many unions began to negotiate widely during this decade. Tiered wage ladders have protected the wages and benefits of older workers while establishing secondary, lower-paying wage scales for newer, younger workers who are just coming into the workforce.

Despite the North American labor movement's occasionally dismal history in dealing with youth workers, unionization remains important to consider for the possibilities that it might have to offer for improving stopgap youth work for two reasons. First, unionization is still one of the most valuable and critical means workers have for transforming and improving their working conditions without having to rely purely on employer voluntarism and goodwill. Although many workplace observers today place their hopes for improved working conditions in North America in employer-driven changes in managerial strategy (especially in the highly touted "high-performance" model), there is little reason to believe that such changes will dramatically affect the low wages, low status, and high stress levels of stopgap youth work in the low-end service sector: Those employers who have positioned themselves in the youth labor market have done so precisely to take advantage of cheap and transient youth workers. Although unionization among stopgap youth workers in North America is rare, a number of unions are operating in the North American youth labor market, and the work these unions are doing with young stopgap workers has so far been almost completely ignored by researchers and policymakers.

Second, over the past few years there has been a shift (some would say a renaissance) in the North American labor movement—particularly in the United States. Faced with an aging and shrinking membership, and increasingly concerned about threats to the social and economic well-being of younger generations on the continent, the North

American labor movement has recently shown renewed interest in organizing among the young. For the first time in decades, union recruiters are becoming a familiar presence on college campuses across Canada and the United States, and over the course of the 1990s, student involvement in labor organizing mushroomed. Like many recent shifts in the North American labor movement, however, this renewed union interest in youth, though exciting, tends to be long on high-profile rhetoric and short on real commitment to confronting genuine past and present problems in the interactions of youth and labor. There is thus a vital need to consider carefully the experiences of youth stopgap workers who already belong to trade unions—to focus not only on the highlights and triumphs of unionization in the youth labor market but also on the failures, shortcomings, and misfires.

THE STUDY

This book explores the significance of stopgap work and unionization for young service and retail workers by describing the work and union experiences of two small groups of young unionized service-sector workers in the United States and Canada. The study that forms the basis of this book consisted of eleven months of ethnographic fieldwork that I conducted in the late 1990s with two groups of young unionized workers: grocery workers in a large U.S. city that I call "Box Hill" and fast-food workers in a similar-size Canadian city that I call "Glenwood." (To protect the privacy of individuals and organizations, I have altered all proper names involved in this research.)

The young grocery workers I studied worked for the three large, multiregional supermarket chains that dominate the Box Hill grocery market. Although some significant differences exist among these chains, I consider them together for the purposes of this study, only occasionally and casually referring to them individually by name as "Good Grocers," "Food City," and "Grand Foods." The union local representing Box Hill's young grocery workers—"Local 7"—had about 12,000 members at the time of my research (about one-third of whom were younger than twenty-five). These members worked in a little more than two hundred grocery stores in the greater metropolitan Box Hill region.

The fast-food workers I studied all worked in the outlets of a single multinational fast-food company in Glenwood that I call "Fry House."

Although many Fry Houses in North America are franchised, almost all of the unionized Fry House restaurants in Glenwood are owned directly by the Fry House corporation. The union local representing Glenwood's young Fry House workers—"Local C"—was a small but diversified service-sector local with members working in the hotel, building maintenance, building security, and restaurant industries in and around the city. At the time of my research, Local C represented about 750 Fry House workers (about two-thirds of whom were younger than twenty-five). These workers worked in approximately fifty different Fry House outlets in the Glenwood region.

I chose the Box Hill and Glenwood sites partly because supermarkets and fast-food restaurants are prototypical places of stopgap youth employment. The grocery and fast-food industries are two of the largest youth employers in North America: In the United States, fully one-third of working teenagers are employed in restaurants or grocery stores, making these two industries the number-one and number-two employers of American teenagers, respectively. For youths between the ages of 16 and 24 who are in the U.S. workforce, one-fifth work either in eating or drinking establishments or in grocery stores (U.S. Bureau of Labor Statistics 1996). Canadian government statistics suggest that the proportion of youth workers in Canada working in the grocery and fast-food industries is highly comparable to that in the United States. In 1986, 15 percent of youth workers age 16 to 24 worked in either restaurants or grocery stores in Canada (Statistics Canada 1989). Because youth employment in the Canadian service sector as a whole has steadily increased over the past decade (Rehnby and McBride 1997), it is likely that this figure is now considerably higher.

I also selected the two research sites in Box Hill and Glenwood because they offered the possibility of studying two different kinds of union experience among young stopgap service-sector workers. In many ways, Box Hill can be said to represent a typical stopgap youth experience of unionism. Although overall unionization rates among young service and retail workers in North America are very low, the grocery industry—the second-largest employer of teenage labor on the continent—is actually a relatively highly unionized industry. About a third of grocery workers continentwide are represented by trade unions; in Box Hill, as in a few other regions of the continent, more than 90 percent of the local grocery market is unionized. If high-school-age workers belong to any union at all in North America, chances are they belong to a grocery union.

Grocery Local 7 in Box Hill can be said to represent a fairly typical youth union experience for two other reasons. Like many North American unions, the local practices what is sometimes referred to as "business unionism" (Moody 1988; Parker and Gruelle 1999). Local 7 staff focus primarily on bargaining for wages and benefits and on policing the union's collective-bargaining agreement on behalf of its grocery membership; they are much less concerned with working to involve, mobilize, or educate members in union affairs. Local 7—again, like many North American unions—also has not had an extensive history of targeting the needs and interests of its younger members. To the extent that young grocery workers are spoken of at all by Local 7 union staff, they tend to be depicted as presenting problems: in the collection of union dues, for example, or in the enforcement of the collective-bargaining agreement.

Fast-food Local C, on the other hand, can be said to represent a fairly atypical example of stopgap youth unionism. The fast-food industry in North America is almost completely non-union. Indeed, my decision to conduct part of my fieldwork research in Canada was motivated by the fact that there are no fast-food union locals (at least, none that have lasted over the years) anywhere in the United States. In Canada, by contrast, a handful of unionized fast-food chains and outlets are scattered across the country. Originally organized in the 1960s and now about fifty restaurants strong, the Glenwood Fry House bargaining unit constitutes one of the largest and longest-lived of these union fast-food units.

Fast-food Local C in Glenwood is further unusual in that it belongs to one of the few unions in North America that embrace what is sometimes called a "social movement" model of unionism (Moody 1988, 1997). Beyond the negotiation of wages and benefits, Local C seeks to mobilize its members, to involve them in union affairs, and to educate them not just about unionism, but also about broad social-justice issues that affect workers throughout contemporary society. During the 1990s, Local C also distinguished itself as being highly oriented to working closely with its youth members. Indeed, the local has gained a widespread reputation in Canadian labor and media circles as being one of the most successful union locals in the country in organizing and working with young stopgap service-sector workers.[4]

THE RESEARCH PROCESS

My fieldwork in Box Hill and Glenwood comprised union and work-place observations; interviews with young workers, shop stewards, and union staff; and the collection of union and company newsletters, training materials, and other such artifacts. Before my study began, I made the decision to conduct my research without official employer involvement.[5] My study was thus based not in the grocery and fast-food workplace, but in the two union locals in Box Hill and Glenwood; it was approved and facilitated not by company management, but by union local staff. Much of my time in Box Hill and Glenwood was spent simply hanging out at the Local 7 and Local C union halls. For the better part of a year, I went to every union meeting, social event, educational program, and conference that I could get to. I traveled with union representatives as they visited their stores and talked with them about how they did their jobs. I attempted to learn as best I could how these two union locals worked with their young members by observing all of the various points of contact between union and worker.

I also talked to young grocery and fast-food workers in Box Hill and Glenwood. Many of these workers I found simply by visiting the stores represented by the two locals. Some workers' names were given to me by union staff and stewards. A few workers I actually met in the union halls. Young workers themselves also frequently put me in touch with co-workers whom they thought would be willing to talk to me.

My interviews, which typically ran a little under an hour and were held in locations chosen by my interviewees (usually a local diner or coffee shop), were unstructured and open-ended. My goals in interviewing young workers were primarily to hear them speak about what mattered most to them in their workplaces and to learn what they thought about their unions. Some interviews ended up being highly focused on one or two issues that were of particular importance to the individual worker, while others were more wide-ranging. In total, I conducted a little more than ninety interviews with young workers (about sixty in Box Hill and thirty in Glenwood) and twenty-odd more with older co-workers, union staff, and shop stewards. Almost all of my interviews were audiotaped and subsequently transcribed.

Because I conducted my research without the official involvement of the employers for whom Local 7 and Local C members worked, I was unable to conduct extensive or intrusive observations in grocery and fast-food workplaces in Box Hill and Glenwood. I did, however, spend much of my time during my eleven months of fieldwork as a casual workplace observer and customer, wandering almost daily through the public spaces of Box Hill supermarkets and Glenwood Fry House outlets. One of the advantages of doing research on low-end customer service work, after all, is that much of this work takes place in an open and semipublic environment. I found that I was often able to chat casually with young grocery and fast-food workers I met while they were on the job and to observe interactions young workers had in the workplace with their co-workers, customers, and managers. When I visited in the company of local union representatives, I was also able to enter stores' private, back-room spaces and talk casually with store-level managers. The experiences and opinions of grocery and fast-food managers, however—like those of grocery and fast-food customers—are not a central part of this study. My focus is on the experiences and opinions of young stopgap grocery and fast-food workers first, and on the relations between these young workers and union staff at Local 7 and Local C second.

THE YOUNG WORKERS OF BOX HILL AND GLENWOOD

Most studies of youth workers in the United States and Canada define this group according to educational achievement and status. There are, for example, studies of high-school-student workers, high-school-graduate workers, high-school-dropout workers, and college-student workers. These groups are often thought to be highly distinct and, therefore, to demand separate study. In Box Hill and Glenwood, however (as elsewhere in the low-end service sector), workforces are composed of youths of all kinds of educational status and achievement. High-school students, dropouts, and graduates, along with community-college and university students, dropouts, and graduates (a handful, at least, of the latter), can all be found at these work sites—and quite often, they are quite literally working side by side. Further, young grocery and fast-food workers in Box Hill and Glenwood have had a wide range of experiences of schooling. Some are, or have been, straight-A students who cram their grocery and fast-food jobs into days filled with school-based extracurricular activities (sports, music, journalism, debating). But there are also those who are, or have been, deeply alienated by their experiences at school and frustrated by being forced to participate in classroom activities at which they are constantly being told they are not very good.

Studies of youth workers commonly use the word "youth" as a proxy for two other, generally unmarked identities—that is, "youth" all too often is taken to mean "male youth" and "working-class youth." (Researchers who study the work experiences of middle-class youths generally say that they are studying "student workers.") In this study, "youth" does not have any such covert gender or class identification. In both Box Hill and Glenwood, large numbers of young men and women are working. A slight majority of youths in the Box Hill supermarkets are male (about 55 percent), whereas a larger proportion of youths in the Glenwood Fry Houses are female (about 70 percent).

Young grocery and fast-food workers in Box Hill and Glenwood come from a mix of class backgrounds. Some, for example, have parents who work as professors, lawyers, and business owners; others' parents work as hospital orderlies, hotel maids, building-maintenance workers, and bus drivers. It is important to note that the mix of middle- and working-class youth workers in Box Hill and Glenwood is typical of youth employment throughout the United States and Canada. Youth work on this continent is marked by the facts that both middle- and working-class youths can be found in the waged labor market and that they tend to work in the same kinds of "youth" jobs, which are more or less discontinuous with the occupations of their parents and with the occupations that most of them will enter as adults. To an extent, workers of different class backgrounds in Box Hill and Glenwood work in different stores in different neighborhoods from one another. But in many stores, youths of different class background work together.

What can be said of class differences among young workers in Box Hill and Glenwood can also be said of differences in race and ethnicity. The workforces at both sites are racially and ethnically diverse. Union staff in Glenwood estimate that 40 percent of the Fry House workforce is visible minority, with significant numbers of workers of East Indian, Filipino, Fijian, and Chinese descent. The grocery workforce in Box Hill likewise has a considerable minority membership of African Americans, Asian Americans, Latinos, and recent immigrants from Eastern Europe and Southeast Asia. Individual stores in Box Hill and Glenwood vary considerably in their local racial and ethnic makeup, but many stores have mixed staffs in which workers of different racial and ethnic backgrounds work side by side. In terms of the educational, gender, class, and racial identities of their workforces, therefore, the Box Hill supermarket and Glenwood Fry House are—as Newman (1999) has said of fast-food restaurants in Harlem—often "living laboratories of diversity."[6]

I assume that most readers will already be somewhat familiar with the basic organization of work in the contemporary supermarket and fast-food restaurant. For not only are most of us regular supermarket—and possibly fast-food—customers, but many of us worked in these kinds of workplaces when we were young. I will only note here that the Glenwood Fry Houses tend to be a little smaller than the average fast-food restaurant in North America, with about ten to thirty-five employees in each outlet. These restaurants are further notable for having a very simple division of labor—again, much simpler than that found in many other U.S. and Canadian fast-food restaurants (Reiter 1991; Leidner 1993). Glenwood Fry Houses have only three job classifications: cook, cashier, and supervisor. In addition to their customer-service role, cashiers in these restaurants share cooking tasks with cooks, as they are responsible for preparing side orders such as fries, salads, gravy, and so on. Supervisors help out with cooking and serving customers and are responsible for a number of managerial tasks (shop-floor supervision, ordering, inventory, scheduling, and so on). A number of cooks and cashiers in Glenwood are trained as "in-charges," meaning that they can act as temporary supervisors when the need arises.

Supermarkets in Box Hill fall toward one of two ideal store types— that is, the "neighborhood store" or the "superstore." Neighborhood stores are characterized by being located in predominantly residential areas and tend to be older and smaller, employing about forty to fifty workers. The superstores are huge, cavernous warehouses that are usually located along major shopping routes or within larger shopping centers; they each employ about eighty to one hundred workers. At least ten different job classifications are used in the Box Hill supermarkets: baggers, stockers, checkers, grocery (dry goods) clerks, produce clerks, deli clerks, bakery clerks, nonfoods clerks, meat cutters, and bakers. Workers in the first eight classifications are represented by Local 7; the meat cutters and bakers are represented by other union locals and are not considered in this study. These Box Hill job classifications are similar to those found in other supermarkets elsewhere in North America (Walsh 1993; Hughes 1999).

Overview of the Book

This book is divided into three sections. In Part I, "Youth and Work," I provide background on the study of youth workers and the conditions of youth service-sector work. In Part II, "Youth in the Workplace," I examine the active and collective presence of young workers within the grocery and fast-food workforces of Box Hill and Glenwood. And in Part III, "Youth in the Union," I describe the experiences young workers in Box Hill and Glenwood have of unionization. My presentation in the first and second parts is fairly straightforward; my strategy of analysis in Part III, however, merits advance explanation.

The day-to-day experiences young workers in Box Hill and Glenwood have of their unions are far more similar than one might expect, given the two locals' embrace, at higher levels of action, of what are sometimes radically different approaches to the practice of unionism. Nevertheless, there are significant differences in young workers' experiences of the two locals, which derive in part from the differences between the business and social-movement models of unionism and in part from differences between what I call (borrowing from Ryan [1987]) an "adult-centered" model of unionism practiced by Local 7 in Box Hill and an "all-ages" model of unionism practiced by Local C in Glenwood. My discussion in Part III deliberately highlights the differences between these two union locals and downplays their similarities for the purpose of describing, succinctly, first, some of the limitations of unionization in the youth labor market; and second, some of the potential that unionization has to offer for improving youths' workplace conditions.

I. YOUTH AND WORK

1 Dead Ends

How are youths positioned in the workplace as workers? What possibilities exist for improving the generally poor conditions of youth work? The two questions that are at the core of this book are strangely absent from most research and theory on youth workers. This is the central irony of the study of youth and work: Youth workers are typically studied through the lens of a "pathway model." Researchers tend to be concerned primarily not with youth work itself, but with the trajectories of youths from school (through the period of stopgap youth work) to career—or with what Christine Griffin (1993: 28) calls the "one Big Question: the incidence and explanation of the inequalities in the move from full-time education to waged employment." Researchers typically focus little on what youths are actually doing in any particular job during their transition from school to career, and more on where youths are initially coming from (in terms of schooling and community) and where they are eventually going (in terms of career and family).

Because the pathway model focuses on youths as they move among workplaces, and not as they act within workplaces, youth-work researchers have tended to ignore the subjectivity and agency of youths *as workers.* Further, details of youth work have often been left vague, because work is seen merely as a backdrop—a measuring stick for determining how far a youth has come in his or her progression toward adulthood. Relying on statistical data of comparative wage levels and job stability, researchers have tended to sketch out a hierarchy of jobs that are tagged as being simply "good" or "bad." They rarely take the time to explore the ambiguities and contradictions of the actual conditions of youth work.

Especially worrisome about the pathway model of youth and work is that it largely ignores the possibility of change in the youth workplace. Indexed as constituting background terrain, the conditions characterizing good and bad jobs are assumed to be natural and inevitable—at least, to the extent that they cannot or should not be changed by and for young workers. The agency of youth employers in particular in shaping the conditions of the youth workplace is widely overlooked. The social-policy concern for most youth-work researchers is not how to improve temporary "youth jobs" but, rather, how to help youths move up (eventually) into stable, well-paid "adult jobs"—a concern that, first, essentially writes off large swathes of the service-sector jobs in which youths now work as being unimprovable, and that, second, begs the question of whether there will ever be enough good "adult" jobs for all youths to move up into.

Discussions of youth and work often invoke the notion of dead ends—of "dead-end" kids working in "dead-end" jobs. What I suggest in this chapter is that the real dead ends in matters of youth and work may lie not in the workers or the jobs but, rather, in the analyses and imaginations of researchers and policymakers themselves. There are at least four distinct bodies of literature in the field of youth and work: youth-labor-market, school-to-work, student-worker, and social-reproduction. Each body of literature has generated critical insights into the study of youth and work—particularly into the fundamental question of why youths in North America tend to work in low-wage, low-status, short-term jobs in the service sector. But each of these bodies of literature is also ultimately limited by the blinders of the pathway model.[1]

THE YOUTH LABOR MARKET

Youth-labor-market theory first developed in the 1970s in the context of concern over high levels of youth unemployment—particularly among non-college-bound high-school graduates and dropouts. In attempting to account for higher levels of unemployment among youths than adults, youth-labor-market theorists outlined the notion of a distinct "floundering" period in the early work experience of the young. Youths in North America, on leaving high school, do not directly enter a primary (adult, stable, career) labor market; rather, they enter a secondary (youth) labor market of low-wage, low-status, short-term, and "dead-end" jobs that are typically found in the service and retail sectors. Periodic, short-term bouts of unemployment are a regular and natural part of young workers' experience in this temporary and seasonal labor market. Most youths, after a few years' time, move out of this secondary youth labor market and into primary (adult) occupations, with few signs of "scarring" from their early labor-market difficulties (Osterman 1980; Freeman and Wise 1982).

Why might such a youth labor market exist? Paul Osterman's *Getting Started* (1980), one of the foundational texts in this body of literature, argues that the youth labor market is essentially created by the combination of youth immaturity and the restrictive hiring practices of primary (adult) employers. "In the first several years after leaving school," writes Osterman (1980: 16), "young people are frequently in what might be termed a *moratorium* period in which adventure seeking, sex, and peer group activities are all more important than work. Some years later comes *settling down,* a stage characterized by a very different set of attitudes about work. This movement from moratorium to settling down is largely responsible for the mobility patterns [in the youth versus adult labor markets]." There is, Osterman argues, a functional match between the needs of "moratorium" youths and secondary employers (ibid.: 24): Because (immature) youths are unwilling to make much of a commitment to work, they take on low-skill jobs that demand little from them; and because secondary employers don't invest much in training their employees (and can afford high turnover), they hire youth workers and put up with their unstable, irresponsible behavior.

Restrictive hiring practices among primary employers also play a central role in reinforcing the boundaries and structures of the youth labor market, Osterman says (ibid.: 25). He recognizes that the terms of causality between youth workplace behavior and labor-market structure are, at best, ambiguous (ibid.: 33): The youth labor market could be created by structures of opportunity set by employers, and youth behavior in the secondary workplace during the "moratorium" period could be "completely demand or opportunity determined." Osterman argues, "When primary firms refuse to hire them, young people are forced into secondary jobs, which by their nature lead to minimal work commitment and unstable behavior" (ibid.).

The idea that there is a distinct youth labor market in North America is a useful one. Explanations of this market that invoke universalist concepts of youth immaturity and instability, however, are deeply problematic. Theorists such as Osterman tend to assume, with little empirical evidence, that minimal work commitment and unstable workplace behavior among youths is a self-evident fact. In consequence, these theorists' explanations often become chicken-and-egg arguments: Youths are irresponsible because primary firms won't hire them, and primary firms won't hire them because youths are irresponsible. As Osterman himself writes, "Probably the best way to characterize the relationship [between youth behavior and labor-market opportunity] is to argue that the modern economic structure permits the expression of characteristic adolescent patterns" (ibid.: 150).

But youth immaturity and instability in the workplace is simply *not* a self-evident fact. My research and numerous other studies of youths at work show considerable commitment and stable workplace behavior among young workers, even among those in low-wage, low-status jobs, where one might not expect to find much commitment or expenditure of effort. In fact, researchers studying young workers often find themselves struggling to explain why these workers say they like their fast-food and mall retail jobs as much as they do, or why young workers work as hard in these jobs as they do (see, e.g., Krahn and Tanner 1996; Newman 1999).

Claims such as those made by Osterman (1980: 25) that the hiring practices of primary employers are "the most important determinant" of the youth labor market are also problematic. Such claims have some merit, of course: If primary employers offering high wages and good benefits in stable jobs with room for advancement were competing for the same group of workers as secondary employers, then secondary employers would never be able to hire anyone by offering the low wages and poor working conditions that they do. But claiming that primary firms' restrictive hiring practices are therefore responsible for the poor conditions of the youth labor market absolves secondary employers of all agency and responsibility whatsoever. The youth labor market exists as a secondary labor market *because* employers in the youth labor market are willing and able to subject youths to low pay and poor working conditions. Framing the youth labor market as the creation of primary employers is a mystification that obscures possibilities for placing direct pressure on secondary employers to improve conditions in this market.

Osterman and other theorists do offer another explanation for the existence of the youth labor market that is much more convincing and useful than the "youth immaturity" argument. Observing that youths and adults constitute relatively distinct groups in the workforce, Osterman recognizes that youths and adults often have different interests as workers, and that these interests are frequently in competition. Youths,

Osterman therefore suggests, end up working in the secondary labor market because "barriers to youth employment . . . have been created to protect the jobs of adults" in the primary labor market (ibid.: 153). That is, adults have used seniority rules, limits on openings in apprenticeships and professional schools, minimum age limitations, and compulsory schooling (which restricts school-age youths to part-time employment) to protect their own interests in the labor market and to exclude youths from stable, well-paid occupations.

The recognition that youths and adults are, or can be, competitors in the labor market is critical. Any society that has an occupational hierarchy of good and bad jobs must relegate some group or groups of workers to performing society's "dirty work," Osterman points out (ibid.: 151). Youths—along with other disempowered groups of workers, such as women and minorities—have been relegated to bad jobs in the low-wage, low-status service sector not solely because of the restrictive hiring practices of primary employers, but also because adult workers (whites and men, especially) are taking the good jobs in the high-wage, high-status sectors of the economy. One cannot talk—as some youth-work researchers do—of moving youths around in a hierarchical occupational structure without considering the effects that such movement would have on other groups of workers.

THE PROBLEM OF FLOUNDERING

Youth-labor-market theorists tend to see this labor market as a natural and functional adaptation of economic structures to the "deeper foundation" of adolescent psychology. That is, they see stopgap youth work as merely a developmental stage that most youths eventually will grow out of (ibid.: 150; Kantor 1994: 446). The arguments of school-to-work researchers directly oppose this viewpoint. The school-to-work literature is dominant in North America today: Its arguments and assumptions stand behind such major policy initiatives as the 1994 School to Work Act in the United States. Policy-oriented and geared toward producing sweeping prescriptions for the economy as a whole, rather than toward providing detailed descriptions of work and workplaces, the body of school-to-work literature is dominated by foundation-sponsored, multi-author reports such as the National Commission on Excellence in Education's *A Nation at Risk* (1983), the Hudson Institute's

Workforce 2000 (1987), the William T. Grant Foundation's *The Forgotten Half* (1988a, 1988b), and the National Center on Education and the Economy's *America's Choice* (1990).

Like youth-labor-market theorists, school-to-work researchers are principally concerned with the fortunes of non-college youth—those high-school graduates and dropouts who become North America's "frontline workers" (or, to use a term generally absent from this literature, the "working class"). Unlike youth-labor-market theorists, school-to-work researchers are concerned not so much with the problem of youth unemployment as with the broader phenomenon of youth "floundering" (or "milling," "churning") in the labor market. "Floundering" refers to the period of stopgap employment during which youths tend to move in and out of the workforce with considerable frequency, "job-hopping" among the low-status, low-wage jobs found typically in the service sector until they eventually settle into more stable, higher-paid "adult" employment. With the increasing disappearance of high-paid, stable jobs for the non-college-educated in North America's manufacturing sector, school-to-work researchers are concerned that non-college youths are finding it more difficult to move out of the floundering period.

Floundering, as the influential report *The Forgotten Half* (1988a, 1988b) acknowledges, is widely thought to result from youth immaturity (a viewpoint that, as seen earlier, youth-labor-market theorists share). Youths, as common-sense arguments go, are not responsible enough when they first finish high school to take on career jobs. Recent high-school graduates are more concerned about their social lives than work; they are interested only in jobs that won't demand too much, that can provide a quick supply of cash, and that they can pick up and drop as fancy strikes. Youths just out of high school, it is popularly said, don't really know what they want out of life and are certainly not ready to settle down. As a result, career employers, who make considerable investments in training their employees, are forced to wait until these workers have had time to "mature." Only employers such as restaurants and retail outlets, which depend on a cheap supply of unskilled and temporary labor, are willing and able to hire the young and give them a chance to develop as workers.

According to the common-sense viewpoint, then, if youths flounder when they first enter the workforce, it is their own deficits that are to blame. The school-to-work literature generally rejects such arguments. Authors in this category look skeptically at claims that youth is a distinct stage that must be waited out. Youths are resources, they say, and as resources they can be either well used or misused. If we don't expect much from our youths, they warn, we will not get much in return (*Forgotten Half* 1988a: 9; *America's Choice* 1990: 43). Youth floundering, according to *The Forgotten Half*, is caused by the misuse of youth assets, not by an accommodation to youth deficits:

> The basic truth faced by too many youth is that regardless of how well schools do their job and regardless of how well high school graduates learn basic skills, most large, established employers seldom hire recent high school graduates for career-ladder positions, even at the entry-level. Such employers typically wait until these same youth, especially males— with no greater educational qualifications and no advanced work skills— reach age 20–22, even 25. In the meantime, young people alternate low paid work and unemployment with a growing frustration that erodes their confidence. (1988a: 26)

Career employers wait to hire youths because they, like many adults in North America, hold false and negative stereotypes of young people as being irresponsible, lazy, self-interested, and antisocial—stereotypes that, *The Forgotten Half* warns, can "nevertheless become self-fulfilling prophecies" (ibid.: 9). But when given the chance, *The Forgotten Half* argues, most non-college youths make "responsible," "resourceful," and "resilient" workers (1988b: 4). Many non-college youths take low-status jobs upon leaving high school not because they are unable to perform, or are uninterested in performing, more demanding kinds of work, but because employers are unwilling to hire them for good jobs. And many non-college youths job-hop not because they are unable to make commitments, but because youths stuck in marginal jobs with no room for advancement justifiably see quitting and finding other employment as their best chance to improve their prospects. Youth floundering, *The Forgotten Half* insists, "reflects the logic of employer economics, not inherent youthful instability" (1988a: 27).

In shifting attention from the supposed immaturity of youth to the attitudes and actions of employers, the school-to-work literature makes a major contribution to the study of youth and work and opens the possibility for changing the early labor-market experience of the young. One might thus expect this literature to focus its policy recommendations on ways to tackle age discrimination against the young: by pressuring employers who do not hire youths to open their hiring practices, and by pushing employers who do hire youths to alter their work organizations (to take better advantage of the educational assets that high-school graduates possess) and improve working conditions (so that youth workers will not have to keep job-hopping). This, however, is not the case, and the school-to-work literature ends up falling short of its initial promise.

Youth floundering, according to the school-to-work literature, may be caused by the prejudicial and short-sighted hiring practices of employers. But both youth floundering and exclusionary hiring practices are *together* exacerbated by the fact that the United States and Canada, unlike other developed nations, do not have structured school-to-work transition systems (such as the German system of apprenticeship) for non-college youths. While colleges and universities help college youths move from school to career, non-college youths are left to make it on their own in the labor market. Because high schools tend to be isolated from large, established employers, youths and career employers are unacquainted with one another when youths first leave school. It is difficult, therefore, for non-college youths to make the leap directly from school to entry-level, career-track jobs.

The policy recommendations of the school-to-work literature consequently focus on developing a network of school-to-work "bridging programs." But these bridging programs—although they no doubt will assist many non-college youths—raise a number of questions. Most bridging programs are designed to improve the skill levels and "work-preparedness" of young workers; they do not focus primarily on dispelling employer prejudice against youth, as one might expect they would. The call for bridging programs to solve the problem of youth floundering thus implies that floundering is essentially a matter of youth deficits. However, the school-to-work literature itself accounts for youth floundering by pointing to prejudice among adult employers. The solution just does not fit the problem.

Further, in turning to bridging programs to take non-college youths directly from school to high-wage, high-status, long-term adult employment, the school-to-work literature implies that these youths can simply be lifted up and over the sea of low-wage, low-status, temporary service-sector jobs in which they now become mired upon leaving high school. But what, then, is expected to become of these low-status jobs? Will they simply disappear? Or will they perhaps become the lot of some other, less fortunate (immigrant?) segment of the population?

One of the most serious limitations of the school-to-work literature in addressing the problem of youth floundering is that the literature never focuses on the service-sector employers who actually hire youths. The literature has been unwilling or unable to consider the possibility of reforming the workplaces where youths now work—either to transform youth jobs into good career jobs or to make these jobs better first jobs (Bailey and Bernhardt 1997). Low-wage, low-status service jobs continue to proliferate in North American economies—at a faster rate than that of most high-wage, high-status jobs. It therefore seems likely that, school-to-work programs or not, large numbers of youths will continue to work in these jobs for the foreseeable future. Thus, this failure to address the question of reforming youth workplaces constitutes a major and undue limitation for both policy and theory.

STUDENT WORKERS

Reading the youth-labor-market and school-to-work literature, one could easily conclude that only non-college-bound high-school graduates and dropouts work and flounder in the youth labor market. Since the 1950s, however, an increasing number of North American high-school and college students have worked while at school—either part time during the academic year or in summer jobs during the off-term. Still relatively rare in many other countries, student labor has become a mainstay of fast-food restaurants, supermarkets, mall retail outlets, movie theaters, and theme parks throughout the United States and Canada. One of the most important contributions the student-worker literature makes is to highlight that it is not just the non-college-bound who work in youth stopgap jobs. In the 1990s, the overwhelming majority of youths across the continent—middle class and working class, male and female, college-bound and non-college-bound—will have experienced some form of paid employment before leaving high school.

The dominant concern of the student-worker literature lies in assessing which kinds of work experience are good and bad for which kinds of students. Popular views in North America have tended to see teenage work as having beneficial effects on youth socialization. Work is said to build character, promote responsibility, and boost feelings of usefulness and self-confidence. Youths who work learn what "real life" is all about, and they learn the value of money and punctuality; they develop "basic communication skills" and "appropriate modes of dress" (Mortimer and Finch 1986: 67). These positive effects are thought to be fostered by work, no matter what kind of job is being done. Even the most marginal jobs, many argue, "require self-discipline, a mobilization of effort, and application to a task" (ibid.). During the 1960s and 1970s, concerns about youth degeneracy and a widening "generation gap" led to support for increased work experience for the young—experience that, it was hoped, would bring youths into greater contact with adults, help them adopt adult perspectives more quickly, and pull them away from their lives of crime, drug abuse, and delinquency (Greenberger and Steinberg 1986: 41–45).

The publication in 1986 of Ellen Greenberger and Laurence Steinberg's *When Teenagers Work,* one of the foundational texts of the student-worker literature, turned popular views of youth work on their head. Greenberger and Steinberg strongly questioned the notion that the kinds of jobs (restaurant and retail) generally available to teens offer rich and rewarding learning activities. Youth jobs, the authors claimed, tend to involve routine and repetitive tasks that require teens to work fast without thinking. These jobs offer limited opportunities for decision-making and teamwork; training is almost nonexistent; and youth workers are more likely to spend their time cleaning and carrying things than using their reading, writing, and math skills (ibid.: 66–103). In fact, the authors claimed, work can actually be harmful for high-school-age students—especially when they start spending long hours at a job. Greenberger and Steinberg presented a host of ills that can come from too much work in fast-paced, high-pressure, meaningless jobs, including negative effects on school performance; increases in delinquent behavior (goofing off on the job, lying, stealing, vandalizing); and increases in the use of alcohol and marijuana (ibid.: 6).

Greenberger and Steinberg's controversial claims helped stimulate a lively and continuing debate over the costs and benefits of teenage work experience. Surveys of the student-worker literature suggest that, when it comes to making claims about the educational and attitudinal effects of teenage work in general, there is no real consensus. Rather, researchers make what is perhaps the common-sense point that the costs and benefits of teenage work depend, first, on the quality of the work (whether it is, or is seen by youths as being, challenging, meaningful, or related to school or future career goals), and second, on the frequency or intensity of the work, measured in the number of hours worked per week. Boring and stressful work and working for more than twenty hours per week can have negative effects on educational performance and youth attitudes; rewarding work and working less than twenty hours per week can have positive effects (Mortimer and Finch 1986; Charner and Fraser 1988; Stern et al. 1990a, 1990b; Lewis et al. 1998).

Beyond expanding the scope of who youth workers are recognized to be, the student-worker literature introduces the critical notion that, in formulating policy on youth workers, considerations such as the importance of schooling and healthy development for youths should be given priority over the interests of youth employers. Unlike the youth-labor-market and school-to-work literature, the student-worker literature focuses attention directly on evaluating and critiquing youth employers. Further, in focusing on youths' student status, the literature highlights one of the most important ways in which young workers are differentiated from adult workers in North America: Youths don't work in the low-end service sector because of their immaturity or inherent instability; many work in this sector simply because they are, or expect soon to be, attending school. That is, youths often position themselves, and are positioned by others in the workplace differently from adult workers as being temporary, upwardly mobile and stopgap workers. Frequently, this is because they see themselves, and are seen as being, if not actual students, then future or potential students.

Despite such critical insights, the student-worker literature is limited by a theoretical framework that defines working youths as students instead of as workers. The literature's proposed interventions into teenage work that is deemed harmful or unproductive focus on pulling youths out of the workplaces where most now work (through the creation of apprenticeships, internships, and the like) or on limiting the kinds and amount of regular paid work that youths are permitted to do. In other words, because youths are seen as students rather than workers, interventions focus on separating youths from work. Although such interventions may be beneficial to many students, student-worker researchers overlook alternative or supplemental possibilities for helping youths as workers and for improving the workplaces in which young people now work. Service and retail workplaces are seen merely as a background through which student workers pass on their way to college or serious, adult, career employment. Indeed, student-worker researchers betray a middle-class bias in their comfortable assumption that most youths will eventually end up in jobs that are radically different from those in which they work as youths (see, e.g., Greenberger and Steinberg 1986: 7).

The student-worker literature also has a worrisome tendency to depoliticize youth workplace behavior. Researchers are concerned about whether early work experience fosters "good" or "bad" attitudes among teenage workers—about whether teen workers become "deviant" or "well-adjusted" individuals. Such questions, however, are politically charged. Youths are typically said to have good attitudes when they do what employers and adults expect and when they show "appropriate" respect and deference to their elders; they are said to have poor attitudes when they resist and question adults' and employers' demands. This literature pays little attention to whether youths are ever justified in resisting or resenting the demands and actions of adults and employers.

Finally, although student-worker researchers debate vigorously the educational and attitudinal effects of student work, when it comes to considering the material parameters of student jobs (hours, wages, benefits), most adopt a functional-match perspective. That is, most accept that what student jobs have to offer materially more or less matches the material needs of most students. In both the student-worker literature and popular discourse, one commonly hears assertions that the material aspects of jobs can be measured differently for adult and youth (student) workers. As Greenberger and Steinberg write, what are "'bad' jobs for adults . . . are in some crucial respects 'good' jobs for youngsters" (1986: 25).

Low-end service-sector jobs typically offer part-time employment, shift work, and irregular and unpredictable hours. Part-time work is inadequate for economically independent adults, and irregular and changing hours are "likely to interfere with the responsibilities of adults" (ibid.). Students, however, need part-time hours and shift work, and they supposedly do not have the kinds of "adult responsibilities" that make irregular and unstable hours a problem. Similarly, low-end service-sector jobs offer low wages and few, if any, benefits—conditions that obviously are undesirable for most adults. But students, many researchers claim, work not out of dire financial need but to earn pocket money for "luxury" consumption. Thus, students can generally "afford to work at, or even below the minimum wage, because they are subsidized by their parents" (ibid.: 26). As for benefits, researchers presumably assume that most students are covered by their parents' health-care plans.

Such functionalist arguments clearly don't hold for college students, who work to help put themselves through college and depend on a decent and regular wage. But even with high-school students, functional-match arguments are problematic. Most high-school students have a range of family, community, educational, and extracurricular responsibilities. Irregular and changing hours are thus hardly less of a problem for teenagers than for adult workers. Student workers may need, and student employers may offer, part-time hours and shift work, but there is no guarantee that needs and opportunities for shifts and hours will match up to students' benefit. As discussed in the introduction, the notion that teenagers don't "need" increased wealth, though highly popular among adults, is itself deeply problematic. Further, the idea that parents should be expected to "subsidize" the wages of their adolescent children—and thereby subsidize the profits of the multinational employers, such as McDonald's and Burger King, that employ their children—in jobs that offer limited educational opportunities is deeply suspect. Many parents in the United States, moreover, are not able to provide health-care coverage for their children. Why should young workers be any less entitled to health-care benefits than other workers?

SOCIAL REPRODUCTION

Social-reproduction theorists—Samuel Bowles and Herbert Gintis, Pierre Bourdieu, Paul Willis, and Henry Giroux, for example—are typically assumed to represent the radical or critical pole of the youth, work, and education literature (see, e.g., Griffin 1993). Indeed, the spirit of social critique that underlies my study of youth workers is directly inspired and guided by many of the classic texts of social-reproduction theory. However, it is important to recognize that social-reproduction theory has had strikingly little to offer, in terms of concrete and detailed research and theory, to the discussion of youth and work. This failure of, or lack in, social-reproduction theory means that there has essentially been no radical or critical pole of any substance in the study of youth workers. There have been only the scattered critical insights of the various mainstream literatures that were discussed earlier.

Social-reproduction theorists have said almost nothing about the youth labor market, the phenomenon of youth floundering, and the student workers who are the focal concerns of the other youth, work, and education literature. When Paul Willis, for example, asked his now widely quoted question in *Learning to Labor* (1977: 182)—"How and why [do] young people take the restricted and often meaningless available jobs?"—he was referring not to the temporary service-sector jobs in which most youths (in North America) work for a spell during and immediately after schooling, but to adult, career occupations. Specifically, he was referring to manual-labor positions in manufacturing. Willis does report that the factory-bound "lads" of his study (which was set in England) worked in the retail and service sectors while they were in school, as cleaners, key cutters, ice-cream salesmen, and supermarket stackers (ibid.: 39). But in a book that is about "learning to labor," Willis has surprisingly little to say about these "lads'" first paid employment experiences—about how they learned the work in these jobs; their experiences performing this work; their interactions with managers, co-workers, and customers; and so forth.

What accounts for the social-reproduction literature's lack of interest in youth work? For one thing, the literature is strongly school-based. Although authors talk about how youth "become" workers, their approach is essentially mentalist—focusing on how youths develop inclinations or aptitudes for certain kinds of work in the context of schooling—rather than materialist. Few studies focus on the actual experiences of getting and learning a job or of performing paid work. Most social-reproduction research is conducted within school, classroom, and neighborhood settings. When work experience is researched in any detail, the context tends to be internships and cooperative-education programs—settings in which youths are still officially students or interns rather than workers per se.

Social-reproduction theorists also overlook youth work because they are primarily concerned with where youths begin their pathways from school to work (in terms of their classroom experiences and their class, race, and gender identities) and where youths end their pathways as adults (in career occupations), but not with where youths pass through in between. Social-reproduction authors are interested in the reproduction of permanent labor-market stratification in capitalist democracies—not temporary conditions of stratification. Although youth work constitutes a marginalized segment of the labor market, it is, of course, a temporary workforce experience for individuals by definition.

It is not just a lack of research focus that limits the usefulness of social-reproduction theory in studying youth workers. The theory itself, strangely enough, is marked by a fundamental conservatism that restricts its ability to recognize the agency of youth workers in the workplace and to address the possibility of improving the conditions of youth work. To explain the reproduction of social inequality in the workforce, social-reproduction analysts rely on "correspondence theories" (Apple 1980). In other words, to address the question of why youths from subordinate social groups regularly take marginal jobs in the absence of extensive physical coercion, social-reproduction theorists attempt to show how the education process instills, either directly or indirectly, the kinds of aptitudes and dispositions that will lead youths voluntarily to marginal jobs and that will "correspond with" or fit the performance demands of these jobs. A consequence of such analyses, as Michael Apple suggests, is that social-reproduction theorists underplay the lack of correspondence and fit between young workers and their jobs and generally overlook the significance of the resistance, initiatives, and struggles in which young workers frequently engage in the youth workplace.

Social-reproduction theory also tends to be oddly uninterested in the possibility of workplace change. At an abstract and theoretical level, of course, social-reproduction theorists call for sweeping "structural" changes in society. But the literature offers almost no vision of how changes might take place at a local and concrete level within specific workplaces, communities, and markets—whether these changes would come from the bottom up, through the collective action of workers, or from the top down, through the intervention of government regulation. In part, this is due to the school-based nature of the literature. When theorists do call for concrete changes, those changes tend to be in the classroom and school system rather than in the workplace. But this lack of vision is due in part to the fact that social-reproduction theory ultimately offers a static and frozen view of the world of work (Wexler

1983; Weis 1990). When they ask how social relations and structures are reproduced, these theorists assume that these relations and structures are, in fact, being reproduced. Social-reproduction theory thus predisposes analysts to look for what stays the same in society and the workplace rather than for what changes—or for what could be changed.

THE STOPGAP WORKER MODEL

Despite their differences, the dominant bodies of literature on youth, work, and education all adopt a pathway model to look at youth and work that offers little vision of the agencies and subjectivities of youths as workers, of the complex and often contradictory nature of work and workplaces, and of the possibility of (local, worker-driven) work and workplace change. This study takes a different approach to the study of youth and work. In this book, I focus on youths in terms of their specific and temporary occupational identities. I am not particularly concerned with where youths are coming from (with what is done in the schools, for example) or with where youths are going—the careers and identities they will develop later in adulthood. My concern is with youths *as workers:* with the work they do, the workplaces in which they work, the employers who hire and manage them, the ways they are positioned as workers in the workplace and labor market, and the possibilities for improving their working conditions.

To focus on youths as workers, however, is not to turn one's back on the pathway model that guides most of the youth, work, and education literature. It is, rather, to view this model from a different perspective. When one looks closely at young workers who work in typical youth workplaces (such as fast-food outlets and grocery stores), it becomes apparent that most of these workers constitute a distinct category of worker. This distinct worker identity is not linked primarily to youths' ascribed characteristics of race, class, or gender (though it is mediated by such factors). Nor is it linked primarily to their educational or student status (though such status, again, plays a mediating role). This distinct worker identity is linked primarily to young workers' age. Young workers in low-end service and retail workplaces in North America tend to position themselves, and to be positioned by others, as temporary, stopgap workers—as just passing through jobs that they hope or expect will be more or less discontinuous with their past and future educational and work paths. In other words, the pathway model, instead of being used by myself as analyst to view youth movements from workplace to workplace, in this study now reappears in the hands of youths as a way of positioning themselves (and being positioned by others) as workers within the world of a single workplace.

In focusing on the experiences of youths as workers, this study is not alone. A handful of in-depth studies of young workers and their workplaces serve as models. Kathryn Borman's *The First "Real" Job* (1991), which describes the post-high-school work experiences of seven young non-college men and women, is perhaps the most widely cited example of these studies. Newman's more recent *No Shame in My Game* (1999) offers a compelling and comprehensive account of the work and non-work lives of young fast-food workers in Harlem. Ethnographic studies of low-end service-sector workplaces, though not directly engaged with the youth-and-work literature, nevertheless offer insightful accounts of the work experiences of the youths who make up such a large proportion of these workplaces (see, e.g., Reiter 1991; Leidner 1993). Indeed, a large body of research in the sociology of work focuses on the work cultures of older workers in manufacturing, crafts, and professional occupations. This study seeks to build on the insights of this research by describing the work conditions and work cultures of stopgap youth workers in the low-end service sector.

The emphasis in this chapter has been on pointing out the dead ends—the gaps and limitations—in the dominant youth, work, and education literature. My intent, however, is not to dismiss these bodies of literature altogether. Each of the four bodies of literature discussed asks important questions that are not asked by any other body of literature (or by this study). Each has also pointed to issues and developed concepts that are critical to any effort to understand the experiences of youths as workers in contemporary North America. The argument presented here is that to understand the nature of youth and work in contemporary North America; to confront workplace discrimination against the young; and to engage with the interests, experiences, and demands of youth workers, it is also necessary—indeed, critical—to develop parallel research and theory on youths as (stopgap) workers.

2   On the Front Lines of the Service Sector

IN THE 1994 film *Reality Bites*, high-flying Lelaina Pierce—college graduate, class valedictorian, aspiring documentary filmmaker—loses her job as a production assistant on a TV talk show, and, after a series of futile attempts to find a replacement job within the media industry, is driven in desperation to apply for work at a fast-food company called "Wienerschnitzel." Lelaina is interviewed for the fast-food job by a cashier in a "Wienerdude" cap, who—while in constant motion preparing food, serving customers, and barking out orders to subordinates—asks: "Miss Pierce, do you have any idea what it means to be a cashier at Wienerschnitzel?" When Lelaina suggests that being a cashier might involve taking orders and handling cash, the Wienerdude laughs:

> *Wienerdude:* No, it's a juggling act. . . . I mean, you got people coming at you from the front, coming at you from the back, from the side, people at the condiment exchange, people at the drive-through, kids on bikes, and all depending on who?
>
> *Lelaina:* Me?
>
> *Wienerdude:* Yeah. . . . You got to be 150 percent on your toes 150 percent of the time.

The Wienerdude then gives Lelaina a math quiz, asking her to add 85 and 45 in her head as quickly as she can. After Lelaina three times comes up with the wrong number—"140? 150? 160?"—the Wienerdude shakes his head and scoffs, "It's not an auction, Miss Pierce. There's a reason I've been here six months." Lelaina, needless to say, is not offered the job at Wienerschnitzel. She does, however, eventually manage to get her life back on track, enjoys some success as a filmmaker, and, by the end of the film, is even able to find true love in an old college friend. Meanwhile, the Wienerdude, after his brief but action-packed cameo, is never heard from again.

This book is about the Wienerdudes of the world. It is about the young workers in those low-end service and retail jobs that are the butt of countless jokes—jobs that, as many would say, "any trained monkey could do." Stereotypes of fast-food and other low-end service jobs (including grocery) typically trade on these jobs' simplicity and simple-mindedness. Indeed, *Reality Bites* finds humor in parodying the Wiener-dude's apparently ludicrous and self-important inflating of the complex and demanding nature of his work at Wienerschnitzel. What this chapter seeks to show is that the Wienerdude is, in many ways, absolutely right: Work in fast-food, grocery, and other low-end service jobs is, or can be, difficult, demanding, and unrewarding. Fast-food and grocery work is high-stress, low-status, and low-wage work. It is work that, on the one hand, is subject to routinization, close surveillance, and management control but, on the other, calls for high levels of self-motivation and investment from workers. It can also be physically dangerous: Grocery and restaurant workers throughout North America face some of the highest risks of all occupational groups of being injured, attacked, or even killed on the job.

HIGH STRESS, LOW STATUS, LOW WAGES

"I would say the stress is the worst thing about it," a young Fry House cashier says of her fast-food job. "Sometimes I get so stressed out, 'cause some days you're in a bad mood yourself, you know, having to deal with people, you just don't want to, you'd rather be somewhere else, any-where except work." High stress levels are the most widespread com-plaint young workers in Box Hill and Glenwood have about their gro-cery and fast-food employment. Stress can be caused by many aspects of grocery and fast-food work: difficult relations with customers and managers; repetitive work tasks; low occupational status and small pay-checks; continual workplace surveillance; and hot, greasy, and often dangerous work environments. But the number-one factor young work-ers point to as the cause of workplace stress is the lack of time to do the work they are expected to do. Either there are not enough workers on shift to cover customer rushes and necessary preparation and cleaning work, or workers are not given long enough shifts to get their work sta-tions ready for lunch and evening rushes and clean up after such rushes are through.

Lack of time lies behind almost all other causes of workplace stress. Young workers regularly endure abuse from their customers. Workers are yelled at, sworn at, and insulted by customers; they are frowned at, glared at, and sneered at; they are ignored, treated as social inferiors, and assumed to be servants whose role in life is to cater to and anticipate a customer's every whim and fancy. There are different reasons for such abusiveness. Young grocery and fast-food workers make easy targets for the displacement of hostility. "Often people come into Fry House," a cashier in Glenwood says, "because they've been yelled at by their bosses, they don't have anybody they can yell at, so they yell at us 'cause they think they can." "Customers go off on some grocery employee," says a stocker in Box Hill, "'cause it makes 'em feel powerful."

Grocery and fast-food workers also incite abuse when their job responsibilities put them in conflict with customers' interests. Checkers in Box Hill, for example, become the target of customers' anger when they are put in the position of having to police company rules on accepting checks or enforce government laws for using food stamps or selling alcohol. In one supermarket, I witnessed a checker politely decline to sell alcohol to a young couple who were clearly intoxicated—as she was required to do by law, under penalty of losing her job. The couple stalked out of the store, and on their way out turned to yell at the checker, "Fuck you! Fuck you, you fucking bitch!" while giving her the finger.

Beyond these various motivations, however, many young workers feel that grocery and fast-food customers are abusive primarily because they fail to appreciate the time pressure under which workers labor:

> That's the worst aspect of it for me, having to explain to people [customers] that, well, this is how it works, because they don't know.... I've said, you're welcome to come back here, take a tour, sit here for an hour, watch us when it's busy, please. Actually, a lady who worked here for about a month, and then she got another job ... she said, "You know, I used to get really mad when I had to wait for stuff, but I have a total new respect for people that work in fast-food. I know what you have do. I know what it's like. I feel so bad for any time I ever blew up at anybody." She says, "I don't know how you guys do it; how you can handle it. I really, really, really admire you guys for that, for keeping your cool the way you do, 'cause it's hard to do."

"They think we're dumb and slow," a Fry House cashier complains of his customers, "but they don't understand. If they came in here and tried to do what we're doing, they'll be about three times as slow as we are."

Young workers are often caught in difficult situations in their relations with customers: On the one hand, they are not given enough time or staff support by their employers to perform at the speed and quality levels their customers would prefer; on the other, they lack the status to be able to persuade customers to respect them for the work that they do manage to do under what are often difficult and stressful working conditions.

Managers are another primary source of workplace stress. Like customers, some managers yell and swear at their young employees, talk down to them, and call them "stupid," "incompetent," and "lazy." Many workers believe that the younger the worker, the more latitude managers feel they have in verbally attacking and belittling that worker. Managers in fast-food and grocery, young workers say, often "go on power trips," order workers around, and "tell you every little thing you do wrong"—all the while, failing to provide encouragement or acknowledgment of jobs well done. Managers criticize workers behind their backs; worse, they dress employees down to their faces, in front of coworkers and customers. Young workers in both Box Hill and Glenwood complain widely of the stress caused by managerial favoritism— by managers picking on workers they dislike and conferring favors on workers they prefer. Many feel that managers will abuse their power by trying to get rid of employees they don't want working in their stores. "When a manager doesn't want you to work there," explains a cook in Glenwood, "they look for things, they kinda set you up so they can give you something bad."

As it does with customer-caused stress, time pressure often stands behind manager-caused workplace stress. Workers, for example, sometimes encounter what they refer to as "office managers"—managers who hide in their offices (claiming to be doing needed paperwork) and avoid helping with rushes. Because stores' labor budgets generally assume that managers will work on the floor when needed, "office managers" put increased stress on already overloaded workers. Workers have to deal with "cheap" managers—managers who (in efforts to keep costs low and earn year-end bonuses) skimp on allocating labor hours. Workers have to deal with managerial error—with managers who regularly screw up when submitting hours to company payroll, so that workers' checks are late or incorrect, or with managers who screw up scheduling, ordering, or inventory tasks. "I notice our managers forget a lot," one Fry House worker complained, "so we have to explain to our customers, 'We have no fried chicken tonight.' 'How can you have no fried chicken when it's Fry House?' 'Well, our manager forgot to order chicken.' It's crazy!"

Managers in the grocery and (especially) fast-food industries come and go with great frequency. Fry House store managers change over about every six months, while area managers change over every couple of years. Store managers in the Box Hill chain supermarkets change over less frequently, but assistant managers come and go every few months. Workers find that they can develop a relationship and system of doing things with one manager, then that manager will quit or be fired, transferred, or promoted. They will then have to start over, building up a new relationship and new system with a new manager. Over time, management instability can be as stressful and wearing as bad or abusive management. "Every time a new manager comes in, they change everything," complains a Fry House cashier. "It's just like being hired. They have to retrain you on everything. It's pretty hard, because once you get into something, you just keep with it. Then somebody else comes in, and they're like, 'No, no! You're doing it wrong; you have to do it this way.'"

Grocery and fast-food work is low-status work. Fast-food work especially carries a stigma, and fast-food workers are stereotyped as being stupid, lazy, slow, and lacking in life goals and initiative (Newman 1999). Fast-food and grocery "youth" jobs (baggers, stockers) are also low in status simply because they are seen as typically being held by young workers. "What's the image of a fast-food job?" a Fry House cashier asks rhetorically. "You get the image of some kid with about a hundred pimples on his face trying to take an order for somebody, and he doesn't understand what to do." Young workers in Box Hill and Glenwood are well aware that if the work they perform were considered glamorous and important, it would be adults and not youths who would be taking on these jobs.

For many young workers, grocery and fast-food work lacks real or intrinsic meaning, interest, and value. "You can't be very proud of yourself as a grocery worker," says a young stocker in Box Hill. "What is your gift to the world [if] you work at Good Grocers your whole life?" The problem with grocery and fast-food work, for many young workers, is that it is difficult to feel a sense of accomplishment or progress. A grocery bagger, for example, explains why she would never want a grocery career:

> It's tough to have a job where it's just a constant flow of people and nothing ever ends or begins, where you're always just providing a service, the same service over and over again. . . . It seems like, to be a checker, to always be saying hello, how are you, have a good day, to always be doing the same thing. I would like a job better where I started and finished something.

In grocery and fast-food work, tasks tend to repeat themselves almost without end. The work is repetitive, mundane, and often boring. Workers may find getting up to and maintaining speed in what are very fast-paced workplaces initially challenging, but once the basic set of tasks has been mastered, workplace learning plateaus, and workers are left with the drudgery of simply executing tasks that long ago became second nature.

Grocery and fast-food work is often said to be "low-skill" work—and, indeed, many young workers in Box Hill and Glenwood slam their jobs by saying that anyone "with half a brain" could do the work they do. Attributions of skill are notoriously tricky, however: They tend to involve assessments of the social standing of a particular job and the kinds of people who hold that job as much as they refer to any absolute and objective measurement of cognitive demands inherent in a given set of work tasks. Young grocery and fast-food workers develop considerable local expertise in their jobs: knowledge of how best to handle individual customers and managers; of how to bend official work rules to get work done effectively and efficiently on the ground; how to make ad hoc repairs and improvisations in the workplace when machines break down, work tools go missing, or the maddening rush of customer demand overwhelms normal working procedures. What can be said of grocery and fast-food work is that such local expertise emerges within jobs that are seen overall—by workers, customers, and managers— as repetitive and low in status, meaning, challenge, and value.

The low status of grocery and fast-food work feeds into general workplace stress. Young grocery and fast-food workers lack a "status shield" to protect them from customer and manager abuse (Hochschild 1983; Leidner 1993). As Robin Leidner (1993: 132) writes, "Customers who might have managed to be polite to higher-status workers [have] no compunction about taking their anger out on [low-status service-sector] employees." The low status of grocery and fast-food work also feeds into low industry wages: Because this work is not considered particularly valuable or important, and because workers in these jobs are considered unskilled and easily replaceable, pay levels in Box Hill grocery and Glenwood fast-food outlets remain depressed. Rabid employer determination to keep labor costs at a minimum, of course, further reinforces and institutionalizes downward pressures on wages.

Unionization has had some impact in Box Hill and Glenwood in raising wages and securing benefits that are unusual in North America's low-end service sector. Wages for some job classifications in the Box Hill grocery stores are relatively high compared with wages in the area's other low-end service industries, and wages in the Glenwood Fry Houses are high compared with those of other fast-food companies in town. Overall, however, wages in these two industries remain low. Even full-time workers earning top dollar in the Box Hill grocery industry stand to make only about the average yearly wage in the United States. The vast majority of grocery workers in Box Hill do not work anywhere near full-time hours—as the grocery industry (like the fast-food industry) mostly provides only part-time work. Grocery wages in Box Hill, furthermore, are divided into three tiers. Only checkers and grocery and produce clerks are paid on the top wage scale. Workers in side deli and bakery departments (who are predominantly women) are paid on a lower, second-tier wage scale, and baggers and stockers (who are predominantly youths) are not on scale, and are paid on a third wage tier, which starts only slightly above the minimum wage.

SURVEILLANCE AND CONTROL

The fast-food and grocery industries traditionally have been characterized by "low-trust" employment relations (du Gay 1996). Because they pay low wages and offer little in the way of enriching work environments and opportunities for job advancement, fast-food and grocery employers generally have expected their workforces to have high turnover rates and their employees to hold only limited commitment to corporate goals. Indeed, these employers hire large numbers of youth workers partly because they expect these workers to be temporary (and therefore cheap). Fast-food and grocery employers have tried to control their temporary workforces primarily through close direction (or routinization) and surveillance of work performance (Reiter 1991; Leidner 1993; du Gay 1996; Ritzer 1996).

Signs of low-trust employment relations are legion in Box Hill and Glenwood. Employers make use of visible and hidden security cameras throughout their work sites. In some Box Hill supermarkets, rows of opaque brown plastic balls, each containing a video camera, hang down over the entire length of the checkstand areas: The opaque covering prevents workers (and customers) from seeing which way the cameras inside are pointing. One grocery chain has even introduced cameras with audio capacity so that managers sitting in store offices can listen in on conversations between workers and customers on the supermarket floor. Fry House, meanwhile, has been known to install hidden cameras secretly as part of "sting" operations in outlets where employee theft or drug use is suspected. Workers who have discovered such cameras say they now wave receipts for meals they have eaten in the restaurants' staff rooms in front of the cameras' invisible eyes.

Employers in both Box Hill and Glenwood are preoccupied with the possibility of worker pilferage and theft. Grocery checkers in Box Hill are often prohibited from serving family members, for example, because they might be tempted to give them special discounts. Checkers can be subjected to discipline for serving family members, even if no evidence of active wrongdoing (e.g., under-ringing the cost of an item) can be produced. As union officials in both Box Hill and Glenwood take pains to tell their members, employers can—and will, if they wish—fire employees for eating even a single grape (or french fry) that they have not paid for or been given by their employer, or for pocketing even a single penny that they find on the store floor.

Low-trust employment relations are initiated early in the grocery and fast-food hiring process. Grocery workers in Box Hill are required to take a drug test (urinalysis) before they are hired. Many workers in Box Hill and Glenwood have also been required to take pre-employment "honesty" or "personality" tests—tests that typically focus on a prospective employee's background, character, values, and beliefs (Duffy 1996; Hays 1997; Lindsay 1998). In these tests, workers may be asked about illegal behavior, such as whether they have taken drugs or stolen anything in the past, or about the behavior of their friends and acquaintances, such as whether they know anyone who takes drugs or steals. They are frequently asked to select adjectives that best describe their personalities, and they are often asked to predict their workplace behavior, such as whether they would pocket money they found lying on the shop floor, or whether they would quit if their hours were cut or changed. Workers who have taken these tests note that the questions "are repetitive sometimes, like the next page would have the same kind of question, to see if you'd change your answer."

As has been described at great length in past studies of the fast-food industry, fast-food, grocery, and other low-end service-sector employers rely heavily on work routinization to maintain centralized control of their dispersed restaurant and supermarket empires (Reiter 1991; Leidner 1993; Ritzer 1996). From cooking to cleaning, bagging to packing, and stocking to selling, work tasks in both Box Hill and Glenwood are laid out step by step, often in minute and painstaking detail. When situations arise that are not covered by such work routines, employers sometimes try to insist that their employees refrain from thinking of their own solutions and obtain managers' official pre-approval of non-routine workplace decisions and actions.

Employers' fear of independent decision-making among workers can be so intense, in fact, that it leads to ridiculous amounts of bureaucratic rigidity, as well as to unnecessary levels of workplace stress. As a young Box Hill deli clerk complains:

> There's no freedom to make decisions there. If the deli manager and assistant manager aren't there, we have to call the store manager. And half the time, they don't know what to do. I had a customer—, we do dinners every night, we put cold ones [dinners] out in the case they can buy. There were two left of meat loaf, mashed potatoes, and corn. The guy wanted two pieces of meat loaf, just one corn and potatoes. It was the biggest hassle in the world. I was there by myself. I called the night manager; she's, "Oh, jeez, I don't know. . . ." She came over and had to make a decision. She said, "I guess we can do it for two dollars for the extra piece of meat loaf." How hard would it be for me to make that decision? It takes an extra fifteen minutes; I have to bother her. It would be so much easier [for me to make the decision myself].

Young workers in Box Hill and Glenwood often do make their own decisions in the workplace: They makes changes in centralized work procedures and do workarounds to get their jobs done. But for many workers, official prohibitions against making their own local decisions in the workplace interfere with their ability to perform their jobs well and make them feel that they look stupid and incompetent in front of their customers.

One of the most politically charged workplace issues during my field-work in Box Hill and Glenwood was employers' intensified use of routinized "scripting" for customer-service interactions. Customer-service scripts used in the grocery and fast-food workplace sometimes spell out for employees required communicative actions (greet the customer, smile, make eye contact, sell suggestively, thank the customer). Sometimes, however, they dictate the exact words and turns of phrase that employees are expected to use. Baggers in one supermarket chain in Box Hill, for example, are instructed that they must not ask customers: "Would you like me to carry out your groceries?" Instead, they must say: "I'd be happy to help you out with your groceries." The chain, which is trying to promote its carry-out service, reasons that the latter, more direct phrasing gives customers less impetus to feel that they should politely decline offers of carry-outs. Staff rooms in both Box Hill and Glenwood are plastered with posters that spell out the companies' "four principles" or "five rules" or "seven steps" for achieving excellence in customer service.

In Box Hill in particular, employers' overly zealous promotion and rigid enforcement of service scripts has created uncomfortable interactions for workers and customers alike. Some young female workers felt great discomfort when they had to smile at and make eye contact with all of their male customers, as they felt that such behavior could all too easily be misinterpreted as signaling personal interest or sexual openness. Many workers found company requirements to thank customers by their proper names inappropriate, and even counter-productive: Some customers disliked having their names used by supermarket clerks who were strangers to them, or took offense when checkers mispronounced the names they were attempting to decipher from charge-card receipts (see also Associated Press 1998; Grimsley 1998; McNichol 1998).

Service scripting in Box Hill occasionally reaches the absurd. In one grocery chain, baggers are expected to listen as checkers read customers' names off charge-card receipts, then also thank customers by name.

As one might imagine, baggers in busy and noisy supermarkets sometimes cannot easily hear what the checkers are saying. Some baggers thus attempt to handle service requirements by mumbling approximations of customers' names, hoping that the customers are not listening closely. In another chain, stockers reported that customers treated them like social misfits because they were required to look up, smile, make eye contact, greet, and offer assistance to customers not only the first time a customer walked down the aisle in which they were working, but each and every time that customer passed. By trying to eliminate decision-making among workers in their interactions with customers, employers risked turning these interactions into empty, disjunctive, and robotic encounters.

To ensure that workers follow service scripts, employers in Box Hill and Glenwood make liberal use of "mystery shoppers." These mystery shoppers are hired at corporate headquarters to pose as customers in company stores. They purchase meals or groceries just like any other customer would; once outside the store, they write out employee and store evaluations based on their visit. These reports comment on everything, from whether an employee smiled, made eye contact, and followed service scripts, to the state of an employee's uniform, the efficiency and knowledgeability of service, and store cleanliness. Some young workers make a game out of "fingering" or "outing" the mystery shoppers, but for the most part, workers do not know who is grading them.

Because mystery shoppers' reports are presented to employees some time (often several days) after they have "been shopped," employees may not be able to recall who the mystery shopper was, even after the fact—and, consequently, they may be unable to judge the accuracy and fairness of these reports. At least one grocery chain in Box Hill requires employees who do poorly on mystery-shopper reports to attend a special customer-service retraining class (which workers call "smile school"). Many young workers are pleased when they receive favorable reports from mystery shoppers, for these provide what is sometimes rare positive feedback from their employers on their work performance. Unfavorable reports, on the other hand, are widely felt to be unfair, because they generally fail to take into account overall and extenuating workplace contexts (a broken fryer, a short-staffed crew) to focus on decontextualized individual performances. Overall, many workers find that ever-possible surveillance by unknown company spies contributes to increasingly stressful workplace conditions.

HIGH-PERFORMANCE WORKPLACES

The current emphasis in Box Hill and Glenwood on customer service is shaped by shifts in the competitive landscapes of the grocery and fast-food industries. In both grocery and fast food, companies traditionally have competed by minimizing costs and keeping prices low. But as these industries have become more competitive and reached market saturation, traditional strategies have come to be seen as insufficient. Grocery and fast-food companies are thus now placing increased emphasis on providing "high-quality" customer service and are focusing on ways to build up and maintain strong loyalty among customers. "Service wars" have come to complement, and even replace, "price wars" as primary loci of competition (Stanback 1990; Walsh 1993).

With this increased emphasis on "high-quality" customer service has come a growing concern with recruiting and training a "high-quality," or "high-performance," workforce (du Gay 1996; *Progressive Grocer* 1996; Bailey and Bernhardt 1997; Rosenthal et al. 1997). Fast-food and grocery employers talk increasingly about seeking workers who, if not exactly skilled, are at least highly oriented to service work in their personalities; workers who will also be committed, enthusiastic "team players," willing to participate fully in drives for company growth and success. In order to provide high-quality service, grocery and fast-food employers recognize, at a certain level, that they need more than just service scripts and mystery shoppers. They need employees who are willing and able to engage fully with customers and make customers' shopping and eating experiences pleasurable and timely.

As Paul du Gay points out, new service-oriented competitive strategies create contradictory impulses in the way low-end service-sector employers seek to control and motivate employees:

> Management is faced with the classic dilemma between the need to exercise control over the workforce, while at the same time requiring its enthusiastic commitment to corporate objectives.... The close direction, surveillance and discipline of labour is more likely to destroy, rather than guarantee, the mobilization of discretion and diligence among the workforce.... [There are] emerging tensions between employment relations

based on "low-trust" substitutability of [low-wage] labour and the importance of "service" in a customer-led retail "strategy." (du Gay 1996: 115)

In Box Hill and Glenwood, such "tensions" have created a split in employers' control strategies. On the one hand, employers continue to rely
on traditional direct-control technologies of routinization and surveillance. On the other hand, they also seek to foster a self-motivating and
self-managing "team" and "competitive" spirit among their employees
that will lead to high-quality service without direct managerial control.

High-performance control strategies have two sides: One is high profile; the other, low profile. High-profile strategies attempt to foster a
team, entrepreneurial, competitive spirit among workers. In company
advertising, employee training, and industry publications, one now sees
constant references to building company "teams" and transforming
employees into "team associates" or "company partners." Workers are
inundated with team and partner rhetoric from the moment they set foot
in the grocery and fast-food workplace. In Box Hill, grocery employers
liberally extend the title of "manager" to so many hourly employees that
it sometimes seems as if everybody in the supermarket is a manager or
assistant manager of something. In both Box Hill and Glenwood,
employers also extend management responsibilities to workers. Glenwood Fry Houses, for example, generally run without a full-time in-
store managerial presence.

Employers in Box Hill and Glenwood seek to foster workplace investment among their employees by sponsoring work-based social events,
such as picnics, outings, company baseball games, and Christmas parties. Most of all, though, employers seek to instill team spirit via a dizzying and constantly changing array of incentive programs. These programs usually involve running individual or team competitions within
or between stores in a single chain: who can sell the most of a new product; whose store can be kept the cleanest; who can raise the most money
for a company's adopted charity. Such programs seek to increase
employees' commitment to corporate goals and to personal excellence
in work performance by offering a combination of material rewards
(cash, coupons, free dinners, prizes) and intrinsic satisfactions (the thrill
of competition, the pride of being the best). Material rewards in these
programs range from the banal (pins, mugs, T-shirts, dinners with the
store manager) to the extraordinary (personal stereo systems, vacations
in Hawaii). Incentive programs are not new to the grocery and fast-

food industries, but their use has become more intensive and their design ever more inventive.

Employers in Box Hill and Glenwood also use a set of lower-profile strategies that are just as critical to the high-performance model. As in the manufacturing sector, which has sought gains in productivity by adopting "just-in-time" inventory and ordering systems, the low-end service sector is seeking high-performance productivity gains via "just-in-time" labor systems (Parker and Slaughter 1988, 1994). Employers in Box Hill and Glenwood use sophisticated computer programs to map business flows over the course of each day, each week, each month—often in increments as small as fifteen minutes. Programs are then used to schedule labor hours ever more precisely, according to minute, predicted changes in service demands.

By relying on shorter and more irregular shift scheduling, companies minimize the possibility of "excess" labor that previously might have been "wasted" during brief lulls in business. The result for workers, inevitably, is a loss of labor hours, an intensification of work, and an increasingly stressful workplace environment. Just-in-time labor systems reinforce team commitment among workers, while helping employers avoid having to rely on traditional methods of direct control. Workers become "self-motivated" and "self-managed" to work hard and cover for one another through a combination of commitment to team identities, as well as the pressure of constantly running out of time to get done the jobs that they expect, and are expected, to be able to do. Harried co-workers, impatient customers, and an employer-fostered sense of investment in team competence and success drive many workers in Box Hill and Glenwood to high-speed and high-quality work performance.

HEALTH IN THE WORKPLACE: ACCIDENTS, INJURIES, AND ATTACKS

A popular stereotype of youth suggests that young people are not particularly concerned with matters of health, illness, and injury. Such issues are thought to be the concerns primarily of older adults; youths, after all, are generally lucky enough to enjoy good health, and thus do not have to worry so much about health problems in their work and non-work lives. In Box Hill and Glenwood, however, these stereotypes do not hold. Accidents, injuries, and attacks are a common part of young fast-food and grocery workers' lives. Teenagers and young adults working in these industries, who expect to have long lives ahead of them, often worry that their jobs, which are supposed to be meaningless, stop-gap places of employment, will have lasting and detrimental effects on their bodies and future life activities. "I've seen the physical side of working at the store," says a teenage stocker in Box Hill. "I mean, this girl, a checker, she's already got tendinitis in her shoulder and stuff. She's twenty years old, and she's already got problems of an older person. And me, I got a backache; I'm eighteen years old. It's just, I don't know, it's not worth it."

In the Glenwood Fry Houses, the most common injuries include burns from the splashing or spilling of hot shortening; cuts; back, head, and knee injuries caused by slipping and falling; and back injuries caused by lifting heavy loads. Burns, especially, are so common that many young Fry House workers have largely come to accept them as part of the job. "My arms are all scarred," a Fry House supervisor says, rolling up her sleeves to provide proof. "That one's from a fryer; that's from a fryer. . . . This arm, I've got quite a bit on. They go all the way up my arms. That's from falling, on the floors. You get used to it, though."

Some young workers in Glenwood complain that they have problems breathing in the workplace—problems that they feel are caused by inhaling flour, grease, or chemicals used in cleaning. Other workers are concerned about rashes and skin conditions that they likewise attribute to working with powerful cleaning chemicals or to working in a hot, greasy environment.

Customers provide further sources of workplace danger in the lives of young Fry House workers. Many young workers describe having been verbally attacked and threatened by customers. "I've had customers threaten my life," says one cashier in disbelief, "because I didn't give them a breast instead [of the chicken leg that is regularly part of a special meal package]." Young workers in Glenwood have been grabbed, punched, and pushed by customers—customers who are typically drunk or high. "I didn't do anything to the customer," a supervisor protests, recalling a particularly nasty workplace injury. "He was drunk in the drive-through and punched the window. The glass shattered in my eye. . . . My whole eye was filled with blood, and I had to go in for an operation. I could have lost my sight."

Several Fry House restaurants in Glenwood have been robbed; some many times. What is of particular concern about these robberies is how low-trust employment relations work to increase the risks young workers are willing to take to prevent robberies. Fry House forbids workers from trying to stop robberies—under penalty of being fired. But the company also has a policy of threatening to fire workers if they have more than a certain amount of cash in their tills when robbed. "You were eight dollars from being fired," one young cashier says she was told by her manager after a drive-through robbery.

Cashiers are supposed to remove cash from their tills regularly and "drop" it into store safes. But cash drops are sometimes forgotten or postponed, as cashiers focus on handling customer rushes. One young cashier, who was robbed by a man holding a paper bag that later was revealed not actually to have been concealing a firearm, articulates a not-uncommon viewpoint among some Fry House workers: If he is robbed again with too much cash in his till, he might as well try to fight off the would-be robber. "Well, if I'm gonna get fired for this guy robbing me, why not get fired the big way?" the cashier says. "Why not get fired for beating the crap out of him, stopping him from taking the money anyways?"

Robberies, customer attacks, burns, cuts, and falls are likewise concerns for young grocery workers in Box Hill. Workers who have been in their jobs for extended periods of time also face cumulative injuries: repetitive stress injuries in arms and wrists; back, hip, knee, and foot ailments that workers attribute to working standing up for long stretches of time and to the pounding caused by walking on concrete supermarket floors; and back and knee injuries caused by repeated heavy lifting. One twenty-four-year-old checker I interviewed, for example, had been working part time or full time at a grocery checkstand for six years. Three years before our interview, she had lost four months of work because of tendinitis in her right shoulder. Although she was back on the job, she continued to feel pain and numbness in her shoulder and arm, as well as aches down her back. Her shoulder movement is now restricted—she is no longer able to braid her own hair. Like other checkers in her store, she frequently takes Advil and Aleve. She tries to be conscious of slowing her pace and alternating hands when scanning groceries but finds that the pressure of customer lineups keeps her moving more quickly than she would prefer.

Both the Fry Houses in Glenwood and the chain grocers in Box Hill have health and safety programs. Workers are officially expected to follow health and safety guidelines and are trained in how to work safely. Many workers, however, find the health and safety guidelines to be of limited use—and even to be an added source of wear and frustration. Guidelines are of limited use because they often focus on individual worker actions, without recognizing the realities of actual working environments. A produce clerk in Box Hill who now experiences considerable back pain, for example, reflects on the value of "safe" lifting procedures:

> I saw the video [on safe lifting procedures]. Of course, it was all perfect on the video; everything was easy to get to. But for example, the other day, I didn't trim celery because I would have had to reach over another case or two, grab it from the side, and pull it out and twist and lift up and over, with my arms out here—a fifty-five pound case of celery. I was just, like: Too bad, no celery; should have broken the load better. I didn't do it. Stuff like that happens all the time. A fifty-pound bag of onions— you gotta lift it straight up with one arm over something.

As a stocker who worked at the same store points out, lifting problems are caused not only by improper "breaking" of the load, but also by the fact that the supermarket's back room is very small. In cramped storage space, needed items inevitably end up in places that are difficult to access, and under pressure of time, one cannot always pull out, then replace, things to get to a desired crate or box. In both Box Hill and Glenwood, young workers complain of the strain put on their work by limited space—as well as by broken, shoddy, and missing equipment. With stores operating under tight spending allowances, managers are not always quick to repair, replace, or improve equipment that does not directly and dramatically affect customers' shopping experiences.

Health and safety guidelines also become a source of wear and frustration because managers often use them to shift the responsibility for accidents and injuries away from the design of the workplace environment and onto individual workers. One young Fry House cook recalls his experiences following a severe burn he suffered at work:

> I was burned in the back of my leg, here, a couple of months ago. It was pretty gruesome. . . . My boss tried to blame it on me—well, not blame it on me, but get mad at me for it, because I'm not wearing the extra type of apron [required by Fry House safety guidelines when workers carry

hot shortening]. But I showed that with the exact burn location, it doesn't cover the apron, so I told him even if I was wearing it that it wouldn't have done nothing. I took two days off. . . . It was pretty bad sitting in the hospital, with my pants down like that!

The cook explains that he—like so many young workers in Box Hill and Glenwood—doesn't always follow safety guidelines because of the time pressure and because of managers' unofficial preference (when push comes to shove) for getting work done quickly rather than safely:

> The Fry House safety guidelines are so much safety, it pretty much takes three times as much time to [follow them] than to actually do the thing. . . . Whenever you clean the fryers, you're supposed to wear apron, gloves. There's a certain kind of way you're supposed to do it. I don't do it, 'cause . . . if you wear all that stuff, it just gets in the way, makes it [take] more time. You need all the time you can get when it gets really busy. If it was really dead, no customers, I would pretty much do it the way they want me to do it, especially if a manager is looking at me, making sure I do it the proper way. But if it's really crazy, they say, "OK. Do it the way you do it. Get it done. We need your help."

Young workers in Box Hill and Glenwood can be disciplined, and even fired, for failing to follow health and safety guidelines at work. Thus, several young workers I interviewed said that they don't always report workplace injuries, especially if these injuries occurred when they were not following proper safety procedures. "I just got my finger cut," says a young deli clerk. "I didn't report it because I didn't have a [safety] glove on. . . . Even if I did need stitches, I probably wouldn't have said it was on the job, because I don't want them to be, like, you're going to get suspended, or you're going to get fired."

THE SIGNIFICANCE OF POOR WORKING CONDITIONS

Grocery and fast-food work is not all bad, of course. Unionization in Box Hill and Glenwood has brought many improvements in working conditions—as will be discussed in later chapters. And as Part II of this book will show, young workers in Box Hill and Glenwood often find meaning, value, and pleasure in their grocery and fast-food jobs—as workers generally do, under even the worst job circumstances (Rinehart 1978; Molstad 1986). Many of these workers, in fact, say that they like their jobs—at least for the short term. Young workers frequently develop positive social relationships in the workplace with customers and managers, and they generally develop strong senses of solidarity with their co-workers.

Why, then, emphasize the poor and demanding conditions of grocery and fast-food work? There are two reasons. First, although fast-food and grocery jobs are generally recognized as being undesirable occupations for adults, many observers tend to make an about-face when it comes to considering youth (and especially student) workers, arguing that these jobs are perfectly acceptable. After all, common arguments go, these are "just kids" who work in such jobs only for short periods of time. This study questions such logic. Working in a bad job for a long time is, of course, worse than having to work in a bad job for a short time. But there is no reason to suspend criticism of poor working conditions just because the workers happen to be young or because they will have to endure such conditions only for a temporary period in their lives.

The second reason for highlighting the poor conditions of grocery and fast-food work is that such conditions are critical to understanding the workplace identity and positioning of young grocery and fast-food workers. Some workplace observers, noting the typically poor conditions of youth work, invoke stereotypes of the young service-sector worker as being a fundamentally alienated and disfranchised worker (e.g., Greenberger and Steinberg 1986; Willis 1998). In Box Hill and Glenwood, such stereotypes do not fit. Although poor work conditions often do lead to feelings of alienation among young grocery and fast-food workers, these feelings frequently coexist with strong senses of workplace investment and worker commitment. What poor work conditions are decisive in fostering is the almost universal stopgap workplace positioning that definitively characterizes young service-sector workers.

II. YOUTH IN THE WORKPLACE

3   Store-Level Solidarities

UNIFORMITY is the hallmark of the fast-food industry. Go into any McDonald's in North America, common wisdom tells us, and it will be the same as any other. This experience of uniformity is usually described from the customer's viewpoint—as George Ritzer (1996: 10) puts it: "The Egg McMuffin in New York will be, for all intents and purposes, identical to those in Chicago and Los Angeles." But uniformity is also claimed to be the experience of fast-food workers (Reiter 1991; Leidner 1993):

> Fast-food restaurants try . . . to make the way workers look, speak and feel more predictable. . . . Employees receive instructions not only about doing the work, but for thinking about the work, the customers, and even themselves as fast-food employees. . . . Training programs are designed to indoctrinate the worker into a "corporate culture" such as the McDonald's attitude and way of doing things. (Ritzer 1996: 84)

Most commentators recognize, of course, that there will be individual variations from centrally designed company programs, but the restaurant crews within which such variations occurs are generally assumed to be more or less uniform throughout each fast-food chain.

One of the most striking aspects of young Fry House workers in Glenwood is that they almost universally insist on the distinctiveness of the individual outlets in which they work. "Our store is different," Fry House workers in Glenwood proclaim with pride. Fry House workers do not (*pace* Ritzer) talk much of sharing in a generic "Fry House" way of doing things: Global corporate culture is more often seen as company PR, something that can be opportunistically embraced or rejected as different circumstances arise. Instead, workers are likely to talk about the "MacArthur Street [store] way of doing things" or the "Lakeshore Boulevard [restaurant] attitude," for example, or about the crew who work the Fry House outlet at Seventeenth and Grand—"Now, those guys are really nuts!"

In claiming interstore difference, Fry House workers are talking about more than the environmental differences between restaurants. It is fairly obvious that fast-food outlets are located in different kinds of neighborhoods that have different clienteles, sales volumes, and patterns of customer flow. Workers are claiming, rather, that it is the workers themselves who create different and localized "ways of doing things" in different restaurants. Although conventional wisdom holds that fast-food workers are unskilled workers who are easily and completely interchangeable, young Fry House workers say that this is not true. Particular individuals matter: Change one crew member and you risk changing the dynamics of an entire store.

Fry House workers in Glenwood thus claim considerably more agency than is usually credited to fast-food workers. These workers are striking in two other respects, as well, for claims of difference and agency are tied up with strong feelings of work commitment and co-worker solidarity. It is not the case that most Fry House workers love the work they do—they don't. Workers complain endlessly of the poverty of their working conditions and often can't wait to get on with their lives and move up into better, more satisfying occupations. Nevertheless, many simultaneously express positive feelings of investment in their Fry House work. Such job commitment is based primarily on a sense of solidarity with co-workers. There are, of course, divisions within Fry House restaurant crews that are based on job titles, personality conflicts, race, gender, and age. Indeed, some crews are polarized along the lines of such divisions. But the significance of internal workplace divisions in Glenwood is often reduced by the organization of Fry House crews, while external workplace divisions sometimes work to reinforce tight-knit restaurant communities.

Fast-food restaurants, and the customer-service industry generally, have been said to generate highly atomized work environments (Rafaeli 1989; Reiter 1991; Leidner 1993). Youth workers are often described as having loose ties to the workplace and as being job-hoppers who are oriented more toward schooling and personal interests than toward work (see, e.g., Osterman 1980). But in the Glenwood Fry Houses, locally differentiated store-level solidarities, though they may be only temporary, are often extraordinarily strong among young fast-food workers. I argue in this chapter that experiences of difference, agency, and solidarity in the Glenwood Fry Houses, though striking, may not be unusual among young service-sector workers. The example of Glenwood may instead call for a rethinking of the popular images of both the youth worker and the fast-food and other low-end service-sector industries.

THREE STORES

Store-level solidarities in Glenwood are readily apparent in the talk of young Fry House workers. Workers commonly refer to their restaurant crew as a "team," "family," or even "a group of friends just hanging out." They point to their co-workers as the most important aspect of their job. "The people is what makes it work or not work," one young cashier says of her Fry House job. "And the people I work with are great." Some workers say that their ties to co-workers are the central reason they have stayed with their Fry House jobs in place of moving on to find other employment. A couple of workers I spoke with in Glenwood had held on to their Fry House jobs even after moving away from the neighborhoods in which their stores were located. Although they now face hour-long commutes to work, they have resisted the option of applying for transfers to closer outlets because of their commitments to workers in their home stores.

When workers claim that their stores are "different" from other Fry Houses, they are in part affirming and bounding their senses of store-level solidarity. It is a way to say that workplace communities matter—that they make a difference. But claims of interstore difference are not pulled out of thin air. Many workers have held positions in more than one Fry House outlet as transfers, trainees, or substitutes. Workers hear reports about other outlets from co-workers and store and area managers. Together, these personal and secondhand experiences lead to the conviction that work is done differently in different Fry House restaurants, and that the people in different restaurants are not all alike. "Every store," as a supervisor puts it simply, "has its own little system."

The interstore differences that young Fry House workers in Glenwood perceive are, to a certain extent, real. Some restaurants simply are not as together as others. But even in Fry Houses with tightly knit crews, there is great variation: Store-level solidarities come in many shapes and colors. To provide some sense of this variation, I will present "snapshots" of three Fry House restaurants. These restaurants are not particularly unusual among Fry House's Glenwood chain; nor do they exhaust the range or types of Fry House work communities. I will call these restaurants the "Sisters Store," the "Green Shirts Store," and the "Players Store."

The Sisters Store is not much to look at. One of Fry House's older restaurants in Glenwood, the store is in a state of disrepair—its walls and windows are yellowing, the ceilings are marked with water stains, and outside, large pieces of asphalt are missing from the drive-through lane. The store is located in one of Glenwood's outlying suburbs, along a commercial strip dotted with other fast-food restaurants, a few banks, and low-rise office buildings. Small and nondescript, the restaurant, even with its lighted tower sign, seems to fade into the suburban background.

Inside the restaurant, however, is a different story. Workers have transformed the decaying building into a warm and open center of community. Almost all the workers at the Sisters Store are women. Some years ago, there were more men in the store, and the atmosphere was different—more water and food fights, less work getting done, and at least one woman who was sexually harassed by a co-worker. But since the men left, the crew has come together: "Even when we're crazy busy, we get along great. Everyone is becoming a little bit like sisters, we're becoming more closely knit."

Workers help each other finish tasks; they cover for those who are having "off days" by taking over on difficult customers and menial chores; and they come in on their own days off to help co-workers in a crunch. Workers try to keep one another relaxed during often hectic work shifts. One cook likes to embarrass cashiers while they're serving customers by loudly singing songs in the back kitchen. "Sometimes it's kinda stressful up front," she says. "I like to put a little smile on their face."

Workers in the Sisters Store range in age from the mid-teens to the late thirties. The younger workers hang out together outside the store, giving potlucks and parties at one another's houses. They buy one another small gifts and sometimes lend each other money for groceries when they're in a tight spot. When a supervisor was promoted to the position of assistant manager, a co-worker baked her a cake—which the whole crew then sat around in the store office and ate. Another worker bought flowers for her manager when the manager won a company award. In what has now become a tradition at the store, workers take their teenage co-workers out for a special bar night when they come of legal drinking age. "I totally love the people I work with," a young cashier at the store says. "I know they would do anything for me, and I would do anything for them." Finding such an intimate community in a temporary workplace can be bittersweet. "I always knew I never wanted to work there for the rest of my life," the cashier continues, "but I'll miss the people if I do quit [this year]. I'll really miss them."

For many workers at the Sisters Store, close ties extend beyond co-workers to include customers. The store has a large group of regulars, many of whom work in the businesses along the strip outside, and some of whom come in almost every day. Workers take time out of busy schedules to talk to their regulars, catching up on events in one another's lives. Workers typically give their regulars "freebies"—extra-size helpings or drinks "on the house." In return, they find they often get deals on coffee and lunches when they visit the businesses where their customers work. A few workers have received gifts and cards from their regulars. Some have become friends with their customers and meet outside of work hours. In such circumstances, the notion of "customer" can become diluted. One cashier laughed as she observed that "some customers don't even buy anything anymore when they come into the store." The food is too expensive (by the standards of fast food) to buy everyday, so these "customers" just drop by to chat.

The Sisters Store is not without its tensions. Workers complain that Fry House is cutting back on providing training hours. Workers with a year or two of seniority express frustration with new hires who have not been properly trained, and thus are slower and less independent in their work; new hires complain they have not been given the opportunity to learn fully how to do the work expected of them. Business is slow, especially in the winter. This means fewer repairs for the store, fewer hours for the workers, and fears of being closed. New hires complain that their hours are cut more than anyone else's during the slow months. In the past, the store has had problems not only with (male) workers, but with managers who come and go—some of whom have caused considerable disruption to the store's way of working. Although relations between workers and the current manager are friendly, workers complain that the manager understaffs the store and regularly screws up scheduling assignments.

From the moment one turns off the freeway and sees the large, stand-alone restaurant, almost completely encircled by a landscaped ring of grassy mounds and small hedges, the Green Shirts Store looks different from the Sisters Store. The Green Shirts store is bigger, newer, and busier than the Sisters Store. A full-size family restaurant with indoor seating, the store serves customers almost constantly—at the drive-through window, over the phone for delivery orders, and along the inside counter at the front of the restaurant. Gleaming and spacious, the store has a modern feel: It is the spitting image of the restaurants shown in Fry House television commercials.

The most remarkable differences between the Green Shirts and Sisters stores, however, are found not in their physical contrasts but in the restaurants' working communities. Workers at the Green Shirts Store articulate a strong "us and them" attitude with respect to their managers and even, at times, their supervisors—a contrast they invoke colloquially by citing the color of the shirts worn by each group in the workplace (managers wear white shirts; supervisors, red; and cooks and cashiers, green). Solidarity in the Green Shirts Store is distinctly color-coded. For example, while workers at many Fry House outlets elect supervisors to be their union stewards, workers at this outlet insist on having a cashier or cook do the job. Workers were incredulous when a supervisor ran for the position during the most recent steward election at the store:

> I thought a shop steward was someone who represents the union and protects you against the white shirts and red shirts. So why the hell would I vote in a red shirt or a white shirt to protect us against [them]?

Needless to say, the cook who ran against the supervisor won the steward job by a landslide.

Even when workers at the Green Shirts Store express sympathy for their managers, they retain their shirt-typing language. "He gets so much slack from the store," one cashier said of her manager. "Chicken's missing, salad's missing, money goes missing, we're short this night, over this night, everyone's telling him to go fuck himself." The cashier says that she is one of the few who listen to the manager when he asks workers to do "extra" job tasks. Why does she listen? Because of the color of his shirt:

You are the boss; this is your job. That's why you have a white shirt [and] I have a green shirt. I'll do what you say. If you go out of reason, I'll tell you to hoof it, but as long as you are in reason.

A recently hired cook at the store says that managers have attempted to counter such "us and them" attitudes in store meetings: "They don't like it when we treat them like they're totally high up, because then people take advantage of it. Like, 'Well, you're a white shirt, so you should do this.' And that's not the way it should be. So they want us to treat them more like they aren't [high up]."

Shirt-typing consciousness in the Green Shirts Store is sometimes coupled with an almost cavalier disregard for official company protocol. Most workers freely help themselves to more food and drinks at work than company policy allows, and a handful of workers run scams stealing money out of drive-through transactions (drive-through skimming is easier than front-counter skimming, because workers' handling of cash in these transactions is less visible to customers, managers, and co-workers). Although other workers resent the tensions that such stealing of money causes in the store, they are resistant to "ratting on" co-workers to their managers. Silent on the matter of theft, workers also cover for one another for unofficial smoke breaks, for leaving the store during a shift to pick up pizza or Slurpees for the crew, or—on particularly slow nights—for hanging out at a bar across the road until a worker at the store signals that extra help is needed.

Despite such activities, it would be a mistake to view the Green Shirt crew simply as a group of oppositional and alienated workers. The store is a high-volume outlet, and workers emphasize their pride in being able to keep up with the pressure—something that workers coming in from other, slower stores often aren't able to handle. Although workers frequently refuse to perform managers' make-work tasks during slow periods, they do work quickly and efficiently during the store's long customer rushes. Workers don't talk much about helping one another in their individual work tasks, but they do talk about working together to create a less stressful environment:

The cooks'll start singing, then everyone'll start singing. Or doing the accents, talking in the accents.... We just make fun of each other. You can't help but laugh; it really takes the stress off you. When it's really busy, you get to go back there [to the kitchen] and start laughing, then go back up front.... We're all doing something silly; all the customers will cotton on, too. It's not so uptight. If we're all uptight, they'll be uptight. If it's more of a calmer, down-to-earth atmosphere, customers calm down, too, which is a lot of help.... [One time], Ralph [a cook] was singing in the back, going on and on, I was just laughing.... So one of the customers said, "I'm trying to order." He starts yelling. [Ralph's] like, "Oh, sorry!" They're yelling back and forth, I'm in the middle.... The customer will be like, "I don't want gravy." [Ralph] will be like, "Oh, yeah. That's not any good anyway."

Workplace fun at the Green Shirts Store, although generally worker-centered, can also involve customers and may alter and even improve the service provided at this particular Fry House outlet.

Workers at the Green Shirts Store do not socialize much outside their store. Some workers say they would be "nuts" to spend any more time with their co-workers than they already do; others just say that it's too hard to fit co-workers in when they have busy schedules and full sets of school and neighborhood friends to see. Nevertheless, workers at the store talk of being "extremely close," and like other Fry House workers, they express a strong identification with their particular restaurant. "I've talked with my [assistant] manager about where she worked before, at other Fry Houses," one young cashier says. "She said, where she was . . . it was totally different. Everything was done the way it was supposed to be, but it almost made it boring." "There was no talking going on, no socializing whatsoever," a co-worker chimes in. "I don't think I'd be able to stand that. I'd want to be able to talk to someone." She adds, "A little chit-chat—I don't see what's wrong with that."

"We're on a big cleaning frenzy right now," a cashier reports from her Fry House restaurant, a small and somewhat decrepit but busy outlet near one of the main stops on Glenwood's subway line. "We're nominated for cleanest store [in the region], and we're really cleaning so we can see if we can win it. 'Cause the more awards you win, the more free dinners you get. It's kinda fun." Although many young Fry House workers are either ambivalent or openly skeptical of the company's many competitions and incentive programs, workers at the Players Store love to compete—and to win. The store has been certified as a "First in Quality" store—a certification that individual restaurants can voluntarily apply for from Fry House and that demonstrates that the restaurant has achieved the highest company standards in customer service, cleanliness, and overall work performance. The store has also won a number of promotional and sales competitions at Fry House, bringing employees free dinners, cash prizes, and other awards.

Workers at the Players Store not only compete and win company competitions; they compete and win in an outlet that, like a number of Fry Houses in Glenwood, has been left without a store manager for more than half a year. One young worker at the restaurant, in fact, contrasts her school and work experiences in terms of the disappearance of authority figures once she came into the world of work:

> Work and school are just two different worlds.... School is people telling you what to do and you do it. Work is more we do what we do.... It's not like there's a manager always over our heads saying, "Now do this, and do this." You just kinda go with the flow.... Once you've been there a while, you know what has to be done, you do it, and it just kinda happens.... If someone's doing something, you help them out. There's not like an authority figure and then the workers.... We're all doing the same thing, except for some of us have less paperwork than others [i.e., the supervisors].

None of the workers I spoke with at the Players Store knew how their store had gotten to be the way it was—although they were well aware of their difference from other stores. The process had essentially snowballed: "We got one award; we thought, great, keep it up, keep it up, keep it up, until we just got better and better and better."

Workers at the store speak of valuing the thrill of competition, the pleasure of being complimented for their accomplishments, and the satisfaction brought by their material gains (which occasionally have been fairly substantial) from winning company competitions. However, more than these factors, they speak of valuing the sense of belonging to a cohesive and committed "team" of workers:

> We all take a lot of pride in our store; I think we really do. We really care about what goes on around there, and how we do financially, and that kind of thing. We all try to make it work the best we can. Actually, I've never seen a store that's that close, that gets along and helps each other that much. It's that teamwork thing we have, which just works for us so well. It's great.

"We're the kind of people in our restaurant," a cashier at the Players Store says, "where if somebody still has garbage to take out and things to clean, and this to do, and that to do, and I'm done everything I'm supposed to do, I'll help the other person out." "Other stores," the cashier adds, "they're not like that." "I know it's pretty weird," reflects another cashier. "But it's fun, you know, and I think that's why everyone's been there so long. Everyone loves the job."

Like young workers at other Fry House outlets, workers at the Players Store have a strong sense of ownership of their store—a sense strengthened by the fact that they work without in-store management and by their feeling that "It's our choice to work the way we do." The ability of workers to take over and possess the social space of their restaurant is symbolized for the Players Store crew (as it is for workers at other outlets) by the private nicknames workers use for one another in the restaurant, by the inside jokes they know and tell, by the gossip and workplace history they share among themselves, and by the fact that workers can listen to their own music while at work.

The drive to succeed in company competitions and the sense of store ownership sometimes puts workers in the Players Store in conflict with customers and corporate management. Company and customers alike infuriate workers when they interfere with in-store efficiency levels. Customers are sometimes indecisive, confused, and slow in ordering their food. "I generally don't like working with the public," says one cashier at the outlet, "because the general populace is stupid." She explains: "They look at a menu board, and then ask you the price of things. They ask you how many pieces of chicken are in a twelve-piece meal, and after a while, you're just like, 'Oh, my god!'" Customers who are recent immigrants and have difficulty speaking and understanding English are singled out in workers' complaints about their jobs. Workers express frustration with Fry House's newly introduced roast chicken, because it is hurting their cooking efficiency: The chicken takes a long time to cook, expires in a fairly short time, and is difficult to predict in terms of how well it will sell. Workers also complain of the occasional stupidity of upper-management decisions. "I swear, sometimes the people that work in the store could run the company better than the people that actually run the company," a young cashier says, "'cause we know what's going on, and we know what people want."

THE MEANING OF STORE-LEVEL SOLIDARITY

What can we make of such variations in workplace communities across the outlets of a single fast-food chain? Are we seeing the failure of a managerial project of centralization of control and routinization of fast-food work? Should we celebrate these different communities as emblems of youth resistance and worker autonomy in the heart of what has often been seen as one of the world's most completely and thoroughly routinized industries?

The story that emerges from the Glenwood Fry Houses is not so simple. The working communities found in the different outlets are not solely the creation of workers; they are the result of interactions among workers, managers, corporate employers, and local environments—as well as the union local that represents these workers. Indeed, store-level solidarities—along with the differences between solidarities that inevitably emerge among stores in a chain when worker identities are focused on co-workers within a single store rather than on the chain as a whole—are, in part, fostered by deliberate company and managerial intervention.

In her study of the routinization of contemporary service work, Leidner (1993: 35) points out that fast-food and other service companies seek not only to routinize the services they offer customers, but also to make routinized services seem individual and spontaneous to customers:

> Since consumers often resent routinized interactions, perceiving them as mechanical and phony, organizations can try to design routines that have some of the qualities of more spontaneous interactions. . . . Sometimes it is the workers' job to deliver with simulated sincerity lines that are clearly scripted. . . . Sometimes the workers are expected to personalize highly routinized interactions with eye contact and a smile, which supposedly constitute "treating the customer as an individual." In other words, the idea is to hide the routinization from service-recipients, to make them believe that the conversation is not scripted.

Leidner focuses on the customer and the service encounter, but her observations are relevant for the service worker and service work writ large, as well. In the Glenwood Fry Houses, company managers seek not only to routinize work, but also to make routinized, chain-store work seem for their employees to be individual, personal, and local.

Fry House employees are literally bombarded with company rhetoric about the importance of being "team members." To a degree, such rhetoric attempts to secure workers' commitment to a global "Fry House team." But more often, the teams in which employees are urged to participate are local and store-based, comprising the co-workers with whom they must cooperate on a regular basis. Companywide competitions and incentive programs typically pit store against store. Which store can pull together and show the most teamwork? Which store can be the best? How does your team rank in comparison with other Fry House teams?

Fry House's sometimes rabid promotion of the team concept draws explicitly on the models of self-managing work teams and other work-participation schemes popular in the manufacturing sector. The high-performance workplace—of a sort—has come to the fast-food industry (Parker 1996; Bailey and Bernhardt 1997). With high performance has come a new managerial strategy for controlling workers and increasing productivity and profits. Companies such as Fry House not only use the forms of technological and bureaucratic control that come through the routinization of work; they also seek to use a form of what James Barker and others call "concertive control":

> [Concertive control] represents a key shift in the locus of control from management to workers themselves, who collaborate to develop the means of their own control. . . . Concertive control becomes manifest as . . . team members act within the parameters of value systems and the discourses they themselves create. These new collaboratively created, value-laden premises (manifest as ideas, norms, and rules) become the supervisory force that guides activity in the concertive control system. (Barker 1993: 411)

Most Fry House outlets in Glenwood operate without a full-time, in-store managerial presence—and some outlets, as with the Players Store, are left for months to run themselves without any store manager at all. Fry House ensures that workers will work hard, first, by deliberately fostering a sense of team membership, store ownership, and distinctive store-based identity among its employees; and second, by using a "just-in-time" labor system, cutting work hours so tightly that workers have to cooperate closely and work hard simply to make it through the workday.

Young workers in the Glenwood Fry Houses are motivated to work in the ways expected in their particular restaurants' communities through the positive desire to be core members of these work communities, and through the negative desire to avoid the ire and censure of their co-workers, should they be viewed as "bad" workers who disrupt preferred ways of working. In both these positive and negative senses, co-workers form the focus of young workers' work attention. Work hard not so much for your corporate employer, Fry House tells its employees; work hard for your co-workers, work hard for your team. This is "your store," corporate owners say, throwing the ball into their employees' court. You can make it as good as you want it to be, and if you try hard enough, you can even become one of the elite stores of the Fry House chain. All workers have to do is ask, and company officials will come to their store, test them, and—if they pass the test—formally certify them as a "First in Quality" store.

Of the Fry House outlets portrayed earlier, the Players Store work community is the easiest to view as a managerially supported work team and as a successful instantiation of the concertive-control model. But in the other stores, too, a sense of pride, co-worker solidarity, and distinctive identity—whether that be the notion that "we cover for one another" in the Sisters Store or the sense that "we can handle the toughest rush there is" in the Green Shirts Store—motivate workers (at times, at least) to work extremely hard in their jobs.

Workplace communities in the Glenwood Fry Houses are not entirely reducible to a managerial agenda of extending workplace control, of course. Young Fry House workers are well aware of their employer's interest in fostering team identities. During interviews, many sought to distinguish their working community from the company's teamwork program. "We're a team," said a cook in the Sisters Store, "but I wouldn't say, you know, 'WE'RE A TEAM!'" By this she meant, among other things, to imply her work crew's ambivalence toward Fry House competitions and incentive programs. Indeed, company competitions and incentive programs, to the degree that they pit store against store, can work to discourage team spirit as much as encourage it: For every store that wins a competition, many more must lose. Stores that find themselves perennial losers can soon grow jaded about such programs:

> There's a lot of people at our store that, when a contest comes out, [they say], "Oh, another one we can lose." 'Cause they put your scores up in the computer, so everybody in [all the Fry Houses in] Canada knows what your score is, and we're always one of the lowest.

Even workers at a winning outlet such as the Players Store insist that their store-level community goes beyond company designs for workplace teams. "We don't help each other out because we saw a training video that says, 'There's no I in TEAM,'" a cashier scoffs. "We help each other out because it's common decency to help somebody out."

More significantly, store-level communities in the Glenwood Fry Houses support practices and attitudes that, if not always completely oppositional to company goals and preferences, are at least separate from and critical of them. Store-level communities generate their own ways of being and doing things in the workplace. These include both the illicit (worker theft, freebies for customers, poaching on company time) and simply the alternative (playing a particular kind of music, organizing the store in a particular way, making local and modest adjustments to dress codes and other official company protocol). Store-level communities generate critiques of company practices. As seen in the Players Store, Fry House workers often argue that they would be able to run their stores better if company managers only listened to them more closely. Fry House workers widely complain of not being paid enough, of not being given enough labor hours, and of not being given enough appreciation or discretion in the handling of abusive customers to put in the high levels of effort in their jobs that they do.

Store-level communities can at times generate collective action among workers in defense of local workplace practices. Fry House managers come and go with great frequency—a fact that has contradictory significance for the strength and development of workers' communities. On the one hand, every time a new manager comes into a store, workers face the need to renegotiate agreements over the terms and practices of their work: We don't care what official company policy says; in this store, we organize our work space in this way, or we sequence work tasks in this manner, or we take our breaks like so. On the other hand, high managerial turnover can also strengthen workers' hand in protecting local practices:

> Usually, because everybody's been there so long, the new [manager] that comes in is always like, "OK, well, what goes on around here? How do

you guys do things?" 'Cause they know we're a store that's been with the same [core] staff for quite a while. . . . Sometimes they'll say, "OK, we're going to try this and do it this way." We'll say, "OK, let's try it, see how that works." If it doesn't work, we'll go back to the old way we used to do it.

Some new managers tread carefully when they arrive at a restaurant, because they know that they must rely at first on an experienced and cohesive staff to keep things moving in what is to them a new and unfamiliar environment.

When new managers fail to respect existing store practices, young Fry House workers can be forceful in their responses. "We're pretty bad for that," a cashier in the Sisters Store says. "The [new] manager comes in; we sit down with them, go, 'OK, look, you can change this and this, but you can't touch this.'" In cases where a restaurant crew decide they don't like a new manager, they will occasionally come together to pressure that manager to leave their store:

> We were trying to get rid of the manager. . . . We made it so bad for him that he had to quit. Not refusing to cooperate, just making it harder, acting in a way, giving him the attitude, but not enough that he can yell at you. Stuff that in the back of his mind, he knows that they don't like doing it and they're not happy. It was pretty much the whole store [working against the manager]. . . . The people that knew he was bad and wasn't good for the store got together.

"It's fun to see," says a cook in another Fry House outlet, who, with six years of work experience under his belt, has seen a steady stream of store managers come and go. "People at our store, they'll complain like that to the [area] manager in a second. If they don't like the new manager, you can tell they're going to rebel right away." "They'll actually stand up [to the manager]," the cook says of his co-workers, and most of the time, "the new manager will crack under the pressure."

Store-level solidarities may thus work both to secure worker consent to employer initiatives and agendas and to spur (locally contained) worker resistance and opposition to these initiatives and agendas. These solidarities are neither accommodationist company loyalties nor broad-based oppositional worker solidarities. They are local, store-based solidarities that exist at the interstices of worker, employer, and manager initiatives. The locally grounded nature of these solidarities is perhaps most clearly articulated in the most forceful critiques young Fry House workers make of their employers. Although workers frequently complain that their employers don't meet their personal needs and interests (in terms of pay, hours, respect, etc.), they often reserve their harshest criticisms for their feeling that their employers aren't meeting the needs and interests of their individual stores.

Workers in the Glenwood Fry Houses constantly ask store and area managers to make needed repairs and replace broken or missing equipment in their stores; managers, with their eyes on tight and strict corporate-determined budgets, are frequently reluctant to respond to these requests unless they feel that repairs and replacements are absolutely necessary. In interviews, many young Fry House workers responded to my questions about the changes they would like in order to make work better for them by focusing first on improvements that could be made in their workplaces—despite the fact that all of these workers identified themselves as stopgap workers who, sooner or later, would be leaving these workplaces. "It's pretty bad when you have to put up cups to prop up the drive-through window," complained one young cashier. "It just makes the store look so cheap, like nobody cares about it." "Maybe [we could get] a new store," a supervisor and college student who knew she would be leaving her Fry House restaurant within a few months said. "This one's a piece of crap. But that's in my dreams, whatever."

DIVISION AND PREJUDICE

Despite the prevalence of store-level solidarities in the Glenwood Fry Houses, there are, of course, differences and divisions that cut across the workforce. Restaurant crews are internally stratified by job category and seniority status. Supervisors in many Fry Houses act as de facto managers, and their responsibilities for scheduling and shop-floor supervision can lead to tension with the rest of their crews. Cooks and cashiers often have semi-separate social circles within overarching store-based communities. Cooks' and cashiers' work tasks are physically and functionally separate, and cooking and cashiering at Fry House are gendered jobs, as the company generally hires men as cooks and women as servers. Cooks and cashiers thus sometimes segregate themselves because they view one another's interactions as being gender-typed. They also sometimes get angry with one another for not pulling their weight on the job: Each side argues that the other doesn't have as much work—or as much "skilled" or "real" work—to do in the restaurant as they do. It is a particularly sore point among cashiers that they are paid slightly less than cooks.

New hires and senior workers can likewise find themselves at odds in the Glenwood Fry Houses. Senior workers (some of whom may still be in their teens) sometimes complain that they have to "babysit" younger and newer workers, because these workers aren't always able to work independently and don't always have the same commitment to their store's success and identity that senior workers do. New hires, for their part, complain that they can't work independently because they have never been properly trained. New hires are also unlikely to feel a strong commitment to their jobs until they feel accepted as full members of their restaurant work communities.

Internal workplace divisions thus exist to some degree in all Glenwood Fry Houses. However, these internal divisions tend to be largely muted by the structural organization of the Fry House labor force and workplace. Tension between supervisors and crews is minimized because many cooks and cashiers are themselves "in-charges" (meaning that they can act as temporary supervisors when needed); many cooks and cashiers share a sense of investment in the success and identity of their restaurants; and many cooks and cashiers are the same age as their supervisors, are friends with their supervisors, and often knew their supervisors before they were promoted to their current positions.

Fry House cooks and cashiers are considerably less segregated than is typically the case with gendered production and service positions in other customer-service workplaces. Because cooking is so highly routinized at Fry House, cooks there do not have the status distinction that cooks in up-market restaurants enjoy. Physical and functional separation of work tasks for cooks and cashiers is actually quite minimal: Cashiers are responsible for many cooking tasks themselves, and thus frequently work in kitchen areas alongside cooks. Food turnover is high and food-production cycles are short in the fast-food industry. This means that the tasks for which cooks and cashiers are responsible are highly interdependent and require close coordination of time and effort. Gendered hiring patterns for cooks and cashiers at Fry House are not as rigid as they are in other service businesses. Fry House, moreover, is increasingly cross-training workers so they can work as both cooks and cashiers.

Divisions between new hires and senior staff in the Glenwood Fry Houses are also frequently minimized—in this case, by high labor turnover. It does not take long for new hires to become accepted as part of a restaurant's core staff (typically a matter of months). Not only do most senior staff see themselves, as new hires do, as stopgap workers, but they also tend to be close in age to their new hires. (In the average Glenwood Fry House, the core staff are in their late teens and early twenties and have about three years of work experience.) Store-level solidarities in Glenwood are therefore supported by an integrated organization of work and muted division of labor.

As in any workplace, Fry House workers bring into the fast-food restaurant external differences and prejudices—differences in age, gender, race and ethnicity, class background, educational status, and personality. Workforce diversity can often add to young workers' work performance and workplace experiences. In many outlets, for example, workers point to the multiethnic, multiracial make-up of their crews as an integral attraction of their work and argue that diverse crews improve the service offered at their restaurants:

> We have pretty much everyone from one part [all parts] of the world [working here]. . . . I'm from Central America; we have somebody from Iran, somebody from Croatia, just different parts. They explain each other's culture to each other. "Oh yeah, in my culture, so and so does this." They open to the other person their culture. . . . Quite often you get a lot of customers, they speak their language, but they're having a lot of trouble [speaking English]; they don't make sense when they order. So if there's a Spanish person, I usually say, OK, and start talking to them, "What would you like?" We have Oriental people working and Filipino and all that. If [customers are] having trouble, we call that person, if that person's on shift, to go help see what [the customers] want.

Indeed, when some young Fry House workers say that their Fry House outlet is different from other outlets, they are referring partly to their restaurant's unique racial and ethnic mix of workers (see also Parker 1996).

But Fry House restaurants are not always pictures of harmony in diversity. Personality conflicts, sexual harassment, elitist attitudes, and age prejudice all emerge sporadically to disrupt and divide worker solidarities. Race tensions, in particular, erupt periodically. Conflicts emerge over workers' differing work habits: Workers accuse others of a different race or ethnicity of not having a "work ethic"; of being overly bossy and domineering; or of being rude and racist in their treatment of customers of different race or ethnicity. Conflicts also arise when race-based joking and ritual insulting among crew members gets out of hand.

Perhaps the most explosive issue related to race and ethnicity in the Glenwood Fry Houses is the use of languages other than English in the workplace. English for many Fry House workers is a second language, and for these workers, the opportunity to speak their mother tongues—Tagalog, Punjabi, Urdu, Mandarin—with co-workers while on the job can help make work more fun and relaxing and easier to handle. For workers who don't understand these languages, however, hearing co-workers speak in what are to them unintelligible tongues can be alienating and even threatening. "I understand them talking [wanting to talk] in their own language," a young Fijian cook—who himself occasionally speaks Punjabi at work—says of his Tagalog-speaking Filipino co-workers. "But sometimes I feel a little bad, ... like hey, they talking about me or what?"

Racial and ethnic—along with other external (age, sex)—divisions do not just fragment store-level solidarities in Glenwood. They also work to reinforce solidarities by excluding certain groups of workers from individual restaurants and causing these restaurants to become increasingly homogeneous in workforce composition. Restaurant homogenization proceeds in two ways. First, managers typically rely on workers' social networks to hire new employees. Workers can thus influence who comes into their restaurant to work, and the people they recommend are often of the same race or ethnicity (or age or sex) as they are.

Homogenization also occurs when workers who do not fit in with a restaurant's core staff are made to feel isolated, excluded, or otherwise uncomfortable, and thus eventually decide to quit their Fry House jobs. One young supervisor who is one-quarter East Indian, for example, transferred out of her first Fry House in part because the majority East Indian workforce there pressured her to date "within her race," and in part because she didn't like her co-workers' habit of speaking Punjabi (which she did not speak) at work. In another restaurant, an East Indian woman quit her job shortly after a Hispanic co-worker left an anonymous letter saying that she had a "very distinctive body odor" and suggesting that she try using deodorant. Exclusion and isolation do not occur only along the lines of race and ethnicity. In a third Fry House restaurant, a woman in her forties quit after only a week or two because she didn't feel comfortable working with—and especially, being supervised by—her predominantly teenage co-workers. As a result of in-migration and out-migration forces, some Fry House restaurants in Glenwood have almost all white, all East Indian, all male, all female, or all youth crews.

Social exclusion in the Glenwood Fry Houses can at times be deliberate, strategic, and conspiratorial. In a couple of restaurants I visited, workers spoke of actively pressuring co-workers whom they felt did not fit in with their work communities to quit or transfer stores:

> It's kind of bad. I hate to say we do this, but there is someone we totally single out at work. . . . We're pretty bad, we sit around and cook up plans to get her to leave. What can we do to get her to quit? It's gotten to the point where . . . [people at work] don't even listen to her anymore. You just ignore her, don't give her any responses, walk away.

Workers claim that they single out individual co-workers because of inadequate work competence and performance: These workers do not or cannot work in the ways demanded by their work communities and are consequently labeled "lazy," "slow," "sloppy," "too serious," or too "by the book" in their work practices. Often, however, workers who are singled out for censure are also separated from their co-workers in terms of external differences of identity. One of the biggest complaints that workers had about the co-worker they were trying to get rid of in the earlier quotation, for example, was that she had been through a series of major illnesses. "She's caused problems with shifts," one cashier explained. "She'll have to go home sick. And she had some illness, she took two weeks off, which put us in a tight situation [with scheduling]."

Store-level solidarities and interstore differences in the Glenwood Fry Houses, then, are sometimes based on workplace exclusion and persecution of individuals and groups of workers. There is a tendency in workplace studies to celebrate workers' communities as being unequivocally positive social forms—especially when these communities are found in highly technological, bureaucratic, and routinized workplaces such as the fast-food restaurant. External social divisions and prejudices in the Glenwood Fry Houses point up the more oppressive aspects of these communities and serve as a reminder that work communities can have negative and harmful, as well as positive, effects on the lives of young workers.

YOUTHS IN FAST FOOD

Three factors particular to Glenwood and the Glenwood Fry Houses likely play a role in strengthening cohesive store-based work communities. First, the Glenwood Fry Houses are small in comparison with other fast-food restaurants, with crews ranging from fewer than ten to a little more than thirty workers. Second, during my research, Glenwood was experiencing high levels of youth unemployment: Young workers were thus staying in their Fry House jobs for longer periods of time than is the norm in the high-turnover fast-food industry. Third, the Glenwood Fry Houses are unionized.

Unionization fosters youth work communities indirectly by making fast-food jobs more attractive to young workers and thereby encouraging and enabling these workers to stay on at their jobs for longer than they otherwise might. Unionization also fosters youth work communities more directly. Local C will intervene in Fry House outlets to insist that incoming managers abide by the collective-bargaining agreement; in some outlets, the local has also intervened to help workers get rid of particularly bad managers. Whereas in non-union stores, the arrival of a bad manager or a series of sudden and unilateral changes in work terms and rules can lead to an exodus of employees, in Glenwood, unionization sometimes helps young workers turn back such adversity and continue in their jobs.[1]

Even with such distinguishing characteristics, however, there is reason to believe that the kinds of store-level solidarities found in Glenwood are also found in other fast-food (and service-industry chain) outlets elsewhere. Newman describes the existence of strong and insular workplace cultures among young fast-food workers in Harlem (although she portrays these cultures somewhat idealistically as being uniform across outlets and as models of worker–manager cooperation and interracial harmony [1999: 102–49]). Leidner argues that "worker culture" is significant in attaching young McDonald's workers to their co-workers and jobs—although she claims that this "peer culture [is] not a unified one that could enforce alternative definitions of adequate work" (1993: 134). Robin Kelley (1994) provides vivid, if anecdotal, descriptions of two strikingly different McDonald's work communities in which he worked as a youth. Finally, Stephen Herzenberg, John Alic, and Howard Wial (1998) report that Taco Bell has experimented with running its stores without full-time managers, relying instead on the development of self-managing teams of workers. Such reduced managerial presence is both a condition that can foster increased solidarity among workers and a strategy that employers are likely to embrace only when employees' store-level solidarities are already strong enough to keep stores running effectively without managers.

The experiences of young Fry House workers in Glenwood may thus have important implications for rethinking popular images of youth labor and fast-food work. Young stopgap workers are often regarded as having limited personal investment in or commitment to their work and as having little agency in their workplaces. The example of Glenwood suggests that solidarity, commitment, and agency are all important aspects of stopgap youth workers' work experiences—although the particular forms that this solidarity, commitment, and agency take can vary considerably.

Sociologists conventionally describe the fast-food industry using the framework of routinization. Researchers point to routinization, along with close managerial supervision and the indoctrination of workers into global corporate cultures, as the key elements of management control in the fast-food workplace. The example of Glenwood suggests that patterns of control and worker–manager relations may be more complicated. Fast-food employers may also seek to control workers—while giving up a measure of their vaunted uniformity—by fostering a sense of local identity, ownership, and control of their individual work sites. From the point of view of young fast-food workers, at least, it may be that interstore differences across fast-food chains are as, if not more, important to their workplace identities and positioning as interstore uniformities.

4   Age in the Grocery Store

> Over the course of the twentieth century, the workplace in which
> young people are employed has become increasingly age-segre-
> gated. Rather than working side by side with adults—adults who
> might serve not only as on-the-job instructors but as confidants
> and mentors—today's young people are more likely than not to
> work side by side with other adolescents. As a consequence, one of
> the most important functions that early work experience may have
> served in the past, namely, the integration of young people into
> adult society, has been considerably eroded. Rather than mingling
> the generations and providing a context for the informal interac-
> tion of young people with their elders, today's adolescent work-
> place has become a bastion for the adolescent peer group.
>
> —Ellen Greenberger and Laurence Steinberg,
> *When Teenagers Work* (1986)

THE CONTEMPORARY youth workplace is often said to be highly
age-segregated. In the alarmist rhetoric of Greenberger and Steinberg
(1986: 79), it has deteriorated into a "bastion for the adolescent peer
group." Invoking the image of the prototypical youth workplace—
the fast-food restaurant—Greenberger and Steinberg raise the specter
of work sites where "sixteen-year-old employees are supervised by
eighteen- or nineteen-year-old 'managers,'" with not an "adult" in sight
(ibid.: 81). "Under these circumstances," the authors warn ominously,
"involvement in a job may not advance the transition to adulthood so
much as prolong youngsters' attachment to the peer culture" (ibid.: 7).
Indeed, Greenberger and Steinberg argue, "It would not be exaggerat-
ing to say that the new adolescent workplace has been just as effective
as the schools in segregating youths from adults" (ibid.: 88).

Looking back nostalgically, Greenberger and Steinberg, along with
many other workplace observers, lament the passing in North America
of an earlier era of workplace apprenticeships—an era in which adults
and youths worked side by side; older generations passed on valued
trade skills, in the shelter of the workplace, to newer generations; and

TABLE 1.   Local 7 Membership Statistics by Age, Box Hill, 1997

	Number of Members	Age Group/ Total (%)
Younger than 20	2,744	23%
20–29	3,505	29%
30–39	2,762	23%
40–49	1,772	15%
50–59	853	7%
Older than 60	396	3%
Total	12,032	100%

Source: Local 7 membership database. Local 7 reports the ages of its members by decade only.

youths entered directly into the workplaces and occupations in which they would remain for the duration of their adult working lives. Whatever truth there may or may not be to this imagined apprenticeship-based society of the past, the notion of a deteriorated, age-segregated youth workplace in the present itself contains a number of largely unreflected-upon assumptions: first, that today's youth workplaces are, in truth, predominantly age-segregated; second, that age segregation is harmful for youths—that is, that youths benefit from the presence of adults in their workplaces and suffer from adults' absence; and third, that adults in a mixed-age workplace will tend to act as "on-the-job instructors," "mentors," and "confidants" to their youthful co-workers.

At first glance, the American grocery industry of the late 1990s would seem to represent a counter-example to the idea that the typical youth workplace is radically age-segregated. As the nation's second-largest employer of high-school-age workers, the grocery industry actually employs about twice as many workers twenty-five and older as it does workers twenty-four and younger (U.S. Bureau of Labor Statistics 1996). In the unionized supermarkets of Box Hill, youths likewise make up a minority—albeit a large one—of the local grocery workforce (see Table 1).

Despite the strong presence of adult workers, however, the contemporary grocery store is in fact highly age-segregated—although not in the simple sense of having an all-youth or even a majority-youth workforce. In the Box Hill chain supermarkets, adults and youths work—

to a degree, at least—side by side. As expected by workplace observers such as Greenberger and Steinberg, young grocery workers in Box Hill often speak of the benefits of the "mingling of generations" in their workplaces and of the intimacy and mentorship they are able to find with their older, adult co-workers. But adults and youths in Box Hill are also often divided from one another through their differential positionings in the grocery workplace. Youths and adults in the grocery store constitute two distinct groups of workers, and these two groups are frequently at odds. For young workers in Box Hill, problems caused by age segregation in the workplace do not arise because the grocery store has become a "bastion for the adolescent peer group." They arise, rather, because young (especially teenage) grocery workers have become a marginalized minority in what is frequently an adult-dominated work space.

THE MINGLING OF GENERATIONS

The (unionized) grocery store is remarkable in many ways in terms of the great diversity in the ages and life stages of its workforce. In the grocery store, high-school students work alongside high-school dropouts, high-school graduates, college students, and college dropouts; they work with young men and women in their twenties and thirties who are starting their own families, making their own homes, building their own lives; with women in their thirties and forties who have been at home raising young children and are now returning to the workforce; with old-timers in their forties, fifties, and even sixties who may have been working in the grocery industry before their high-school-age colleagues were even born; and with retirees, as young as forty but more often older, who have had careers and lives elsewhere and who, attracted by union pensions and health-care benefits, have now come into the grocery industry to finish out their working years. All of these workers, in their great diversity, work together in single stores under the shared identity of being grocery-company employees.

For the youngest workers entering the grocery industry, this diversity of age and life stage in supermarket work communities can be a dramatic and welcome contrast to prior or concurrent experience with highly and narrowly age-stratified school-based communities. Although some young workers in Box Hill find—to their great disappointment or utter delight—that work communities are much the same as school communities, many more find significant differences between the two. Young workers often speak of their move from school to grocery as a form of liberation, because the grocery community provides new opportunities for developing relationships with a whole range of older people.

Young grocery workers in Box Hill speak with pride and pleasure of the work and social relationships they have formed with co-workers and managers in their late teens, twenties, thirties, forties, and up—workers who, most significantly, are all older than they are. Many young workers see these relationships as confirming their sense that they have reached a developmental stage beyond their chronological age. "I'm mature for my age," a young stocker says, in what was a common refrain among young Box Hill workers. "I mostly hang out with older people at work." "I had to grow up real quick; I had a shitty life," says a young deli clerk, who feels she has finally found a social group in her mixed-age deli crew. "I get along better with older people better than I do with people my own age," a bagger says quite simply.

Forming relationships with older co-workers can be both exciting and tentative for young workers, who may initially feel hesitant about approaching "adults" in the workplace—many of whom are in such very different life stages—as peers and friends:

> I was intimidated by [being young at work]. I smoke outside, and someone else from the store would come out and have a cigarette, especially adults, people in their thirties and forties. I'd always feel so awkward; it's like I'd want to say, "Come down and join me." But you know, you can't say that to them. But most, they'd come down anyway and talk to me.

One young deli clerk describes how, even though she feels close to an older co-worker, she still isn't sure whether it is appropriate to ask her to go out socially. "Rosemary [is] almost fifty years old," the eighteen-year-old clerk explains. "Every time I work with her, we find out how we're exactly the same. I call her my mom; I have so much fun with her. . . . I would love to go out [socially] with her, but she's thirty years older than me. How do I say, you know, 'Do you want to go out and do something?'"

Entering the grocery community can be liberating for some young workers because the social categories and divisions and the cultural capital that were so important in high school often have much less significance in supermarket work. Older workers, especially, simply do not participate in such high-school-based economies of meaning. As one young clerk puts it, it no longer matters exactly how old you are when the ages of your co-workers are all over the map. It no longer matters exactly what clothes you wear when your co-workers are all in uniform, share the fashion tastes of different age groups and generations, and simply don't have so much vested in clothing styles as do students in high school:

> In school, you have to worry about peer pressure, about trying to fit in, trying to worry about what other people think, wearing the right clothes, driving the right car. To me, that's just a lot of BS. [At work,] you don't have to worry about what other people think, you don't have to worry about—, you wear uniforms. . . . [That's because] all sorts of people become grocery workers, there's the high-school crowd, you've got your people with families. I think it's all sorts of people, all sorts of age groups, all sorts of ethnic backgrounds, a whole bunch of different people who can come together. And not—, you don't have to worry about how old that person is, or where that person comes from, what kind of family they come from. . . .
>
>   I don't like cliques; I was never in one in high school. That's the one thing I hated about school was the cliques and the way you needed to fit in. At work, there's no cliques. . . . You might have your deli people, but it's not like they just stick with deli people, they won't associate with other people in the bakery or floral [department]. . . . You don't have your cliques or your groups, your skaters over here. We've got all different kinds of people in there. We've got your gossip, we've got your redneck. Nobody cares what you are, and I like that. I like that.

Many other young workers in Box Hill made similar observations. A stocker, for example, described his misery at school—where students were concerned that "so and so wears this brand of jeans, while so and so wears this brand of jeans"—and his comparative relief at being able to hang out with co-workers in their twenties and thirties who don't particularly care who wears what kind of jeans. These are people "you can learn from," the stocker says. "They have life experience."[1]

Indeed, the "mingling of generations" in the mixed-age grocery store can provide young workers not only with new, more diverse and open social relationships, but also with valued learning experiences. Older workers, as well as managers, can act as mentors and confidants to their young co-workers—as Greenberger and Steinberg and other commentators on the youth workplace hoped they would. Older workers teach younger co-workers tricks for getting by and succeeding in the grocery workplace, but they also share their knowledge, experience, and feelings about life outside of and beyond grocery.

For example, a teenage stocker and high-school dropout who wasn't sure what he wanted to do with his life—but who was toying with the idea of becoming a trucker—found a friend and counselor in a fifty-year-old grocery clerk who also worked at his supermarket:

> Elizabeth has been like a mom to me. She used to drive trucks, so I talk to her about truck driving a lot. She's a real nice lady. . . . She's given me a lot of good advice. She probably thinks I don't listen to her, but I do. She doesn't want me to be a trucker. She told me to quit smoking, too! I told her I wanted to get a tattoo on my right arm, she's like, "No, don't do that." I won't listen to her on that one, though. If I get enough money, I'm getting one. . . . But she's outstanding, she's the kind of friend you want.

For many young grocery workers, the "older" co-workers whom they look to learn from may actually be only a year or two older than they are—workers who are just out of high school or who are a grade or two ahead of them. Young workers in Box Hill sometimes talk about how they have been able to meet and befriend older youths in the supermarket whom they feel they would not have been able to meet as easily in their schools or elsewhere. Friendships with older youth co-workers can bring valued access to information about education and employment paths beyond high school, as well as access to new social worlds—to local party or club scenes, drug connections, sexual relationships, and so on.

Youth Marginalization in the Workplace

Young workers speak about age in the Box Hill supermarkets in terms of the opening of opportunities and social interactions, but they also point to age as a factor in their workplace exclusion and marginalization: Many young grocery workers in Box Hill find themselves either on the periphery or altogether outside their grocery stores' central working communities. Youths are marginalized in grocery communities in two principal ways: first, through the departmental organization of the supermarket; and second, through the career structure of the grocery industry.

Unlike in the Glenwood Fry Houses, where work communities are formed primarily at the store level, work communities in Box Hill tend to be based on departments (or job titles): checkers, produce clerks, grocery clerks, deli clerks, bakery clerks, stockers, and baggers all tend to work, socialize, and identify first and foremost with workers from their own departments. This prevalence of departmental over store-based work communities and identities in Box Hill is perhaps to be expected, given the size of most supermarkets. The smallest supermarkets in Box Hill, after all, are almost twice the size of the largest Fry Houses in Glenwood, while the largest grocery stores are more than twenty times the size of Glenwood's smallest Fry Houses. In large grocery stores, many young workers do not even recognize all of their co-workers, let alone know their names or share work histories and practices with them.

Strong departmental identities follow not solely from store size, however. They also follow from the spatial, social, and economic organization of work in Box Hill supermarkets. Supermarket departments each have their own defined work spaces: Checkers work at the "front end" of the grocery store; deli, bakery, and floral clerks work in "side departments"; and produce and grocery clerks work "in the back." Such spatial separation is reinforced by functional separation—what John Walsh (1993: 132) has identified as the "relatively low interdependence among [supermarket] departments." Side departments often have their own cash registers, for example, so workers there can serve and sell to customers without needing cooperation from workers in other departments. Moreover, unlike the Glenwood Fry Houses, where there is considerable cross-training of workers, grocery workers in Box Hill (with the exception of stockers) work exclusively in their own departments. Indeed, grocery workers are divided from one another in Box Hill by large differences in the relative status and wages of separate departments—ranging from meat cutters and produce clerks at the top to stockers and baggers at the bottom.

Departments in the Box Hill supermarkets, finally, are strongly segregated by gender—checking and side-department work are widely seen as women's work, while produce and grocery (dry goods) department work are seen as men's work—and by age. Bagging jobs, though held by increasing numbers of retirees and adult immigrants, remain clearly identified in Box Hill as jobs for high-school-age (or younger-than-eighteen) workers, both male and female. These jobs are so strongly age-typed, in fact, that youths who are still working as baggers when they turn eighteen often start to feel self-conscious about still having a "kiddy job." Stocker jobs are also identified as youth jobs—as jobs primarily for men in their late teens (women in their late teens tend to work in side departments). The remaining jobs in the supermarket are all negatively age-typed: deli, bakery, and floral jobs are generally seen as not being jobs for workers younger than eighteen; and checker and produce- and grocery-clerk jobs are typically seen as not being jobs for workers younger than twenty.

Because of the departmentalization of supermarket work, young workers in Box Hill—especially teenagers—often find themselves separated from adult workers in terms of their work responsibilities, pay, status, spatial location, and social networks. The wages for baggers and stockers place young workers in these departments in a class far below the adult-dominated classifications of checker and produce and grocery clerk: Baggers are paid just 40 percent and stockers just 50 percent of the top department wages in the supermarket. (By comparison, only a 5 percent differential separates the wages of the top and bottom job classifications in the Glenwood Fry Houses.) Baggers' and stockers' work tasks, similarly, are widely seen in the grocery store as being simpler, less skilled, and less important than the work tasks performed by those in adult-dominated departments.

Bagging places young workers quite literally on the outer edges of grocery work communities: Baggers work primarily at the front end, and even outside, of supermarket buildings, in adjacent parking lots (collecting grocery carts). "It's such a big store," one young bagger says, explaining why she has little knowledge of her co-workers in other departments:

> Most people, you don't really see them. . . . It took me a couple of months to realize where certain people did work. I just knew they were around occasionally. They're back behind doors in the back, and I'm sorta stuck up front.

Baggers have greater freedom of movement in the supermarket than many of their adult co-workers—who are largely confined to check-stands or department counters. But equally, baggers have no space in the supermarket to call their own: The space in which they move is almost entirely public space. In the spatial symbolism of the supermarket, baggers are still semi-outsiders to the world of the workplace, whose movements remain concentrated in those areas consigned to supermarket customers.

Stockers, too, experience something of this blend of homelessness and freedom of movement in the grocery store. Stocking work can bring stockers into contact with workers all over the supermarket, but it can also isolate stockers from their co-workers, because they spend much of their time working by themselves, filling shelves on the supermarket floor. Consequently, stockers, like baggers, can sometimes be left "out of the loop" in the circulation of information among older and more experienced grocery employees. "The only reason I'm plugged in," an eighteen-year-old produce clerk says, "is because of the position I'm in [having a job in the produce department], which is unusual [for a teenager]":

> Stockers, they are like jerked around all the time [by managers] just because they're low, they're young. . . . I know so much about what goes on, how things should be run, just from being in the back room with all these people that have been there forever. I know all this stuff, hearing em talk about it. . . . They [stockers and baggers] have no clue as to what's going on. . . . There's a big separation between older people and younger people [working in the store]. . . . Most [people my age] are baggers, stockers. They're separated, they don't talk to any of the older people. Older people are just people they see working, not to talk to or say hi to—stockers a little bit more, but baggers especially.

The produce clerk tries to pass along information when he can to his friends who are still working as stockers and baggers: "If someone says, 'They're making me do this,' and I know that's not the way it's supposed to go, I'll say, 'You shouldn't. Don't do it. It's not your job; it's not your responsibility.'" For some stockers, the clerk even says, "I'll talk to managers [on their behalf]." But beyond this, according to the young produce clerk, young stockers and baggers in his store are often left in the lurch.

Young workers in Box Hill are also marginalized by grocery-industry career structures. Unlike fast-food jobs—which in the Glenwood Fry Houses, as elsewhere, are seen as being prototypically "youth jobs" (despite the presence of older workers)—grocery jobs in Box Hill are seen as being held by two distinct categories of people: "lifers": older, long-term employees who constitute the core of the grocery workforce and who usually work as close to full-time hours as they can during the weekdays, and "students," or younger stopgap and peripheral employees who are prototypically high-school students working part time during non-weekday hours as they make their way through school. Many grocery workers fall between these two categories, of course, but the categories normatively structure how workers identify themselves and are identified by others in the grocery workplace. The grocery workforce, in terms of age and life stage, is distinctly two-tiered (Hochner et al., 1988; Hughes 1999).

As with departmental divisions, career-status differences generally form an open-ended focus for Box Hill workplace communities—that is, younger, temporary workers tend to work, identify, and socialize more with other young, temporary workers than they do with older, permanent workers (and vice versa). Career-status differences, in fact, introduce a temporal dimension to the age geographies of the grocery store. Whereas teenage women may work in the same supermarket bakeries and delis as do older women, for example, younger and older workers in these and other departments often work different shifts: Older, permanent workers tend to work weekday shifts, while youths and students are most likely to work irregular hours in the evenings and on weekends. Between 3 P.M. and 5 P.M. on weekdays in Box Hill, and between the Friday and Saturday day shifts, the average age of workers on the grocery shop floor can drop suddenly and dramatically.

In some Box Hill supermarkets, career-status solidarities, like department solidarities, can produce social divisions and hostility between younger and older workers. As a young deli clerk explains of her fractious supermarket deli staff, the combination of (worksite-external) age prejudices and (worksite-internal) age-based shift divisions can make workplace interactions between workers of different ages and life stages particularly nasty:

> The morning crew [in the deli] and the night crew don't get along, and the morning crew is older ladies, and then the night crew is younger people.... They don't like each other, they always telling on each other: day crew didn't do this or night crew didn't do that. It's like two generation gaps between them, because there's old people in their forties, and then young people in their twenties.... They [the older workers] talk about us, like, "They talk too much and they're lazy." ... You'd think old

people would wanna give young people some wisdom, you know. Not them; they want to keep it all to themselves and act mean toward us, snotty, give us the shoulder, talk behind our backs. . . . They talk, too, you know—they talk, laugh, they be eating food while they make the party trays [which they're not supposed to do]. . . . We just don't tell on them because we don't care.

Popular discourses that portray youths as lacking a work ethic or sense of responsibility color some older workers' views of their younger co-workers. For their part, younger workers sometimes tread on popular discourses of the universal possibility of individual upward mobility in America and look on older grocery co-workers as having personally failed in some way in their career trajectories. "The deli," this young deli worker, a student who is training to become a nurse at a local Box Hill college, says derisively of her older deli co-workers, "is their *life!*"

In addition to such prejudices about the work performance and work orientation of youth workers and lifers, beliefs about preferential managerial treatment and feelings of job competition can further entrench age-based divisions in the workplace. Older grocery workers in Box Hill often express sympathy for their younger co-workers and feel that store managers abuse younger workers because they have not yet learned how to stand up for themselves in the workplace. But, on the other hand, some grocery workers in Box Hill—both young and old—feel that younger workers sometimes are actually treated better by supermarket managers than are older workers.

There are several reasons that young workers may occasionally receive preferential treatment in the grocery stores. The deli clerk quoted earlier, for example, notes that managers in her store cut younger workers more slack, grant younger workers more favors, and praise younger workers more than they do older workers. The reason, she suggests, is that "we're the younger ones coming in, and they [the managers] want to keep their people at Good Grocers." In other words, some young grocery workers may be able to get their way more often with managers than can older workers because the managers may be interested in trying to keep young workers—as self-identified temporary workers—from leaving their employ. Managers may neglect older workers because, as long-term or permanent workers, they have no special need to be persuaded to stay on. Or, alternatively, managers may actively prefer younger workers because they tend to be less expensive and (possibly) fresher—that is, less jaded and tired by accumulated work experience.

Casual conversations with store managers and union staff in Box Hill suggest that managers may occasionally be willing to cut young middle-class workers, in particular, more slack than they do older workers. Union representatives claim that managers of supermarkets in middle-class neighborhoods let their young workers (who tend to come from middle-class families in the surrounding neighborhoods) get away with more than do managers of supermarkets in poor and working-class neighborhoods. Reps offer several reasons for this discrepancy: managers in middle-class neighborhoods generally face tighter labor markets, and thus do what they can to hang on to their workers; managers in middle-class neighborhoods are likely to know and respect the parents of the youths who work in their stores and are thus loathe to cross or upset their young employees; and managers in middle-class neighborhoods see the young workers in their employ as being grocery workers only temporarily—they fully expect these workers to grow up to become members of the middle class and, consequently, to become future valued customers (see also Hughes 1999).

While temporary and permanent grocery workers in Box Hill tend mutually to reinforce the differences (and in some cases, the divisions) between them, it is the permanent grocery workers who stand at the center of supermarket social networks. (Permanent workers also dominate grocery union positions and agendas, as will be seen in Chapter Six.) One of the clearest symbols of this dominance can be found in the planning of supermarket social events. Although held infrequently (a couple of times a year, usually), store social events constitute direct representations for young workers of their peripheral status in grocery work communities:

> We [our store] had a little party at the Blue Moon Club [this Christmas], but minors weren't included. So I felt kinda bad, you know. I was going to go, but then I read on the paper, "No minors allowed." I can understand why, because [the party was held at] a club that serves alcohol. I mean, it was no hard feelings by any of us because it was, like, half of us [underage workers] probably wasn't going to go anyway. But I was going to go. So it was just, like, oh well, you know, Thursday night, we can go out and do something else.

At supermarkets throughout Box Hill, young workers complained that store social events were held in places that they were unable to get to (because they did not have cars); that older workers would disappear at store social events into bars that didn't allow minors to enter; or that younger workers simply weren't encouraged by managers and older workers to attend store social events.

At one supermarket, a couple of teenage stockers responded to this sense of social exclusion by organizing a separate store party for younger workers:

> We said, forget this—we're throwing a party for underaged employees, for just us, on our own time. We planned it ourselves, used our own money. It was not affiliated with the store; we had to do it ourselves.

"There's so much tension in our store," one of the stockers explained, "we could really use a store party, where everybody's mixing together, having a good time." If their store wouldn't throw a party that included younger workers, the stockers decided, they would have to do it for themselves.

The exclusion of young stopgap workers in Box Hill from store social events primarily has a symbolic significance—and young workers, as seen here, can sometimes create their own matching social events. Likewise, the marginalization of some young grocery workers from in-store social and information networks can, to an extent, be made up for through the creation of parallel and adjacent networks among young, temporary workers themselves. But the marginalization and exclusion of young stopgap workers from union positions and agendas in Box Hill—a marginalization and exclusion that both follows from and leads to marginalization and exclusion of young stopgap workers within grocery work communities, as will be discussed in Chapter Six—limits young grocery workers in ways that they, having no alternative avenues of collective, formal representation, are simply unable to overcome.

THE GROCERY BAGGER

Youths in the Box Hill grocery store are not just a distinct social group. They are a marked social group. Youth behavior in the supermarket is constantly commented upon, judged, and, quite frequently, complained about by older workers, managers, customers, and union staff. The behavior of young workers, moreover, is on display in the workplace as representing some essential nature of youth. If an adult grocery worker is lazy, late, careless, or irresponsible, or if he or she likes to play around, that worker's behavior is rarely said to reveal some truth about adulthood. Rather, that worker is likely to be called a bad or, possibly, a disgruntled or alienated worker. If, on the other hand, a young grocery worker exhibits the same set of behaviors, these are likely to be said to be caused by that worker's youth—and by implication, by his or her immaturity. Similarly, a young worker who shows himself or herself to be a responsible and serious worker is likely to be called not just a good worker, but a worker who is particularly "mature for his (or her) age."

This manner of evaluating the work behaviors of young grocery workers serves, of course, to maintain and reinforce popular and negative stereotypes about youth as workers. Youths are frequently said to lack a work ethic, to have poor work attitudes, and to lack commitment to their jobs; youth labor is generally seen as being unskilled labor and, therefore, as lacking in value and status. In this section, I analyze how structures internal to the supermarket construct youth as a relevant (and subordinate) social category in the workplace and work further to maintain and reinforce these popular stereotypes. The key site for this internal workplace construction of youth as a meaningful category is found in the job position of the grocery bagger, for it is the behaviors and stances of high-school-age baggers, more than that of any other group of young grocery workers, that are the object of attention and concern when stereotypes of youth start getting bandied about in the Box Hill supermarket.

Bagging, as I have noted, is clearly identified in Box Hill as a youth job. As a rule, Box Hill supermarkets claim not to hire teenagers younger than eighteen for any other position. Many stores invoke state and federal child-labor laws as central reasons for this de facto segregation of high-school-age labor in their workplaces: Child labor laws prohibit workers younger than eighteen from working with dangerous machinery, and most other jobs in the supermarket involve some such "dangerous" work (e.g., with ovens in the bakery, meat slicers in the deli, trash compactors and balers in stocking jobs).[2] Some baggers thus blame the state rather than their employers for their inability to move up into other (higher-paying) grocery departments:

Once I turn eighteen, I can work in all of the departments. I can't use most of the equipment till I'm eighteen. . . . If it was an ideal job . . . I would be able to put things in the garbage can [and be a stocker]. I'm not allowed to touch the garbage crusher, 'cause I have to be eighteen. Which is like, yeah, I'm going to throw myself in there. . . . I don't think when I turn eighteen I'm gonna get a brain. I kinda thought I had one already. But I guess the law thinks I have to be eighteen to have one.

Grocery stores' invocations of child-labor laws to restrict high-school-age youths to bagging positions are actually quite arbitrary. In practice, Box Hill supermarkets do employ minors in departments other than bagging, and although some do so in violation of child-labor laws, most easily accommodate these laws by asking minors to leave those few tasks that they are legally prohibited from performing to their older co-workers. Child-labor laws, in this context, are thus significant to Box Hill employers primarily for their role in legitimizing and naturalizing—through invoking the authority of the state—arbitrarily restrictive hiring practices. High-school-age youth, by way of government law, come to be defined in the Box Hill grocery store as being inherently able to do nothing more than bagging work.

The bagging work that high-school-age youths are consigned to perform is the lowest-status, lowest-paid, least-independent, and—at least in its official job description—least-demanding, and most boring work there is to do in the supermarket. One of a bagger's primary responsibilities is to assist checkers (with bagging groceries, running price checks, exchanging damaged items, finding products that customers couldn't find on the shelves, and returning products that customers decide they don't want). This means that baggers, unlike other grocery workers, in effect have two sets of bosses: checkers and store managers. It also means that baggers are rarely able to get through a shift without having some other worker tell them what they should be doing. Baggers' general checker-assistant role is ripe for abuse, for it is all too easy for checkers to treat baggers as personal go-fers whose only responsibility is to wait on them individually, hand and foot.

In addition to being general checker assistants, baggers are also store janitors, responsible for emptying trash cans, doing clean-ups and floor sweeps, and—most disliked of all—cleaning staff toilets. For many Box Hill baggers, these janitorial duties are a stark reminder that their rank in the supermarket is, as one bagger put it, the "lowest of the low":

> The baggers here . . . they don't get respect. They do everything, garbage, hey, do this for me, do this for me, bag here, bag there, carts. When you're a bagger, you're the slave of the store.

"Bagging is basically doing all the little things no one else wants to do," says one bagger. "If a job's worth doing, it's worth doing, but if it's not, we give it to the bagger kind of thing." Slavery, in fact, is widely used by young Box Hill workers as a metaphor to refer to the position and role of baggers in the grocery store. When high-school-age youths are identified solely as baggers, and when bagging is identified as proto-typically (high-school-age) youth work, the characteristics of bagging jobs all too easily rub off on people's evaluations of (high-school-age) youths as workers: These youths come to be seen and treated as a class below the rest of the grocery workforce.

The identification of baggers as high-school-age youths—and the cor-responding identification of managers and checkers as adults—often leads to manager–bagger and checker–bagger interactions that are mod-eled on parent-child interactions. Baggers in Box Hill widely complain that they are talked to at work as if they were "four years old." Some complain of micro-management and the tendency of managers and older workers to hyper-explain work tasks to them:

> [Baggers] are usually treated as not being very intelligent. . . . Sometimes they [managers] dumb things down a lot, like, "You need to go, and there's the mop in the broom closet with the bucket of water, and I want you to mop the floor. Do you want someone to help you with it?" I'm like, I can mop the floor. "Do you know how to do a floor sweep?" I'm like, yeah, I just take the broom and run it across the floor. . . . "Do you know what a go-back is? Do you know where these items are? Do you want a map? Can you do this? Do you want me to get someone else to do it?"

Many grocery workers in Box Hill also feel that baggers are disciplined and ordered around by managers (and some checkers) in ways that never would happen to older workers in other departments. One young bakery clerk, for example, was particularly upset by her store managers' way of treating baggers as if they were small children:

> When I say they [baggers] are treated like the manager is their mom or dad, it's well, "You know what you should be doing!" I've seen 'em yell at 'em, in front of customers, away from customers. In my opinion, there

should never be a time that a manager should ever yell at a worker; that is just not appropriate. I mean, mommy does that, but managers don't.

By their very job position in the supermarket, baggers are singled out for differential age-based treatment. Their behavior in the grocery store thus often responds to a different level and type of management than is experienced by older, adult workers in other departments.

The flip side of managers' (and checkers') treating baggers as children is that managers, older workers, and even young workers themselves often come to expect and accept that young baggers will, in fact, act like children in the workplace. Managers sometimes tolerate behavior among baggers—food fights, "goofing around" on the job, or disappearing into neighboring arcades to play video games while supposedly collecting carts in the parking lot—that they would not be likely to tolerate nearly so well among older workers. Many young grocery workers in Box Hill who started as baggers and since have been promoted to higher positions say that it was only with their promotions that they really became—and felt, for the first time, expected to be—committed and serious workers. As one stocker (and reformed bagger) puts it: "As baggers, you're just kids. All you are is a bagger. Nobody really cares what you do or where you are."

There are other, more indirect ways in which the bagger position reinforces popular negative stereotypes of youth workers. Managers and older grocery workers often complain that youths/baggers are lazy and unmotivated at work. Baggers, however, point out that it is the structure of their work scheduling and responsibilities that can cause such impressions:

> [Checkers] are always complaining to the manager about us baggers, saying that we're lazy. I think, there's only two baggers working at one time, or one, and there's four checkstands open. We can't bag for all four of them at the same time.

There are never as many baggers on the grocery floor as there are checkers: thus during customer rushes, checkers often feel that baggers aren't doing their work properly because they find themselves having to bag some of their customers' groceries on their own. During lulls, baggers find themselves in a Catch-22. If they leave the checkstand area to take care of other tasks, they frequently find themselves paged over the store intercom as soon as a checker has a customer whose groceries need bagging—and they are often accused when they return to the front-end area of "disappearing" and "goofing off." If, on the other hand, they wait around the checkstand area for customers to come through the checkout lines, they are just as likely to be accused of "counting tiles [on the ceiling]" and "slacking off."

Managers and older grocery workers sometimes complain that youths/baggers are not committed to their jobs and are more oriented to their lives outside the workplace than they are to store work communities. However, as I noted earlier, baggers are physically and socially marginalized in the grocery store. Their very job position militates against full membership and involvement in the workplace community. Two other factors contribute to such workplace isolation. First, turnover in the grocery store is largely concentrated in the bagging department. Many baggers, possibly because of the poor conditions and subordinate nature of bagging work, quit after only a week or two. Grocery workers in other departments say they feel as if baggers are always coming and going, and they often take much longer to introduce themselves and interact with new baggers than they do with new workers in non-bagging departments: Many wait until baggers have been on the job for at least a good number of weeks.

The second factor limiting baggers' workplace involvement is store managers' tendency to hire more baggers than they really need. Managers are loath to sacrifice flexibility in their scheduling options and are also well aware of the high turnover among baggers. Thus, they tend to overload on hiring baggers. As a consequence, baggers often find that they are unable to get as many hours as they would like, and some find—particularly during the slow winter months—that they can be working as little as one four-hour shift per week. Such managerial overhiring and underscheduling do little to foster strong workplace involvement among baggers.

Baggers are paid the lowest wages in the grocery store—only slightly above minimum wage—and are thought by many grocery workers to be responsible primarily for the repetitive task of bagging customers' groceries. Low wages, low status, and young age, however, conceal the fact that baggers actually perform some of the most important work in the grocery store. As one Box Hill bakery clerk observes:

> Baggers are the worst paid [in the supermarket]. They're just baggers.
> And [yet] they talk to customers all the time. They talk more to cus-

tomers than we do, cause they have to take 'em out and load 'em up [carry customers' groceries out to their cars]. They see what their cars looks like, see who's in the car, basically get to know the family. They're just baggers, but they should be paid more.

All of the Box Hill chain supermarkets now emphasize improving customer service as a key competitive strategy, and baggers play a critical role in this strategy. Baggers are responsible for "carry outs," which puts them in a position to talk with customers as they leave the store and to provide customers with their all-important final impressions of their supermarket visits.

Baggers do far more than carry-outs. Many baggers in Box Hill are of minority backgrounds and speak languages other than English: Spanish, Russian, Thai, Tagalog, Vietnamese, and so forth. When customers need help with translation, it is baggers who are often called on for interpretation duties. Similarly, when customers have other special service requirements, it is often baggers who are called on to help out. Several baggers I interviewed, for example, said they regularly helped senior citizens walk around their stores and find everything they needed. The very performance of these and other such services—let alone their value—is all too often overlooked because of a self-perpetuating tautology that links young age with low value (or low skill) with low pay.

The job category of bagging in the Box Hill supermarkets, then, (re)produces identities, stances, and behaviors that clearly match the identities, stances, and behaviors that are popularly and negatively attributed in our society to young workers. One telling sign of the closeness of this reproduction is that many grocery workers in Box Hill—even those who are sympathetic to high-school-age workers or are themselves young and have worked, or are working, as baggers—have a hard time telling when certain behaviors and stances are caused by the bagging position and when they are caused by the baggers' youth:

> You don't see a lot of us doing other jobs. You see most of the teenagers in there [the supermarket] as baggers or stockers. You don't see them working in the deli, or at the checkstand, or in the meat department, because who's gonna hire somebody my age, a teenager, to work in those big positions? They're [teenagers] put in those positions where they're treated—, they're at the lowest part of the triangle. . . . I think if a teenager goes in there and they're treated like a teenager, how are they supposed to grow and become more mature, more an adult? . . . But a lot of 'em [teenage baggers] *aren't* mature; a lot of 'em don't want to work,

either. I mean, I don't know if that's the cause of the way they're treated or what. But a lot of 'em don't—, they just want the bagger position so they can goof off and do nothing and get paid to just sit around and talk to one another. I don't know. I guess it just depends on the individual.

Do young baggers act out, avoid working, and fail to take their jobs seriously because the work they are asked to do is shitty work and because they are treated so poorly in the grocery store? Or do they act out and not take their jobs seriously because they are young and not yet ready for real responsibility? Attempts to separate out youth as an essential identity from institutional structures and social settings are bound to be futile and self-defeating, for age itself is a social production created through interactions in the context of social institutions (Laz 1998). In Box Hill supermarkets, (high-school-age) youth is actually constituted by the position of grocery bagger—in the context of other work-site-external and -internal age-shaping and -constituting structures. To be a high-school-age youth in the Box Hill grocery store is, after all, to be a grocery bagger, and to "act one's age" as a high-school-age teenager is to act as a grocery bagger acts.

AGE SEGREGATION IN THE CONTEMPORARY YOUTH WORKPLACE

It is instructive to compare the nature of age segregation in the Box Hill supermarkets and the Glenwood Fry Houses, for age segregation in the youth workplace is not always and everywhere the same. The Glenwood Fry Houses come much closer than the Box Hill supermarkets to being the "adolescent strongholds" described by Greenberger and Steinberg at the outset of this chapter: More than two-thirds of the Glenwood Fry House workforce are younger than twenty-five. It is far from clear, however, that young fast-food workers in Glenwood suffer the effects of age segregation more—as Greenberger and Steinberg suggest they should—than do their counterparts in the Box Hill chain supermarkets.

There are parallels in workplace age structuring in Glenwood and Box Hill. Most Fry House restaurants have older (mostly female) workers in their thirties, forties, and fifties as part of their crews. On the one hand, these workers often become friends, mentors, and allies of their younger co-workers. On the other, these older workers are sometimes set against younger workers. As noted in the previous chapter, new hires and senior workers in the Glenwood Fry Houses sometimes come into conflict over work performance, commitment, and scheduling. Older, adult workers sometimes have negative views of the work ethic of their younger co-workers. Young Fry House workers, for their part, occasionally complain of older workers trying to claim authority in the workplace simply because they are older—even though younger workers may have more seniority and Fry House work experience. Young Fry House workers also sometimes look down on their older, adult co-workers for working in a job that they see as being fit only for youths who are on their way to bigger and better careers. As in Box Hill, older workers in Glenwood tend to work weekday shifts, and younger workers evening and weekend shifts, so that inter-shift conflicts are at times overlaid with age-based prejudice.

Despite such parallels, though, the significance of age and age difference in Glenwood contrasts radically with Box Hill. First, youths make up the majority of the Fry House workforce: In most outlets, adult workers constitute a small, if important, minority. Second, youths and adults in Glenwood are not segregated by departmental divisions. Although supervisors tend to be slightly older than cooks and cashiers, there are plenty of teenage supervisors in Glenwood. No Fry House job category has a clear age marking. Adults and youths in Glenwood work in the same job categories and are not differentiated in terms of status, pay, space, or work responsibility.

The third contrast between Box Hill and Glenwood is that, whereas the grocery workforce in Box Hill is symbolically split between "lifers" and "students," fast-food jobs in Glenwood are generally seen by workers as entry-level jobs—primarily for youths, but also for recent immigrants (see also Parker 1996). This is not to say that there are no long-term workers in the Glenwood Fry Houses: There are workers in Glenwood with more than twenty years of Fry House experience. Indeed, some young stopgap workers in Glenwood themselves stay with their Fry House jobs for three, five, or even eight years before moving on to jobs and careers elsewhere. But there is no core–periphery structure in Glenwood of (older) lifers and (young) stopgap workers. Fast-food jobs in Glenwood are quintessentially youth (and increasingly, immigrant) jobs; young stopgap workers are generally at the center of each Fry House restaurant's working community.

The central positioning of young Fry House workers in their restaurant communities has clear significance in Glenwood for age relations within the workplace. Although in most Fry Houses, older, adult workers are full and often dominant participants in youthful workplace communities, in outlets where young and adult workers are experiencing tensions, it is generally adult workers who end up being marginalized and excluded—and who are positioned by their younger co-workers as a marked social group whose behaviors are to be observed, complained about, and commented upon. The young Fry House workers' central positioning has perhaps even greater significance outside the workplace, in union-member relations and activities. As will be discussed in Chapter Seven, youths in Glenwood, as core members of their restaurant crews, have to some degree been able to move into leadership roles within their union. And as a clear majority in the Fry House workforce, youths in Glenwood have also caused Local C to pay close attention to their workplace interests in its collective-bargaining and contract-administration practices.

5   Stopgap Work Cultures

> [One] way of dealing with a tedious and unrewarding job is to see
> it as a stop-gap measure that merely fills in time until you can go
> on to better things. This kind of adaptation involves a low commit-
> ment to the job, planned instability, and not having to accommo-
> date your sense of self to your job.
>
> —Jane Gaskell and Marvin Lazerson,
> "Between School and Work" (1981)

> Early jobs are often not part of an institutionalized career path but
> instead represent a particular type of "stopgap job"—a job which is
> often dominated by workers who, for life-cycle related reasons,
> have marginal labor market and job attachments. The youth in
> these jobs are frequently combining employment with school atten-
> dance and may, depending on the circumstances, continue in these
> jobs for a period after leaving school or between schooling spells.
> . . . Stopgap jobs are poor predictors of later job type and status.
>
> —Valerie Oppenheimer and Matthijs Kalmijn,
> "Life Cycle Jobs" (1995)

YOUNG GROCERY and fast-food workers in Box Hill and Glenwood are, for the most part, stopgap workers. Young workers at these
sites expect or hope that their grocery and fast-food jobs will be temporary places of employment and largely discontinuous with their adult
careers and identities. They see their jobs as being "youth jobs"—and
little more. To call these young workers "stopgap workers," then, is to
characterize their subjectivities as workers and describe the way they
position and orient themselves in the workplace. As Gaskell and Lazerson suggest, stopgap work orientations among young workers are
essentially "ways of dealing" or "strategies of coping" with tedious,
low-status, and low-wage work. It is, after all, easier to accept such
work if one believes, or reminds oneself, that it is only temporary.

Though they may be "ways of dealing" and "strategies of coping,"
stopgap work orientations among young grocery and fast-food workers

in Box Hill and Glenwood are not altogether unrealistic. In past eras, the "myth of the temporary stay" was a central part of the early work experiences of young working-class men and women as they moved directly from school into manufacturing jobs—jobs that, despite these workers' best intentions and highest aspirations, often did become permanent or long-term places of employment (Chinoy 1992 [1955]; Pollert 1981). But grocery and fast-food jobs in the 1990s are not the manufacturing jobs of the past. Middle- and working-class youths alike enter grocery stores and fast-food restaurants looking for temporary employment, as age more than class shapes who takes on such work. Although some youths do "get stuck" in grocery and fast food, most eventually move on to other occupations and identities, some of which will be working-class and some middle-class.

Thus, young grocery and fast-food workers are also stopgap workers because the majority are likely to work only temporarily in these jobs, and most will move on to other careers and identities that are more or less discontinuous with their youthful places of employment. To an extent, stopgap work orientations match stopgap work realities. To call young grocery and fast-food workers "stopgap workers" is to characterize the likely place of grocery and fast-food jobs in these young workers' life courses. As Oppenheimer and Kalmijn write, stopgap jobs are distinguishable by being "poor predictors of later job type and status." Youths in North America work predominantly in a narrow band of low-end service-sector jobs; when youths move into adulthood, however, the occupations in which they work are all over the map (Jacobs 1993; Myles, Picot, and Wannell 1993).

There is a third sense in which young workers in Box Hill and Glenwood are stopgap workers: Their employers expect them to work only temporarily in the grocery and fast-food industries. Both grocery and fast-food employers these days make noise about the costs of high labor turnover and the need to improve labor retention at their work sites. But these employers are mostly talking about their desire to improve stability in stopgap workforces—to have workers stay in their jobs for a year or two rather than a week or two—and not about any wish to create fully careerist workforces or to take on the social and financial responsibilities that such workforces would bring. Grocery and fast-food employers have positioned themselves in the youth labor market for a reason, of course: These industries consider the ability to rely on a steady supply of young, temporary workers who can be paid low wages highly cost-effective and highly profitable.

In this chapter, I present a general framework for describing the stopgap work cultures of young grocery and fast-food workers in Box Hill and Glenwood. Workplace cultures have been described in the sociological and anthropological work literature primarily for older workers in professional, crafts, and manufacturing occupations—but rarely for young workers in the low-end service sector. My concern is to describe how young workers, as stopgap workers, are positioned and position themselves within their places of work. I focus in particular on the issue of how stopgap work cultures shape the nature of youth consent and resistance to the grocery and fast-food work process.

Stopgap status is commonly thought to be linked with increased passivity in the workplace. As James Tucker writes in his study of young, temporary, college-bound and college student workers, for example:

> Transiency . . . allows aggrieved employees, knowing they will depart the organization at some time in the near future, to endure unpleasant experiences. It is simply not worth exerting energy on matters that will disappear in the normal course of events anyway. Besides, if the problem is unbearable, the option of departing prematurely and securing employment elsewhere is often available. (1993: 40)

As can be seen in this chapter's epigraphs, stopgap status is also typically assumed to engender low levels of workplace investment among young workers—"low job commitment" in the words of Gaskell and Lazerson, and "marginal job attachment" in the words of Oppenheimer and Kalmijn.

There is a core element of truth in associations between stopgap status and workplace passivity and disengagement. However, as I have suggested in previous chapters, these portrayals of stopgap work culture are much too simple. Young stopgap workers can work "temporarily" in grocery and fast-food jobs for months and even years. Although stopgap status may frame their overall participation at these work sites, day-to-day interactions within the workplace tend to foster other forms of work agency, investment, and engagement among young workers. In Box Hill and Glenwood, stopgap youth work cultures are shaped by at least two additional work orientations: a "peer group" work orientation that involves having and valuing close ties with one's co-workers and that often leads to the blurring of work and leisure activities in the workplace, and a "local investment" work orientation that consists of a sense of local expertise in and ownership of the work site and labor process. Stopgap, peer-group, and local-investment work orientations alternately compete with and mutually reinforce one another in the work lives of young workers.

STOPGAP WORK: "IT'S NOT FOR LIFE OR ANYTHING"

"I started working here when I turned fifteen," a young Fry House cashier says. "I had this thing where my cashier number was eighteen, and that was the year I was supposed to leave Fry House and go somewhere else." The cashier, now eighteen and a half (and just out of high school), explains that since the day he started work at Fry House he had planned a point of departure—to come no later than two weeks after his eighteenth birthday. Much to his disappointment, that deadline has come and gone with no change in his employment status. "I'm looking for a change," the cashier says, "but it has to be a good change, a smart change, a change for the better, for better pay, and not just to go back down and work my way up again."

Young workers in Box Hill and Glenwood have all sorts of ways to time themselves out of their grocery and fast-food tenures. For some, it is a particular age that they reach; for others, it is a stage of their lives—they want to be working somewhere else by the time they finish high school or college. And for some, it is an absolute length of time. In the Glenwood Fry Houses, for example, some young workers use the fact that seniority-based wages stop increasing after three years' tenure as a good measuring stick for when they should be looking to find new occupations. After all, they reason, if seniority-based wages stop increasing after three years, this is probably the point by which their employers and union representatives expect them to be leaving their Fry House jobs.

Timing out is a central part of young workers' stopgap work orientations. Almost universally, these young workers express their convictions, expectations, or hopes that their grocery and fast-food employment is strictly temporary. "It's just a job, not a career." "It's not what I want to do for my whole life." "It's a kiddy job." "It's not a real job." "It's just for now." "I'm definitely gonna be outta here; I'm not a lifer." "It's not for life or anything." Occupations and organizations all have their own age grading and timetables for tenure and mobility. There are occupations that workers expect to have for years—for life, even—and there are occupations in which workers are still considered young in their thirties and forties. But in grocery and fast food, young workers age quickly and expect to have their jobs for only short periods of time during discrete (and early) stages of their life courses. "I feel old already," says a twenty-four-year-old Fry House cook as he looks at his predominantly teenage co-workers and his six years of Fry House work experience. "It's like I've been there forever. I gotta leave now."

Stopgap work orientations are further distinguishable for their double-sidedness. On the one hand, young workers see grocery and fast-food jobs as being good—or, at least, acceptable—jobs to have for short periods of time while they are young or in school. Part-time and irregular (evening and weekend) hours, in particular, make grocery and fast-food work attractive to student workers. As many observers of the youth workplace point out, what is a bad job for most adults can be seen as a good job by youth workers. There is, however, another side to young workers' stopgap work evaluations: As stopgap workers, young workers also see grocery and fast-food work as being bad—and even terrible—work that they on no account would want to have as an adult career. Real jobs, good wages, interesting work, and job security are to be found later, elsewhere, and in other industries.

Grocery and fast-food employers in Box Hill and Glenwood benefit enormously from their young employees' stopgap work orientations, because these orientations frequently foster increased worker passivity and consent in the workplace. Young workers simply do not make the demands on their grocery and fast-food jobs that they expect to make on their later career sites of employment. They are passive not only because of their sense of transiency, but also because they accept—to a degree, at least—the popular North American ideology that positions youth workers as a separate class of workers who deserve less than adult workers do. Good jobs are predominantly the privilege of adulthood. Young workers must be content at first to spend their time in a tier of lower-quality service and retail employment. Dreams of meaningful work must be deferred. The bargain—the terms of such deferment—is that young workers will allegedly be able to find the kinds of jobs and occupations that they truly desire once they reach adulthood.

When young workers evaluate their grocery and fast-food jobs a, being good jobs, they do their employers the favor of comparing themselves not with the rest of the workforce, but with other youth workers. Measured against the non-union restaurant and retail jobs where many of their young friends work, unionized Fry House and grocery jobs, not surprisingly, look pretty decent to young Box Hill and Glenwood workers. They generally accept that, as young workers, they cannot expect to enjoy the working conditions and rewards they could demand if they were adults. Wages especially are widely interpreted through the lens of age. "They had me start out at six bucks an hour," says a Box Hill stocker, "and *for my age,* that was a lot of money. I mean, not many people at sixteen make that much" (emphasis added). "I'm getting paid what I deserve," says a Fry House supervisor. "I mean, maybe I should be getting paid twenty dollars an hour, but the money is good enough *because I am young*" (emphasis added).

Grocery and fast-food employers can not only count on their young stopgap employees to evaluate their jobs lightly; they can also generally rely on the fact that most of their young employees will not make demands to turn these casual service-sector jobs into well-paid, secure, and meaningful careers as they get older. As stopgap workers, young workers largely accept that there will be discontinuities in their employment paths into adulthood. Although the career goals of young workers in Box Hill and Glenwood are all over the map, ranging from the highly specific ("I want to be a medical illustrator") to the vague and unknown ("I don't know what I want to do with my life"), most of these workers are fairly certain, at the least, that they do not wish to turn their grocery and fast-food jobs into lifetime employment. To move up into the more rewarding and lucrative occupations of adulthood, most young workers accept and expect that they will leave the grocery and fast-food industries behind. Thus, it is not just young workers' acceptance of grocery and fast-food jobs as being good jobs that helps secure their passivity and consent in the workplace; it is also, paradoxically, their rejection of these jobs as being fundamentally bad jobs.

The flip side to this story of stopgap passivity and consent is that young workers in Box Hill and Glenwood, as stopgap anti-careerists, are hardly doe-eyed about accepting or embracing everything their grocery and

ıst-food employers have to offer. Young workers are often highly negative in describing their jobs, and when they explain why they do not
want grocery or fast-food careers, they fire off what are sometimes blis-
tering attacks on what they see life in these industries as being like:

> I look around at some of the people in grocery who have been in this
> stuff for a really long time . . . and they look depressed. And the man-
> agers, the closing managers, a lot of them have been there for a while, . . .
> they just look pissed off, they don't look happy with what they're doing
> with their life. Maybe they're making good money, grocery managers
> and store directors. . . . But would I wanna be stressed out and have to
> deal with thinking, "I don't wanna be at work this day. I don't wanna
> be here?" I wanna have something I enjoy to do for a living, something
> I really love to do, that I'd be happy to come to work everyday. . . .
> Whatever it takes, I'll do that to get to that level.

Young workers, it is important to point out, do not focus primarily on
low wages when they explain their stopgap orientations—for wages,
they imagine, would increase at least marginally if they moved up in
the industry ranks. What they cannot imagine changing—and what
they complain about most when explaining their stopgap orientations—
are the working conditions in grocery and fast food: the high stress and
low status; the irregular hours and unstable scheduling; the repetitive-
ness and lack of intrinsic interest and challenge.

Young grocery and fast-food workers, after all, are not stopgap workers solely because they are young; they are also stopgap workers
because of the poor work conditions that have been created by their grocery and fast-food employers. Witnessing these work environments
from the ground level and from a point in their lives at which most
believe themselves to have other and better career options, young stopgap grocery and fast-food workers can be some of these industries'
harshest critics. In Box Hill, especially, where there is a core of permanent grocery workers, young workers point to what they see as the
damaging effects of grocery work on the bodies and souls of lifers as
being the living lessons of what happens if one works in grocery for too
long. "Lifers look older than they really are," says one young stocker.
"Lifers are all alcoholics," quips another. "It really changes people," a
young checker says of the grocery business in general. "People become
bitter because they put up with crap for so many years. I don't want to
be like that."

Anger, critique, and alienation among young stopgap grocery and fast-food workers can create challenges for their employers. Although neither the Box Hill chain supermarkets nor the Glenwood Fry Houses show any signs of desiring fully careerist workforces, employers at both sites do regularly seek to recruit tiny minorities of their young employees for promotion into career and management ranks. As is the case with the grocery and fast-food industries continentwide, employers in Box Hill and Glenwood sometimes find it difficult—in the context of stopgap work cultures and poor workplace conditions—to persuade even a small number of young employees to consider grocery and fast-food work as legitimate career options (see also Hughes 1999). Quite aside from such career recruiting efforts, dominant stopgap work cultures also make it hard for employers to persuade young employees to stay in their jobs for extended temporary durations or to consider their jobs as anything more than casual forms of employment that they can pick up and drop at will.

Stopgap workers' anger, critique, and alienation can also foster subversive and oppositional workplace behaviors that can make these workers hard to manage and control. Seeing their jobs as only temporary and expedient, some young workers do not feel the need to take their grocery and fast-food work overly seriously. Young stopgap workers sometimes slack off and adopt cavalier attitudes toward company policies, programs, and goals—in a way they say they would not do if they saw their jobs as leading into career work:

> I'm a slacker. I'll be honest: I goof off all the time. . . . [I cut] corners, in speed, I guess. . . . I go for speed, not quality, to a point, [because] you can't leave everything dirty, it's gotta look good; everything that has to be done gets done. . . . The goal is to get time to sit on your ass, doing nothing. . . . Some people are different. I'm a slacker, what can I say?

> *Stuart:* Why are you a slacker?

> It's not like I don't care about the place. I wouldn't want it to burn to the ground or anything. But basically, it's I'm not going to be there forever—like, I'm not going to work my way up the Fry House corporate ladder.

And because they see their jobs as only temporary and expedient, some young workers are more inclined to quit (or threaten to quit) than give in to disliked management demands. In Box Hill, managers are occasionally exasperated by baggers who, rather than work a Friday or Saturday night shift they have been unable to get out of, will simply up and quit their jobs—often without telling anyone. On the other hand, a number of young workers I spoke with in both Box Hill and Glenwood said they had successfully used threats to quit to force managers to back down in confrontations, without ever having to lose their jobs.

If it is true, then, that transiency can lead to workplace passivity, it is also true that temporary, stopgap status can foster increased senses of agency and authority among young workers. If workers are planning to quit their jobs in the near future in any event, then the risk of being fired for standing up for their rights may not seem so daunting. "I'm young," a young Box Hill produce clerk proclaims. "I'm not afraid to tell him [the store manager] what I think at all, because I don't need this job nearly as much as they [older workers] do."

If young stopgap workers further see themselves as being bound for greater things than grocery or fast-food work, they may come to reject assumptions of their subordinate status in their workplace interactions with customers, managers, and adult workers:

> If they [customers] are really bitchy, if they have that tone, I'll talk to them in that tone and be sarcastic about it. It's a two-way street. I'm not going to treated as someone lesser than they are. The thing is, people think that just because you're working in a fast-food place, that you're nobody, that you're not doing anything with your life. If they knew that I went to university and that I was actually doing something with my life, then maybe they would have more respect for me. I've had people talk to me in a rude way; they're like people from the street, and I'm probably more smart and more intelligent than they are.

The young Fry House cashier quoted here claims workplace authority not because she is a fast-food worker, but because she is a university student who hopes and expects one day to become a corporate lawyer. Many young stopgap workers in Box Hill and Glenwood likewise adopt what are essentially elitist attitudes that simultaneously accept that grocery and fast-food workers should have subordinate status in society while rejecting such subordinate status for themselves because of the mitigating influence of their stopgap identities.

Many young stopgap workers in Box Hill and Glenwood leave their grocery and fast-food jobs quickly and easily: after a few months or a couple of years, they move on with their schooling, with other stopgap jobs, and, eventually, with their future careers and adult identities. For some young workers, however, transitions out do not come as quickly or easily as they might have hoped or expected. Indeed, one of the greatest fears of some young stopgap workers is the danger of becoming "stuck" or "trapped" in what are supposed to be only entry-level, temporary sites of employment. After all, in both Glenwood and Box Hill, there are adult workers for whom fast-food and grocery work has become a long-term, if not permanent, occupation.

For many young workers, stopgap work orientations not only place a time frame around their employment status; they also act to make their jobs seem ever less desirable as time goes on: A clock of declining job satisfaction starts ticking almost from the moment these young workers are hired into their jobs. A twenty-three-year-old cook in Glenwood who has over seven years of work history with Fry House, for example, describes how the meaning of his fast-food employment has changed over the years:

> When I was fifteen, it was a cool job, because I guess from working in high school, if you worked, if you had a job when you were fifteen, . . . that was kind of a cool thing because most of my classmates didn't have jobs. If you had a job, especially one that paid higher than the minimum [wage], it was something that was really cool to have at that time. . . . It was a good job, it was nice and stable. I guess I would be a person who doesn't like changes very much; that's why I've been working there. I kept my job, I didn't go out to look for other jobs.
>
> But as high school ended, the job became less and less cool. . . . It gets very repetitive. I guess that's what a fast-food restaurant is all about: fast production, repetitive product. . . . It was more or less, as you move on to university, people get into other work [that is] more related to what they were doing [in college classes]. I couldn't see myself—, I don't think anyone going to university saw themselves as working in a fast-food restaurant. . . .
>
> We joke about it a lot now. There's another cook at my store that started when I did. . . . We keep joking, we're gonna be here for the next twenty years, when we're fifty, we're still going to be working there. . . . If you were to look at it, I've been there more than a third of my life. . . . I'm not saying Fry House is a bad place to work. I'm just saying it's still in the image of a fast-food chain. . . . When you're in your twenties, working in Fry House is something that's kind of loser. . . . I want to move on definitely sooner or later. . . . When I graduate [from college], hopefully I can find a job other than Fry House.

Personal inertia, tight job markets, accumulated consumer debts and financial responsibilities, and limited educational accomplishments are all factors that can conspire to prevent a young stopgap worker from leaving his or her fast-food or grocery job to look for other, possibly more lucrative and rewarding forms of employment. This is especially true in the Glenwood Fry Houses and Box Hill chain supermarkets, where unionization has secured benefits and raised wages at least a degree above those which are commonly available in other entry-level service and retail jobs in town.

In an intriguing article titled, "Managing Aging in Young Adulthood" (1992), Carol Rambo Ronai describes how strip-tease table dancers, working in an industry that is oriented toward young workers, must, as they get older, either negotiate their departure from table dancing as an occupation or find a "niche" in which their age does not detract from their right and ability to continue working in the table-dancing milieu. Managing aging and occupational timetables are likewise a preoccupation of young stopgap grocery and fast-food workers—who, like table dancers (albeit in a different vein), also work in youth-oriented industries. Many young workers, as I have already noted, develop strategies for "timing themselves out." Other workers, having missed their expected points of departure, work to renegotiate the boundaries of stopgap youth membership. A twenty-four-year-old bakery clerk in Box Hill who found herself once again working in a stopgap service-industry job after she had graduated from college, emphasized her relief to find that she at least wasn't the oldest worker in her store who still identified as a stopgap worker: "It makes me feel a lot better to know that there are people I'm working with that are thirty and disgruntled like I am. *I still got a couple more years!*" (emphasis added).

Finally, some young stopgap workers attempt to manage their aging and occupational timetables by trying not to become too comfortable or attached to their jobs and work communities. One eighteen-year-old stocker I spoke to in Box Hill, who had seen his own father end up an embittered lifetime grocery employee, was painfully anxious about the dangers of "getting stuck" in his first job—even though he had held his grocery job only for a little more than six months:

This is my first job. . . . It's cool; it's a job. . . . But I don't want to take it too seriously, because then I'll be stuck there all my life. But if I just, when I'm there, just do what I need to do, try to keep my mind on other things. 'Cause my dad has been working in grocery stores all his life; he's been there since sixteen. He's a produce manager now. . . . So like, I'm kind of afraid; I don't want to do that. I see all these other people in my store; they been checking for twenty-six years. It's like, no thank you, I don't want to do this for the rest of my life. . . . A lot of people bicker at work. I'm over here 'cause I don't want to get into it. You know, I BS with them, shoot the breeze. . . . But I try not to have too strong opinions, 'cause I don't want it [grocery work] to be too important to me. . . . I wanna follow my dreams.

Recently, the young stocker's employer held a softball tournament for all of the local stores in the chain. "It was fun, I had a good time, I admit, unfortunately," the stocker said ruefully. "That's one thing I'm starting to fear," he explains, "'cause I'm making friends with everybody there, going and doing stuff with them, and I'm going to enjoy going to work, and then I'm going to be stuck."

PEER GROUP RELATIONS: "IT'S THE PEOPLE"

In my interviews with young workers in Box Hill and Glenwood, I heard over and over some variant of the phrase "It's the people" as these workers explained why they—at times, at least—actually enjoyed working in their grocery and fast-food jobs. As I have described in previous chapters, co-worker solidarities, whether organized at the store level (as in Glenwood) or the departmental level (in Box Hill), are central to young grocery and fast-food workers' work experiences and identities and are critical in fostering a strong sense of workplace engagement among many of these workers. Although co-worker solidarities are sometimes centered on relations that young workers have with older, adult co-workers, most often young workers' workplace social relations are shared with other young stopgap workers.

It would be easy, as some workplace commentators do, to blame young stopgap workers' invocation of peer-group social relations as the primary basis for valuing their grocery and fast-food jobs on these workers' alleged youthful immaturity—on their occupying a "pre-adult" or "pre-career" stage in which social relations with friends are more important than serious and challenging employment (e.g., Osterman 1980; Krahn and Tanner 1996). In Box Hill and Glenwood, however, peer-group work orientations among young workers are shaped fundamentally by the organization of work and control in the grocery and fast-food industries themselves. Such orientations, therefore, can in no way be read as reflecting directly some essential nature of adolescent youth.

If young workers in Box Hill and Glenwood valorize social relations with age-group peers in the workplace, it is important to recognize that they do so, first, because they are able to: A distinguishing characteristic of the grocery and fast-food industries, as two of the continent's largest employers of youth, is that their workplaces tend to be filled to the brim with young people. Young workers' appreciation of being able to work in the youth labor market is sometimes reinforced by prior and reported experiences of adult exclusion of youths in other workplaces. A number of young workers I spoke to had previously worked in office environments—often in the offices where one of their parents worked. Even though these office jobs were often higher status—and in some cases, higher paying—than grocery and fast-food work, these young workers said they preferred grocery and fast-food work because they found that, as youths, they had been isolated and excluded in adult-dominated office settings.

Moreover, young grocery and fast-food workers valorize socializing and having fun with co-workers in their workplaces in large part because they are actively encouraged to do so by their employers. As I discussed earlier, employers in Box Hill and Glenwood constantly push the rhetoric of team spirit and team competition as part of their effort to raise workers' productivity. In addition to this rhetoric of teamwork, Box Hill and Glenwood employers also constantly push the message that "the grocery store/fast-food restaurant is a fun place to work."

Such messages are motivated by two principal factors. First, as youth employers, supermarkets and fast-food restaurants seek to orient many of their control and motivation strategies to a predominantly teenage audience. Because these employers (like many North Americans) see teenagers as being primarily oriented to "fun and friends," they attempt to portray work and the workplace as fitting in with a fun-loving youth culture. "Have you seen the Fry House training videos?" a young cashier in Glenwood asks me as she shakes her head, laughing:

> Oh, they're bad. They're so cheesy; they're just, "Hi, I work at Fry House and I'm so happy!" I mean, it's kind of funny. It's true, in a sense—it's like, we're kind of like that, but not to that extent . . . ! We make fun of them [the videos]—the little rappers, they do some rap in there some-

times. It's so funny. They try to make it look cool, but it just doesn't look it. Right! Ah, they're trying!

Internal workplace structures thus work to reproduce work-site-external ideologies of youth. In what may often be a self-fulfilling stereotype, teenage workers are actively positioned within the workplace by their own employers as being more oriented to fun than work. The second reason that grocery and fast-food employers try to equate work with fun is that, as customer-service businesses, they need their employees to be able to provide "sincere" and happy, welcoming, friendly service to the customers they serve. It is much easier for workers to provide "sincerely" happy service, of course, if they really feel that they are happy and having fun in their workplaces.

Grocery and fast-food employers in Box Hill and Glenwood foster peer-group work orientations among their young employees indirectly as well as directly: Young workers' peer-group orientations are reinforced by their stopgap work orientations, which, in turn, are themselves reinforced by the industry work conditions that have been created by grocery and fast-food employers. Because they see their jobs as only temporary and stopgap, young grocery and fast-food workers do not demand the meaning and reward from these jobs that they would expect from adult, career employment. They consequently become more willing to embrace peer-group relations as being a primary site of value, identity, and practice in their (stopgap) low-wage and low-status service-sector jobs.

Peer-group work orientations, like stopgap work orientations, play a central role in the organization of young workers' consent and resistance in the grocery and fast-food workplaces. Strong peer-group relations among young workers often work to the benefit of grocery and fast-food employers. Workers' valorization of social relations within the workplace can help mitigate dissatisfaction with low wages, low status, and boring and repetitive work (Krahn and Tanner 1996). Co-worker solidarities can also foster a strong sense of workplace engagement among young workers and motivate them to work hard in their grocery and fast-food jobs—as was discussed at length in Chapter Three.

On the other hand, strong peer-group relations can also lead young workers to challenge, suspend, or ignore employer regulations, policies, and demands. Co-worker solidarities can lead to the development of local and alternative work practices among young workers and can, at times, move workers, individually and collectively, to challenge employer initiatives and interventions in their workplaces. In looking to the workplace as a site for socializing and fun, and in blurring the lines between work and leisure, some young workers do not take their work as seriously as their managers feel they should, as they allow leisure activities to creep steadily into their work time. Grocery and fast-food employers encourage their employees to maintain friendly and chatty store environments. Often, though, workers get more caught up in talking with one another and with their customers than they are with performing the various other work tasks that are expected of them. In both Box Hill and Glenwood, managers constantly feel obliged to tell young workers to "stop talking and get back to work."

Playing on the job is also a common part of the workplace experience for young grocery and fast-food workers. Food and water fights, for example, are frequent. Indeed, for some young workers, the food-based service and retail workplace seems to present an almost endless series of opportunities to engage in extended rounds of horseplay—as in the following story, told by a young stocker in Box Hill, about one of his most memorable "work" experiences:

It started originally that we were in back. We had two hours to face the bread [to neaten the bread displays by pulling all the loaves up to the front of the shelves in order to eliminate unsightly gaps].... We're just like, "Eh, let's do something; we're bored." So we took a half-hour break. We were out back on the loading dock; there was a bag of mildewing bagels that we decided to play golf with, with a broom that was back there that was broken.... We're smacking bagels out into the parking lot. We're having fun, and then he [a fellow stocker] goes out to start picking some up, and I start throwing 'em at him. He throws 'em back at me, then I went running inside....

I'm like, "I'm gonna go to the bathroom." And apparently he knew a little trick on how to open the bathroom door and threw an egg in there. I'm like, "Oh, you're going to get it." You could hear him laughing all the way out there.... So I went into the back room, and he was doing the dairy.... I hold up the dozen eggs; I flip it open. He's like, "Hey man; better be careful." So I start lobbing eggs at him, and then he grabbed a dozen eggs, we started going back and forth, the dairy's covered with eggs. Then I went running out the dairy door, and he threw a carton of milk, and that splattered on the floor, and I went running out the main doors. That's when he lobbed the egg. It missed me and splattered at a

manager's feet. It was like, "Oh man, this is not going to be good." . . .
He's [the manager is] real quiet; he's like, "Get a mop."

In addition to food and water fights, young workers play tag at work;
they ride grocery carts in the parking lots; they lock one another in
walk-in freezers; they untie one another's aprons; they play basketball,
football, and hockey in the back rooms; and they race and try to toss
one another off stockroom forklifts and power jacks. Workers eat, drink,
smoke, and occasionally do drugs together, all on employer time. Sexualized play—joking, teasing, gossiping, flirting, pinching, slapping,
and so on—is widespread in the grocery and fast-food workplace. As a
young Fry House cashier in Glenwood put it, flirting and joking on the
job "makes the work more fun, more livable, like you can be there, it's
not like, 'Ach, work, oh no!' Like I look forward to it."

Young grocery and fast-food workers' valorization of workplace
social relations is not without its limits, of course. Supermarket and
restaurant solidarities are sometimes broadly divided by both worksite-internal and -external differences in worker identity. Sexualized
play in the workplace easily and frequently deteriorates into sexual
harassment. In these multiethnic, multiracial workforces, joking and
teasing can likewise rapidly unravel into racial and ethnic work-site
tension and hostility. Workplace gossip slides all too smoothly into character attacks and simple meanness that can alienate workers and turn
them against one another.

Young workers' valorization of workplace social relations is also limited by their stopgap work orientations. As seen in the previous section,
some young workers deliberately restrict and distance themselves from
their co-workers' interactions for fear of becoming overly attached to
and comfortable in their stopgap jobs. For other young workers, meanwhile, the appeal of workplace socializing and fun quickly starts to lose
its luster as they near or pass the points at which they, as stopgap workers, feel they should be leaving their grocery and fast-food jobs far
behind.

LOCAL WORKPLACE INVESTMENTS: "THAT'S MY KITCHEN"

"When I wasn't bagging," a young Box Hill stocker recalls of his first
year of supermarket employment, "I'd be up there cleaning. I even got

the nickname of Mr. Clean." The stocker tells the story of an entire day he once spent cleaning the floors of his supermarket's back rooms:

> I took a nine-hour shift, scrubbing the hell out of both [staff] bathrooms, the break room, and the managers' room. I had to totally strip the floor, then I had to wax it; most of my shift was spent scrubbing the hell out of the floor. Those floors looked new. Then I went in there and I waxed them; they looked awesome. I took pictures, I was so proud of my floors, man.

"About a month and a half later," the stocker says, "this kid went in there and used bleach on *my floors*. I coulda killed him" (emphasis added). The stocker yelled at his errant co-worker, complained to his manager, and tried to insist that the co-worker take another full shift to restrip and rewax the now tarnished floors. "Nine hours," groans the stocker as he remembers the incident, "right there, wasted."

Despite (but also because of) their stopgap work orientations, many young workers in Box Hill and Glenwood express a strong sense of local investment—of local ownership and expertise—in their grocery and fast-food workplaces. A sense of local ownership is expressed most simply in the way young workers casually refer to "my kitchen," "my customers," or "my floors," or collectively to "our store" or "our department." Although they work in corporate-owned chains that have highly centralized control systems, young workers in Box Hill and Glenwood generally experience corporate owners as being physically and socially distant from the stores and departments in which they work. It is workers who actually inhabit, fill out, and take possession of company-owned property.

The work that workers perform subtly shapes and reshapes company spaces so that grocery and fast-food workplaces, over time, come to reflect the activities and identities of the workers within them. Workers can point to their regulars—to the customers who come into their stores and ask for them individually by name—and say that those are "my regulars that I got started here." Workers can point to display cases and produce racks, to floors and parking lots, to prepared meals and repaired machines, to sales figures and customer counts and say that it is their work that made these things look the way they do. Workers take possession of their local work sites through consumption as well as through production—through the familiarity of repeated use of work props and tools. Workers have cash registers, mops, refrigerators and freezers, four-wheelers, and power jacks that they use day in and day out, that they use more than anybody else does, that they know the particular quirks of better than anyone else, and that they come to see as in a sense belonging to them.

Local-investment work orientations are further based on a strong sense of local expertise. Workers in Box Hill and Glenwood claim a knowledge-based authority in their workplaces that is derived not from official job training or certified trade skills but, rather, from the simple fact of their "being out there." "We're in the trenches doing all the hard work," a Fry House cook says of his restaurant's work crew. "You [managers] could [should] listen to us . . . get some advice from us, 'cause we know what's going on in the store." Many young workers in both Box Hill and Glenwood, in fact, view their corporate employers' centralized work policies and procedures as being hopelessly out of touch with the day-to-day realities of the grocery and fast-food business and develop their own "workarounds" to get the work that needs to be done in their stores done right and done on time.

In Glenwood, for example, Fry House recently introduced a Computerized Cooking Schedule (CCS), which, using calculations based on a store's past sales, tells cooks how much chicken to cook at different times of the day, on different days of the week. Cooking the right amount of chicken is a tricky business for Fry House cooks: Chicken takes anywhere from fifteen to forty minutes to cook and lasts only an hour or so once cooked. Cook too much chicken and a store's "overcook" waste skyrockets; cook too little and a store will lose customers. Although the CCS can be helpful for new cooks, most of the more senior cooks I spoke to viewed the CCS skeptically:

> They have a little chart saying this is how much you should have of this product at this time, and it's usually pretty wrong. I mean, we know; we're there five days a week. We know what we need, and what [different] days are [like]. Sometimes it may surprise you—it's busier one day, dead another day, you never know with fast-food. . . . They think there's a science, but there's not. You just gotta go with the flow of how the evening's going.

Many Fry House cooks rely on their past experience in their stores to add or subtract chicken from what the CCS tells them to cook. "The cooks at our store cook just by instinct," says one cook. "They cook whatever's needed."

Similar stories are told by young grocery workers in Box Hill. Some grocery chains, for example, distribute centralized "schematics" showing the types and quantities of products they want stocked in dairy cases and on produce racks and tables. Clerks frequently make their own adjustments to these schematics (often in opposition to company policy), however, because they know that some products simply don't sell very well in their stores:

> They send us pictures of the rack that's put in right; we're supposed to make ours exactly like that. They want every single store to be the same, but you can't do that with tiny neighborhood stores [like our store]. . . . Say we're carrying large oranges and small oranges, and their schematic has these big displays of both of them, and the smaller ones are cheaper. In our neighborhood . . . they're going for the cheaper stuff; the big ones aren't selling hardly at all. So we widened out on the small ones; we keep the big ones small so we wouldn't throw 'em all away [when they went unsold].

"You gotta know your store," says a young dairy clerk. Otherwise, he explains, you'll forever be short on some products and long on others, throwing them away when they are unsold beyond their expiration dates.

Although managers and centralized control systems can often block the application of workers' local expertise in Box Hill and Glenwood, local-investment work orientations among young workers are generally supported and fostered by grocery and fast-food employers. Employers at both sites encourage employees to think of their workplaces as their own, to work as if they were the owners of their stores and departments, and to make their stores and departments the best they can possibly be. Younger workers especially, who view their jobs in the context of their transition from youth to adulthood and through a contrast with high school, can be highly receptive to such messages. As Gaskell and Lazerson argue:

> Being at work means being seen as and treated as an adult. School, on the other hand, defines students as children. It is a "people-processing" or custodial institution, preparing youth for adulthood, defining them as not yet fully responsible. . . . A formal consequence of moving out of an institution where you are being "processed" into an institution where you are doing the processing is that the work is clearly for someone else's benefit; that, after all, is why it is paid. . . . Producing something for someone else, something that [is] really valued, [makes] young people feel responsible and grown up. Instead of producing essays or bookends that no one

[cares] about, they [are] producing work that [matters] to someone else beside themselves. (1981: 89–91)

"Accomplishing an externally defined if routine task and getting rewarded for it," Gaskell and Lazerson (ibid.: 91) add, "is a public definition of competence [that] provides a public identity that compares favorably to the identity of the non-worker." The more ownership and investment young workers have in their work, the more "adult" they may see themselves (and may be seen) as becoming.

The receptivity of young workers to employers' exhortations to invest themselves fully in their stopgap jobs may be further fostered by their orientations to future work identities. Growing up in North America, young workers are inundated with meritocratic ideologies that link hard work with future success. Even though young workers see their grocery and fast-food jobs as stopgap jobs and not career paths, many still believe in the importance of developing strong work histories and identities early on. Young workers who expect to go on to college, and to one day enter the professions, sometimes seek a head start in their stopgap youth jobs on developing the professional (self-motivated, committed, hardworking) behaviors that will be demanded of them as adults in careers.

Employers also foster young workers' local workplace investments indirectly and by default. Both Box Hill and Glenwood employers keep store budgets trimmed to the minimum in order to maximize company profits. This frequently means that broken equipment goes unrepaired and missing equipment goes unreplaced. And this, in turn, means that young workers are quite literally forced to care for their stores and departments on their own as best they can. In Box Hill and Glenwood, young workers fix broken appliances, locks, taps, and switches; they tape up busted mops, brooms, and dustpans; they prop up drive-through windows that no longer stay open with pencils, straws, and stacks of paper cups. Some stores and departments, in fact, are able to keep running on tight budgets largely because their workers are willing and able to come up with ad hoc repairs, innovations, and adjustments so they can do their jobs effectively.

Employers therefore clearly benefit from their employees' local workplace investments. Because of their employees' willingness to intervene locally, employers are able to get away with small store budgets, as well as with what are often inadequate centrally designed work procedures.

Further, workers' sense of local ownership, expertise, and agency frequently motivate them to work hard in their grocery and fast-food jobs (Burawoy 1979; Miller 1988).

A sense of local ownership can even lead workers occasionally to "forget" the corporate structures of control that shape their workplaces. In one interview I conducted in a grocery-store staff room, a young stocker told me that he liked to greet all the customers he met when he was stocking shelves on the grocery floor. "Is that Good Grocer policy?" I asked. "That's my policy," the stocker replied. "So they didn't tell you that you had to do that?" "No—," the stocker started to answer. But he then looked up at a Good Grocer customer-service policy notice that was posted on the staff-room wall behind me and read aloud through the "Six Steps to Excellent Service." One of these steps required employees to greet all customers wherever they were in the store. "I was wrong," said the stocker. "I guess it is their policy."

But locally invested employees also create headaches for employers. Young workers in Box Hill and Glenwood pester their managers for workplace improvements and often resist following the letter of company protocols and work procedures. Although this can work to the advantage of company bottom lines in the long run, it can also be more costly for employers at times—and, most critically, it represents a limit and check on centralized employer authority and control. Despite company policies dictating that "the customer is always right," locally invested employees in the service workplace often assert increased authority over their customers. Seeing their workplaces as their own, some young workers feel at liberty to adopt and enforce independently sets of standards for behavior in their workplaces that they expect their customers to respect and follow:

> There's a lot of times that I'll ask them [customers] if they want ketchup or something; they're like, "Yeah." I'm like, "It would be nice if you said, 'Yes, thank you,' or 'Yes, please.'" Most of 'em, they smile, "Yeah, right." It's like, "No no no no no! It would be nice to have some manners." Or when somebody makes a big mess on the counter with their food, there are some jerk customers, they'll strew their food all across the counter, then I have to go clean it up. I'm always, when they're leaving, "Thank you very much for cleaning up your mess." A couple of times I've said, "I don't get paid for cleaning up your mess." They'll kind of clean it up; they'll try really hard.

Locally invested employees, finally, can come to demand better working conditions and higher wages for themselves. Although young grocery and fast-food workers, as stopgap workers, often accept low wages as a natural part of stopgap youth work life, as workers with a strong sense of local expertise, they question and challenge their low status, low wages, and lack of voice in the workplace. "They're so high up there," a young Fry House cashier says, voicing a typical complaint. "Like the Fry House company, the presidents, they just look at the money and the big planes they're sitting on and stuff. I personally don't think they look at who's really making the money for them very much. They don't take into consideration the stuff we do and the crap we go through."

Local workplace investments interact in contradictory ways with stopgap and peer-group work orientations. Peer-group relations and local workplace investments often combine to forge strong store-based and department-based solidarities. But peer-group relations can also limit young workers' sense of workplace investment, as workers become more caught up in socializing and having fun with co-workers at work and less concerned with their actual work and workplaces.

The story is similar with stopgap work orientations. When talking of their grocery and fast-food work within the framework of stopgap employment, young workers in Box Hill and Glenwood are willing to focus on the challenges of their work, on the interest, the variation and local nuances, the tricks of the trade and the hidden (tacit) skills that they need to excel in the grocery and fast-food workplace. But as soon as young workers start thinking of grocery and fast-food work as possible sites of career employment, and begin contrasting this work with the "real jobs" they hope to find as adults, all such excitement typically begins to fade. Young workers then tend to focus on the unskilled nature of their work and on the limiting and routine nature of jobs in the contemporary grocery and fast-food industries. "It's just like the same thing everyday, really," a stocker in Box Hill sighs. "Fill the milk, fill the beer, fill the pop. It gets kinda old. You get good at it, and then it's the same thing, everyday."

YOUTH WORK CULTURES

Between the twin stereotypes of the alienated youth worker and the happy teen worker can be found the actual identities and experiences of contemporary young stopgap workers in North America's low-end service sector. Youth work cultures, as evidenced by the examples of Box Hill and Glenwood, are neither fully oppositional nor completely accommodationist. They are stopgap work cultures, harboring not just passivity and alienation but also workplace investment and engagement. Youth work cultures emerge in the context of employer-created structures of workplace control, but they are not only not reducible to these structures of control; they also place limits on them.

Youth work cultures are distinctive from the work cultures of other groups of workers. Unlike the work cultures of professional and crafts workers, for example, youth work cultures have a distinctly local (and non-institutionalized) base of knowledge and identity. Youth work cultures are also shaped strongly by age: stopgap status is highly age-correlated; peer-group social relations that are so central to these cultures take on forms (e.g., style and content of conversation and interaction) tied closely to workers' age; and local workplace investments are often strengthened by young workers' negotiation of personal paths out of schooling and into adulthood.

Youth work cultures have significance for thinking about whether and how to pursue reforms in the youth workplace. Youth service-sector workers are stopgap workers and therefore are generally uninterested in, and sometimes even adamantly opposed to, turning their youth jobs into careers (i.e., without radical transformations in workplace environments). But this does not mean that youth stopgap workers are uninterested in pursuing workplace change, for young stopgap workers also have strong senses of workplace investment and worker solidarity. In Box Hill and Glenwood, young stopgap workers show themselves to be interested in taking steps—on a day-to-day and informal basis, at least—to change and improve their work and workplace conditions.

The young grocery and fast-food workers of Box Hill and Glenwood are unionized workers, of course. But there is little reason to expect youth work cultures in non-union sites to be radically different, because these cultures, as I have argued in this chapter, are shaped primarily by stopgap youth status and employer systems of workplace organization and control—not by union presence. Indeed, the critical question that will be explored in Part III of this book is not the extent to which youth work cultures in Box Hill and Glenwood are fostered and shaped by unionization (although this clearly does happen at these sites) but, rather, how successfully the two unions in Box Hill and Glenwood have been in connecting with and supporting the youth work cultures in their bargaining units that are independently vibrant and strong.

III. YOUTH IN THE UNION

6   Outsiders in the Union

> If we were to be totally honest, we'd probably have to say that we
> don't have the hearts and minds of all of our younger members.
>
> —Grocery Local 7 Political and Education Director

WHEN THE POLITICAL and education director of Grocery Local 7
in Box Hill concedes that his union might not have the hearts and minds
of "all" of its younger members, he makes a considerable understate-
ment: Local 7 does not "have the hearts and minds" of a great number
of its younger members. This is not to say that young grocery workers
in Box Hill don't generally prefer working in a union job to a non-union
one—they do. Most appreciate their union for the wages, benefits, and
sense of job security it provides. They look down on comparable youth
jobs—in fast food, especially—that pay only minimum wage, offer no
benefits, and impose the arbitrariness and precariousness of an "at-will"
employment contract. But beyond such baseline appreciation of unionization, young workers in Box Hill articulate a deep sense of alienation
from their union.

Young grocery workers in Box Hill often have little sense of who
their union is and what it does. They express frustration and anger with
union policies, actions, and inaction. They have almost no involvement
in union activities and minimal contact with union personnel. Even
with the core union currency of wages, benefits, and job security, many
young workers express dissatisfaction. Wages, for the most part, are
still low—particularly in the job classifications in which most youths
work. Benefits are not available to some young part-time and temporary workers. Job security and union protection often remain in the
realm of the imaginary rather than experienced reality, for few young
workers have actually witnessed concrete union intervention to protect
their own jobs or the jobs of co-workers. Many young workers in Box
Hill, in fact, feel that their union primarily serves the needs and interests of their older, adult co-workers, not the needs and interests of youth.

To the extent that they consider and acknowledge the problem of youth alienation in the local, union staff in Local 7 almost invariably construe the phenomenon as reflecting the nature of contemporary young workers. They complain that youths don't learn about unions in school, for example, and so don't fully understand the value of unionism, or they claim that youths are temporary workers, oriented to their lives outside work, who have little time for and care little about unions—or, for that matter, any other workplace institution. But these kinds of explanations are of limited merit. Many schools in Box Hill do teach students about trade unions (albeit typically in the context of early-twentieth-century U.S. history). And, as argued in Part II, even when they are stopgap workers, young workers can be highly invested in their workplaces and strongly motivated to put in extra effort and initiative while on the job.

In this chapter, I approach the phenomenon of youth alienation in Grocery Local 7 by focusing on factors internal to the structures, practices, and industry contexts of Local 7 itself that—along with external factors shaping young workers in Box Hill—contribute to such alienation. For youth alienation in Grocery Local 7 reflects not primarily problems with young workers; rather, it reflects problems with unionism—at least, with the particular form of unionism exemplified by Local 7. The story of youth and labor that emerges from Box Hill is a cautionary one: Unionization in this setting, as is unfortunately often true of unionization elsewhere in North America, has not been the force for reducing the workplace and labor market marginalization of young workers that it could and should be.

INTRODUCING YOUNG WORKERS TO THE UNION

Any union that works in the high-turnover youth labor market faces constant pressure in introducing new members to the union. Unions with more stable workforces often rely on contract negotiations (typically held every three years in North America) as the primary occasion for members to become involved with and to learn more about their union. But unions that work with stopgap youth workers simply cannot afford such luxury. In Local 7, in the three years between contracts, thousands of young workers will have joined and quit the local's membership.

Local 7 is one of the few unions in North America to recognize and address the problems caused by high turnover among youth workers through the creation of an outreach program that is explicitly oriented to new union members. Since the early 1980s, the local has run monthly "new members meetings." The goals behind these meetings are high-minded—they seek to educate new members (who tend overwhelmingly to be youth workers) about the union and unionism in general. But they are also expedient. Until 1998, the local did not have an automatic dues-checkoff clause in its grocery contracts and thus had to spend large amounts of time, money, and effort in collecting dues monies from members. Educating new members about their union was seen as a strategy for increasing the willingness of these members to pay dues voluntarily, without having to be chased down by union representatives.

How do these new members meetings work in introducing young grocery workers in Box Hill to their union? To answer this question, I describe a typical new members meeting, which was held one summer morning in the Local 7 union hall. I base this description both on notes of my personal observations and on an audiotape recording that I made of the meeting.

The main meeting room in the Local 7 union hall resembles a traditional school classroom: Rows of hard-backed chairs face a large table that sits at the room's front end. In a corner next to the table stands an American flag. A few decorations line the room's colorless walls: a mock traffic sign reading "Scab Crossing"; a flyer that pronounces "Union Beer Only"; a series of heritage posters depicting "Images of Labor"; a copy of the local's first grocery contract, negotiated in the 1930s.

It is 8 A.M. on the first Wednesday of the month—the day that the local holds its introductory meetings for newly joined members. Six of these members now sit scattered around the room: two young men side by side who came to the meeting together; a young mother rocking a crying baby; three others seated a respectful distance apart. As is the norm with these meetings, the members are young—in their late teens and early twenties. Four other people are in the room, as well: myself, the local's political and education director, and the two union reps who will be running the meeting. Apart from the reps' asking the young workers to sign in as they arrive at the hall—so they can be properly credited with a discount on their union initiation fees for attending—nobody is speaking.

At a little after eight, the two union reps start the meeting. Their presentation is closely scripted—even the jokes and asides are shared and recited by other union reps as they run simultaneous new member meetings at other sites around the city. Money is the first order of business: union money. Rules are spelled out slowly, almost tediously. Members are told when, where, and how to pay their union dues. "It's your responsibility," the first rep warns her silent spectators, "to get the money in by the first of the month." One month of missed payments leads to a delinquency notice and a five-dollar surcharge; two months brings suspension from the union and a heftier reinstatement fee. Those who have not yet paid their initiation fees and first months' dues are welcome to do so at the meeting's end.

We move to benefits. The second union rep takes over, and the tone of the meeting changes. The rep is excited, he speaks in a volume that seems, perhaps, as if it might be more appropriate for a packed auditorium. He gestures wildly, he grows red in the face. He is here to sell his audience on the union. "We feel," he pronounces, "that we have one of the best insurance programs out there. We've done comparisons on the major companies in the area, and ours beats them hands down!" "And the best thing of all," the rep now moves in with his punchline, "is you're gonna pay nothing for this coverage. It's entirely employer paid!" The rep then races through a dizzying array of benefits, acronyms, eligibilities, restrictions, conditions, and types of coverage: medical, dental, family, vision, hospitalization, time loss, COBRA payments, preferred provider organizations, prescription drugs, claim forms, life insurance, worker compensation, member assistance programs, pensions.

The baton is passed back to the calm and orderliness of the first union rep, who now comes to the young workers assembled to speak of the problems of workplace discipline. Grazing—eating product that is not paid for—is a no-no. You will get caught, and you will be terminated. Failure to record—not ringing up merchandise immediately—will lead to termination. Store security will get in your checkout line just to see whether you are doing what you are supposed to do, and if you fail to record, they will walk you off, and you will be terminated. Under-ringing—charging less than what an item costs: You're taking money from the store, and that is called theft. Don't put your job on the line. Drugs and alcohol: No drugs and alcohol on company property. Period. Time-card violations: Working off the clock is illegal. Leaving early and having somebody else clock you out is stealing time from the company—which is considered the same as stealing money. You can and will be terminated.

Back now to the second union rep and a discussion of union privileges (listening to the two, I am given the sense of a good cop, bad cop routine). Unions give you just-cause job protection, access to grievance and arbitration procedures, and the right to union representation at disciplinary meetings. Non-union workers have none of these. Unions give you a say in what goes in your contract—the employer cannot dictate the terms of the contract. Indeed, the rep goes on to say: "If you leave here with nothing else, leave here knowing who the union is. We're not the union; we're your hired hands. You folks are the union, you tell us where and how you want this union run." "You have a voice," the rep proclaims to the group of young workers, who, at this, their first union meeting, have yet to say or be asked to say a word.

There is just a little business left on the meeting agenda: political action and the need to give money to support the union's lobbying activities. The oratory of the second union rep is in high gear now. It is crucial that we, the active workers of America, lobby our congressmen to vote for the bills that affect the working class. Employers, the rep decries, are spending billions for corporate interests. Nobody's rights are sacred when Congress is in session. We must hold our congressmen to task, make sure that they work for us, not against us; that they help us, not hurt us. We have been able to defeat bills that would have severely hurt grocery workers in America. But don't think they're dead forever, folks. They'll be back, you can bet on it, and we'll be facing the same thing again. It is crucial that we have your money so we can fight to protect your rights.

A little more than forty minutes have now passed, and the reps have been talking non-stop. Finally, the first rep opens the floor to the seated members: "Do you have any questions at all regarding this all?" But the moment is not to be. The rep pauses for only a second before starting to wrap up the meeting, when the second rep breaks in:

First rep: Do you have any questions at all regarding this all? [One-second pause] If not, thanks for—

Second rep: I have a question. Do we have any baseball fans out there? How about football? Basketball? Any of these sports I mentioned, you all have something in common, you all have a contract that spells out your wages and working conditions. These people make millions of dollars a year, but they realize the importance of having a contract.... All too often, we middle-class America, we have a tendency to listen to our managers, listen to our corporate America: "Trust us; you don't need a union; we'll take care of you." OK. That's it for our presentation today. Thanks for coming.

With this, the meeting ends. Five of the young workers disappear immediately, leaving as silently and separately as they had come. One worker stays briefly to ask a question about why the union returned her initiation-fee check and then leaves, too. After the meeting has ended and the members have left, the union officers gather together to assess how the morning has gone and to explain to me some of their objectives. "I just hope," the first rep says to no one in particular, "that it sinks in. That they get it."

Other new members meetings run by Local 7 have slightly more interaction between union members and officers than the meeting described here. In some meetings, reps ask members their names and provide brief spaces for questions. Young workers are occasionally able to chat casually with union reps and co-workers from other stores before and after these meetings. But in general, new members meetings are fundamentally non-interactive and non-participatory affairs. They are centered on monologic presentations of the union to its members by union staff. They do not seek to create spaces in which members themselves talk, act, reflect, critique, strategize, form new links, or enter into new projects.

The union practice modeled by the new members meetings contradicts the union staff's rhetoric about having a member-centered, member-driven union. In new members meetings, union staff have a voice; union members are silent. Union staff act and initiate; union members sit passively by. The new members meeting also presents a narrow, financially focused, technically oriented, and authoritarian image of the union local. Emphasis is placed on discipline—in the collection of dues and proper workplace behavior—and on money and the provision of financial benefits. The portrait limned out in these meetings is one of the union as dues-collecting machine, rule-making body, and benevolent insurance company.

Young workers' reactions to Local 7's new members meetings are fairly expectable: They tune out. The young workers I interviewed in Box Hill who had been to a new members meeting—a minority of all Local 7's youth members—almost invariably described these meetings as boring and as events that were endured solely to receive a reduction on initiation fees. Many said they had a hard time recalling what was even spoken about at these meetings. "I can't remember much from it," a bagger says. "Just the fact that everything was very serious about being disciplined. I wasn't used to that."

Young workers complain that new members meetings do not seem oriented to the interests of younger union members. "It really is hard," one young bagger explains, "for someone to sit through a meeting learning about health care when they're insured through their parents still, or retirement, which they don't get for another thirty years." A teenage checker describes how she quickly stopped listening to the reps' presentation as they droned on about family benefits the union provided: "I was just like, 'Oh, this isn't for me; this meeting is not designed for someone my age.'" Young workers complain, further, that new members meetings do not give them the "real deal" about the union. The meetings explain little about what the union does, how it works, where their dues money is going, or how they can actively use their contract in their workplace. Instead, the meetings go over "basic stuff" that young workers feel they either already know or could easily read in their contract booklet. As such, new members meetings are seen by many as being a "waste of time."

Finally, young workers, complain that they have little opportunity in new members meetings to talk, ask questions, or express viewpoints. One young checker, who had worked as a supervisor in a non-union drugstore before entering the grocery trade, compared staff meetings at her previous job favorably to the new members meeting she had attended:

> I went to meetings all the time at my other job. In a way, I felt more like I could open up and speak, because . . . it was open to the floor. . . . I felt like I could speak up and voice my own opinion and they were going to

listen to me. . . . See, then again, I've never been in a union, either. This is
the first time, and I had no clue [about what to expect].

If Box Hill youths, then, have any ideas about unions as being organizations that help workers gain a voice in the workplace before they
are hired into the locally unionized grocery industry, Local 7's new
members meetings work quickly to put such notions to rest.

ADULT-CENTERED UNIONISM

Youths are often thought of in terms of media: We regularly hear references to the "MTV" or the "Internet" generation. Labor activists and
staff sometimes talk as if the only problem that comes between unions
and youth is one of communication packaging: Find the right vehicle
or medium, and all will be well. "Unions and youth, huh?" a Local 7
union rep asked me when I described to him my general research interests. "You know, we're planning on setting up a Web page for the local.
All the young people are on computers; they're brought up on it." Put
up a Web page for the local, the rep tells me, and we'll really be able to
start making links with the younger members. Other labor staff search
for a youth lingo or dialect into which they can translate their own
union-speak. Throughout my research, labor personnel repeatedly
asked me which words, discourses, and cultural referents were current
among today's younger generation—as if there was some youth mas-
ter code just waiting to be cracked by an intrepid labor researcher or
union organizer.

Focusing on communications difficulties as a source of youth union
alienation is not entirely misplaced, as I suggested in my discussion of
Local 7's new members meetings. In labor circles, however, there is a
danger of assuming that communication problems are the primary, or
even the only, internal source of youths' alienation from the union.
When young workers—and the parents of young workers—in Local 7
complain about having to join the union and pay high dues, Local 7 staff
generally assume that these individuals are misinformed about the
value of unionism and that the local simply needs to do a better job of
communicating what this value is to its members. However, young
workers' complaints about Local 7 are not always misinformed: Local
7 is an adult-centered union that frequently neglects the interests and

needs of its youngest members. Substance, not just form, is at the heart of youth–union problems for Local 7 in Box Hill.

Local 7 discriminates against its youth membership in two ways. First, its contract provisions favor long-term and full-time (or, at least, half-time) workers over temporary and part-time (or less than half-time) workers. Youth grocery workers tend to work far fewer hours per week for much shorter tenures than do adult grocery workers. As a consequence, youth grocery workers in Box Hill tend to pay more and receive less from their union than their adult counterparts:

- *Youth grocery workers in Box Hill tend to pay higher union-dues rates than adult grocery workers.* Monthly dues rates in Local 7 are calculated as a percentage of a worker's hourly wage and do not take into account the number of hours a worker works per month. Part-time workers, consequently, pay a higher percentage of their monthly earnings in dues than do full-time workers.
- *Youth grocery workers in Box Hill are less likely to be eligible for union-negotiated health-care benefits than are adult grocery workers.* Health benefits in Local 7 are available only to those who work more than fifteen hours per week, and the benefits kick in only after three months of employment. Student workers and workers who take on grocery work for short periods of time (i.e., as a summer job) are thus often excluded from union health plans.
- *Youth grocery workers in Box Hill are less likely to be eligible for union-negotiated pension benefits than are adult grocery workers.* It takes five years for a worker to become vested in Local 7's pension plan. The vast majority of youth grocery workers stay in the industry for a far shorter period of time than five years, and are thus excluded from pension benefits.

Grocery employers, the union, and (long-term, full-time, and half-time) adult grocery workers all benefit directly from excluding youth grocery workers from the union's health and pension plans. For even when youths are not eligible for benefits, contributions are still made to these plans in their name—for each hour of labor they work. Local 7's health and pension plans are thus supported by a "youth subsidy." Because of this youth subsidy, the union and its adult membership are able to negotiate increased health and pension coverage for themselves, while grocery employers are able to limit their contribution rates per employee.

Local 7 also discriminates against its youth membership through its "youth" job classifications—the stocker and bagger positions. As I noted earlier, although other age groups do work in these classifications, the industry clearly sees both positions as youth jobs. Most baggers are high-school-age teenagers, and most stockers are young men in their late teens. Because of the separate bagger and stocker job classifications, many youth grocery workers in Box Hill receive lower wages and enjoy fewer workplace protections than do adult grocery workers:

- *Grocery baggers earn only 40 percent of the top grocery wages in Box Hill, at a rate that is only slightly higher than the minimum wage.* In fact, during my fieldwork, baggers who worked ten hours or less per week (which is not unheard of in Box Hill during the school year) actually earned less than the minimum wage in take-home pay—thanks to the local's wage-based, as opposed to earnings-based, dues rates.
- *Grocery stockers earn only 50 percent of the top grocery wages in Box Hill, and are actually paid less for doing the same work as workers in other, adult-dominated classifications.* Stockers can perform any job in the grocery store except checking. Stuck at an essentially flat wage, stockers can work for years performing work tasks for which other, typically older grocery clerks can earn as much as double what a stocker is paid.
- *Baggers and stockers are explicitly excluded from certain contract provisions.* Although other grocery workers in Box Hill, for example, must be paid extra when they are asked to come in early or stay late after their scheduled shifts, baggers and stockers are denied unscheduled overtime premiums. And although other grocery workers are guaranteed a minimum of four hours per work shift, stockers are guaranteed only two hours of work per shift, and baggers have no minimum shift length whatsoever. Consequently, Box Hill grocery employers have an incentive to use these workers as an "on-call" workforce, scheduling them for short shifts and asking them to stay on longer as business demands.

It is critical to recognize that the marginalization of youth interests via the bagger and stocker classifications in Local 7 is neither natural nor inevitable. Rather, it is the direct result of years of age-based discrimination on the part of both Box Hill grocery employers and Local 7 union staff. Indeed, youth interests in Box Hill's grocery chains were not always marginalized to the degree that they are today. Such marginalization has emerged gradually over the local's sixty-year history.

The local's first grocery contracts, negotiated in the 1930s, had no separate bagger or stocker classifications. Youths entering the grocery trade went directly onto a single wage scale, starting as "beginner clerks" and winding up as "journeyman clerks" twelve months later. Grocery employers in Box Hill, however, repeatedly pushed in contract negotiations over the years to create a separate classification for young student workers. Employers essentially based their demands on the age-prejudiced argument that it was simply absurd, or "not right," to have youths who were still in high school earning top dollar in the grocery trade. In the mid-1950s, Local 7 staff agreed and negotiated the local's first separate job classification for young grocery workers.

The original youth job classification in Local 7—colloquially known as the "box boy" classification—provided for a separate, lower wage to be paid to grocery workers who were eighteen-and-a-half years old or younger and who worked twenty-four or fewer hours per week. The age cut-off for the box boy classification was determined by Local 7 staff visiting Box Hill high schools to find the average age at which youths graduated. Box boys, in these early contracts, could do any of the work in the grocery stores that older grocery workers did. They were paid less than older workers only because they were young and worked part time.

In the 1960s, Box Hill grocery employers pushed through a second age-based wage tier in their negotiations with Local 7. In addition to teenage box boys, the new grocery contracts now provided for a "junior clerk" classification, in which grocery workers who were younger than twenty-one were to be paid a separate and lower wage than older grocery clerks. Once again, the sole basis for the new wage differential was age-based discrimination.

The box boy and junior clerk classifications of the 1950s and 1960s have gone through a complex series of permutations to become today's bagger and stocker classifications. Three general changes are particularly significant. First, by allowing young grocery workers to be paid a lower wage in Box Hill, Local 7 created an incentive for employers to substitute youth for adult labor. To protect the jobs of older grocery workers, Local 7 has sought over the years to limit employers' use of youth labor by restricting the kinds of work that baggers are permitted to perform in supermarkets and the percentage of overall supermarket labor hours that can be worked by stockers. Second, Local 7 has allowed wage differentials between baggers and stockers and top grocery earners to widen gradually over the years. When first introduced, the bagger (or box boy) position earned 66 percent and the stocker (junior clerk) position earned 88 percent of the top grocery wage.

The third general change, which occurred during the 1980s, involved stockers and then baggers losing their explicit age designations. This was not motivated in any way by an attack on grocery-contract age discrimination on the part of Local 7. Rather, Box Hill's grocery employers pushed for this removal of age restrictions in part, at least, as a response to demographic changes in the United States: Fewer teenagers were available to work, and bagging and stocking positions were becoming harder to fill.

Whatever its motivation, the removal of age designations from the bagger and stocker classifications might seem to have been a boon for teenage grocery workers in Box Hill. It was not. Baggers and stockers in the Box Hill supermarkets continued predominantly to be teenage workers. But whereas baggers and stockers previously at least had been guaranteed promotion to higher-paid positions in the grocery stores once they reached a certain age, the removal of age restrictions meant that they had lost any such guarantee. Baggers and stockers can now be stuck in their low-wage positions indefinitely.

The particular history of contractual ageism in Local 7 has created a peculiar situation in which many union staff and activists feel angry that the bagger and stocker classifications no longer have age designations. The current president of the local, for example, explained to me that she would like to see a return to the age-grading of past contracts so that baggers and stockers will not be stuck for long periods of time on low-level wage tiers. That, she explained, would "give them a light at the end of the tunnel." Thus, paradoxically, many union personnel in Local 7 are driven by a strong sense of workplace social justice to call for a return to explicit forms of age discrimination in grocery contracts. Treating teenage grocery workers as a separate, lower class of worker has now come to seem natural to many older workers in the industry. What is seen as unnatural is the removal of a promise that youths can progress, as they move into adulthood, into full grocery citizenship.

The practice of adult-centered unionism in Local 7 is now, and probably has always been, a self-perpetuating phenomenon. The more youths are marginalized in Local 7 contracts, the more marginal are the positions that they occupy within grocery-store hierarchies and communities. The more marginal youths become in grocery-store communities, the more marginalized they tend to be in terms of their union participation. The more marginal youth participation in union activities and contract negotiations becomes, the more newly negotiated contracts are likely to marginalize youth interests. The current split in Box Hill supermarket work communities between a core of permanent lifers and a periphery of stopgap youths thus follows from and reinforces a long history of youth marginalization within Local 7.

An Outsider in the Workplace: The Union

Young grocery workers in Box Hill do wicked impersonations of Local 7 union reps. "I met my union rep once," a teenage stocker named Luke told me, explaining that the brief meeting constituted the full extent of his contact with his union:

> I was up front [in the grocery store] bagging; it was really busy. I was walking to put a cart out in the cart-dock area. I'm walking out, and the union rep's coming in. She looks at my name tag [Luke comically shoots his head forward and down, staring at a spot on my shirt as if attempting to read my name tag]. It's like a robot, you know, when she's talking to you. She's like [Luke puts on an artificially friendly voice]: "Hi . . . , Luke? I'm Sheila Davis, I'm a union rep. Here's my card if you ever need to talk to anybody." And that's it. She leaves. I'm like, OK, whatever, 'bye. I don't care. I have no use for the union.

The story is repeated by young workers all over Box Hill. A union rep walks into the store one day, after months of their never seeing anybody from the union, and, as a complete stranger, uses the worker's name tag to assume some kind of artificial casual familiarity. The rep urges the young worker to get in touch if he or she has any questions or problems at work, but—often without even breaking stride—keeps walking right past the young worker and out of his or her life, rarely to be seen or heard from again. Often the rep plays Santa Claus and hands the young worker a pen, box knife, or schedule pad complete with the local union insignia. These gifts are presented as freebies, but given the high dues and steep initiation fees young workers pay and the lack of other visible returns from the union, some young workers see these "freebies" as the most expensive pens and box knives they have ever bought.

Local 7 has minimal shop-floor presence in Box Hill grocery stores. The union is not a part of young workers' working communities, and it is generally seen by young grocery workers as a workplace outsider. Maintaining a regular and effective shop-floor presence is difficult for any service-sector union, because these unions generally represent workers at small work sites spread out over large geographical areas. Local 7's 12,000 members are dispersed in more than two hundred supermarkets in a 1,100-square-mile area. But in the context of such adverse conditions, the culture and structure of Local 7 does little to help the union strengthen its position within the grocery workplace.

Local 7 has a weak and undeveloped shop-steward system. Prior to the 1980s, the local had no steward system at all. By 1997, the local had stewards in only about one-fifth of the supermarkets it represented. Moreover, the steward system that Local 7 launched during the 1980s was minimalist in nature. Union staff were wary of giving too much power and authority to shop stewards and nervous about the possibility of workplace disruptions that could be caused by meddling, ill-informed, and uncontrolled stewards. Thus, unlike other union locals that give stewards the role of handling initial stages of workplace grievances, Local 7 allocates its stewards only a passive, observer role. Stewards are supposed to be the "eyes and ears" of the local in the workplace and an information conduit between union staff and membership. They are expected to report workplace issues and events to union reps, introduce the union to new hires, and, when possible, answer members' questions about their contract rights and responsibilities. They are not expected to be proactive in the workplace.

Union reps in Local 7 do little to make up for the absence of a strong steward program. A union rep usually visits each supermarket for about one hour once or twice a month. Not only are reps' store visits short and infrequent, but their structure and purpose generally minimize young grocery workers' chances to interact with the reps while they are in the store. Reps work a regular workweek and thus tend to visit Box Hill supermarkets in the daytime on weekdays; young grocery workers tend to work on weekends and weekday evenings.

Reps are evaluated in their job performance (by the union president) primarily in terms of their "numbers"—how many outstanding initiation fee and union dues debts they have in the stores for which they are responsible. They are not evaluated in any systematic way on, for example, how many formal or informal grievances they have resolved for union members (activities that are obviously difficult to evaluate and measure), how many work-site problems they have brought to the union's attention, or how many members they have brought into union activities and programs. This means that when reps visit Box Hill supermarkets, their primary objective is to determine who has been hired, terminated, and promoted in the store by cross-checking union records with in-store work schedules—that is, their primary objective is not to learn about workplace conditions in a particular store or about the employees' most pressing needs and interests. Consequently, the bulk of a rep's time in the supermarket is often spent in the store office rather than on the floor and in talking to managers rather than workers.

Local 7 reps typically do a quick walk-through around the supermarket floor on each visit, during which they introduce themselves to workers and hand out business cards and other union paraphernalia. But the workers with whom reps stop to have conversations longer than a quick, "Hello, my name is ... ," tend to be older workers whom the reps are more likely to know. It is rare for a rep to talk at any length with a young stopgap worker during a store visit. If a rep does seek out a young grocery worker, it is usually to ask him or her to pay his or her union dues or initiation fees.

The lack of a strong union presence in Box Hill supermarkets has important implications for the relationship of young grocery workers to their union. It is difficult for young workers to gain access to information about their union and the collective-bargaining agreements within their own workplaces. Some young grocery workers have never even received a copy of the union contract booklet. Thus, there is a fair amount of ignorance as well as misinformation among young grocery workers in Box Hill about what their union-negotiated rights and privileges are and what they can do if these rights or privileges are denied them by their managers.

Even when they are aware of their workplace rights, some young workers hesitate to contact their union for help with problems because they see the union as a workplace outsider, a strange and unknown entity, and—at best—a white knight who may be able to intervene in the moment but who won't be around for the long term to help deal with possible repercussions of its interventions. Some young workers fear what the union will do if they report a workplace problem. "I don't want to get anyone fired," says a young deli clerk who was being harassed by one of her managers. "I just want to have everybody sit down together and talk things over." The clerk called her union rep with the hopes of securing assistance in setting up such an informal meeting, but when the clerk described the situation to her union rep, "his voice got really serious." Not knowing the rep very well, and not trusting what he might do, the clerk decided—in spite of what was a rapidly deteriorating work environment—that she would prefer to try to deal with the harassment herself, without union assistance.

Young grocery workers sometimes also fear what their employers will do if they complain to the union about workplace problems. A teenage bakery clerk explains why she has never gone to the union to complain about a broken and unsafe oven that has already sent two co-workers to the hospital with burns, and that her employer has still not fixed months after the problem was first reported:

> Everybody knows, if you go to the union too often, and the managers find out, they're going to find a reason to fire you. If you're going to the union a lot, they're going to get sick of that. You're going to end up fired because you were one minute late twice in a row, or something [like that].

Many young workers in Box Hill suspect that, if their managers decide to single them out for discipline and dismissal, their union won't be in the workplace every day to help them out. Unions' outsider status can thus create a sense of a strategic economy of grievances among some young workers, in which workers delay involving the union in workplace problems until they encounter that perennial future and hypothetical workplace situation that really is insurmountable.

Finally, this outsider status fosters the sense among many young workers in Box Hill that their union is out of touch with workplace realities and that Local 7's leadership doesn't really care about workers' daily grind in the supermarket business. "One thing I've never seen a rep do," complains a grocery clerk who had worked in his store for more than two years, "is go in and see: Are there stools for everybody to stand on? Is everything working? Are things broken? I never see anybody come in and check." Young grocery workers across Box Hill argue that, to be effective and useful for them, the union needs to come to their stores more often:

> I think the union needs to come in and make employees feel that they're worth something. . . . I feel they need to come in and work with the employees, work in the store, actually get behind a checkstand at night, at midnight, see what we're going through. They need to come and stock, get down on their hands and knees, see the situations we deal with.

For the moment, as one young deli clerk says resignedly, "people's job environments aren't the best. And unions don't know that because they're not there everyday."

STAFF-CENTERED UNIONISM

Few young grocery workers in Box Hill ever become involved with their union. Many never even make it to a new members meeting, let alone participate in union activities beyond this entrance point to the local. During the eleven months of my fieldwork, only a handful of grocery workers younger than twenty-five ever attended Local 7's bimonthly general membership meetings, and only a couple of youths showed up at these meetings more than once. At the local's annual summer picnic, the only youths in sight were the children of older grocery workers.

The reasons for youths' lack of union involvement have as much to do with Local 7's practice of unionism as it does with any essential nature that can be attributed to contemporary young stopgap workers. For young grocery workers in Box Hill, Local 7 appears as an institution that is socially, symbolically, and geographically distant from their own work lives. Simple physical inaccessibility alone acts as deterrent to youths' union participation. Local 7's general membership meetings are held in the local's union hall in an industrial area of central Box Hill that is poorly served by public transit and that is far from the residential suburbs where the bulk of Box Hill grocery workers live and work. Especially for young workers without a car, the local hall is out of the way and difficult to visit.

Those young workers who do make it to the Local 7 union hall and who do express an interest in becoming more involved with their union find that few union activities are available in which grocery workers in Box Hill, young or old, can actively participate. Contrary to the union staff's rhetoric about having a member-centered, member-driven union, Local 7—like many unions in the United States—practices a staff-centered form of unionism. Virtually all of Local 7's meetings, programs, and activities are organized, coordinated, and dominated by Local 7 staff. In this respect, the local's new members meetings work exceedingly well in that they accurately model the kinds of union practices that characterize the local as a whole.

In reality, members' alienation and disengagement from their union is not really a problem for Local 7 staff. Rather, it is business as usual—a sign, even, that all is well with the local. As the local's president explained to me: "I wouldn't know what to do if a thousand people showed up for a [general membership] meeting. I'd feel scared, like I must be doing something wrong." Typically, only sixty to eighty out of the local's 12,000 members attend the bimonthly membership meetings. Union staff view member participation as a "barometer of how good a job we're doing"—but in quite the opposite way from what one might expect: Low turnout at meetings can be interpreted by union staff as meaning that members must be reasonably happy in the stores; larger turnouts signal problems.

Local 7's bimonthly membership meetings constitute the primary occasions for member participation in the local. When union reps tell newly joined young grocery workers in new members meetings that they "have a voice" in their union, they tell these workers that, "at general membership meetings, you can raise your hand and get up and voice your concerns, and let the president know what your feelings are." "This," reps promise young workers, "is how you get it [your opinions] out." Yet the primary function of general membership meetings is not to have members talk to union staff, but to have union staff present to union members reports of what the union has been doing since the previous meeting. As much as 90 percent of the time at a general membership meeting is taken up by union staff talking about their own activities, thoughts, and goals. Opportunities for members to introduce their concerns, desires, and ideas are usually relegated to a rushed "new or unfinished business" slot at the very end of the meeting—at a time when many members need to head home or back to work.

There are few other regular forums or opportunities in Local 7 for members to have a say in how their union should be run. Local 7 has a women's committee, but this committee is not for female grocery workers; nor does it address issues of concern to women working in Box Hill supermarkets. The committee is for female staff members at the local, and it focuses on issues of concern to women working in unions. Local 7 has a political-action committee. But when union staff describe this committee to members at general meetings, they do not invite members to participate in shaping the local's political agenda and programs. Instead, they ask members for their money, for donations to support this staff-run committee in strategizing and acting on behalf of the membership.

During my fieldwork in Box Hill, Local 7 was involved in its triennial contract negotiations. The local's staff-centered practice of unionism was strikingly apparent throughout the negotiation process. Membership involvement in contract negotiations was minimal. There were no open forums for members to negotiate the contract demands that the local should make; nor was there ever an opportunity to debate whether to accept the final contract proposal recommended for membership approval by Local 7 union leaders. Indeed, neither the local's nor the employers' original contract demands were ever made known in detail or entirety to union members. Negotiations were conducted almost solely by Local 7's union president and secretary-treasurer in an atmosphere of quasi-secrecy: Even the rest of the union staff were often in the dark as to the exact state of ongoing negotiations. No member-based bargaining committee was ever formed.

Members' input into contract demands was essentially limited to responding to a multiple-choice questionnaire that the union mailed to all of its members. The questionnaire asked members to rank in importance a series of nine contract issues that had been pre-selected by union staff. No space on the single-page questionnaire was made available for members to write in issues that were important to them but that were not included in the multiple-choice questions. Many members who sent in their questionnaires scrawled their own demands and opinions in the margins and on the back of the form, but in the tabulation of the questionnaires, these informal insertions went unrecorded and were thus lost to the negotiation process.

The tabulated results of the union questionnaire were never made public to Local 7 members. Instead, these results became the basis upon which Local 7 leaders could claim that their actions in the contract negotiations were based on the membership's wishes. The results of the questionnaire became the vehicle through which ownership of the "voice of the membership" could be transferred from members to union staff. A few members here and there might have felt that the union was not addressing important issues in its negotiating, but it was the union leaders—not these members—who had the results of the questionnaire in hand and who, consequently, could claim to know best what the membership as a whole wanted.

Membership voting on the final recommended contract proposal was likewise restricted. Details of the proposal were not released to the membership until the day on which contract voting took place. Only when members came to Local 7's polling stations could they view the proposed contract. At that point, many union representatives were on hand to explain to each member why the contract was a good one and why he or she should vote for it. Thus, not only did Local 7 grocery workers never have a chance to discuss the contract proposal with co-workers in their stores or go to a general membership meeting to hear the proposal debated; they also quite literally had no time to sleep on the contract proposal—to mull it over before coming to a deliberated decision.

When the recommended contract proposal was put to a membership vote, it was small surprise that the proposal was overwhelmingly approved by Local 7 members. On the day of polling, a fair number of young grocery workers came out to vote. But neither they nor their older co-workers had much to do with the basic shape and nature of the new contract that Local 7 was in the process of adopting for the next three years. Like most other union activities and projects in the Box Hill grocery local, the contract—as strong or weak as it might be—was at heart the work of Local 7's staff.

YOUTH–UNION DISJUNCTURES: "STINGING" THE BAGGER

Young grocery workers in Box Hill demonstrate an interest in altering the conditions of their work and in making work for themselves more meaningful and enjoyable. Local 7, on the other hand, for the most part practices a dollars-and-cents form of unionism that focuses on raising members' wages and benefits but largely fails to address the issue of working conditions in Box Hill supermarkets. Some of Local 7's interventions, in fact, actually work to worsen conditions in the name of protecting grocery workers' wages.

The "wages only" versus "working conditions, too" disjuncture between union and youth in Box Hill is emblemized by an endemic "problem" in Box Hill's supermarkets: young baggers' working outside their job classification. Local 7's union rules prohibit baggers from performing work outside an explicitly defined and narrow set of responsibilities. As noted earlier, Local 7 has deliberately restricted the work that baggers may do in supermarkets to protect the wages of higher-paid job classifications, from stockers up. Union staff argue that if young baggers perform more job responsibilities than those laid out in its contract, then it is in the baggers' best interest to be paid a higher wage.

To prevent baggers from working out of classification, Local 7 occasionally conducts "sting" operations, in which union staff go to a store to see whether they can catch any baggers doing work they're not supposed to do. If the union can show that a bagger has been told directly by a manager to work out of classification, then it can demand that the bagger's employer pay that bagger stocker wages for all hours worked during the week in which the offense occurred. However, as union reps sometimes warn young workers at new members meetings, classification violations often come down to a bagger's word against a manager's word. In such cases, it is the bagger who is at risk of being held responsible and disciplined for violating the union contract.

Baggers regularly work out of classification in Box Hill supermarkets. According to the Local 7 grievance department, the reasons for this have to do, first, with baggers' wanting to get ahead and be upwardly mobile—baggers perform extra work for their managers in hopes of promotion—and second, with baggers' not understanding or respecting the union contract. In other words, the union's project of improving the grocery workplace is being frustrated by wrong-headed, selfish, and ignorant high-school-age workers.

Talking to young baggers in Box Hill, however, reveals reasons for working out of classification that go beyond simple brown-nosing, ignorance, or anti-union sentiment. One is that doing stocker work can be more interesting and meaningful than bagging work, and it can help pass the time at work more quickly:

> My title is bagger, but baggers do some stocker stuff. I've been doing that. It's pretty hard. It's not really cool; that's why a stocker gets paid more. . . . But being a stocker, the time flies by, 'cause you're constantly working. And when you're a bagger, it's pretty laid back; you're not really doing anything. When you're a stocker, you're pretty important; the store needs you. You're constantly being asked to do something. The first time I was stocking, I kept hearing my name over the intercom: "Can you do this? Can you do that?" [The worst part about bagging] is just boredom. . . . It's not fun at all. I just watch the time. . . . When it's not busy, as a bagger, you got nothing to do, so you just hang around. But as a stocker, you're constantly working. I like that part of being a stocker.

Bagging is the most boring, unrewarding, and disempowered work there is in the supermarket. Local 7 has been so successful in restricting the work baggers can do that it has helped make bagger work an eternally tedious occupation. When baggers take on stocker work to increase their workplace pleasure—even when they are unjustly denied increased wages by their employers—they are rejecting as insupportable Local 7's wage-supporting strategy of impoverishing the youth work environment.

A second reason baggers offer for working out of classification is their commitment to their work team and their interest in helping coworkers out:

> [The union] makes it so that there's only certain things I can do, which means that legally I can't go help in floral. I can get fired 'cause it's not in my contract, which is kind of dumb. And I can't—, like if a stocker's behind, I can't help him stock. It's not in my contract, and I'll get fired if a union person sees me. . . . So it's very limited. I think it's kind of silly. . . . If we're behind, I don't see why I can't help out.

For some young baggers, Local 7's restrictions on working out of classification diminishes the quality of their working environment not only by making their work more boring but also by making their work less collaborative. It is not necessarily always because of selfishness that baggers reject the Local 7 contract. Ironically, they may also do so because of an increased sense of workplace solidarity.

In Box Hill, there is little constructive dialogue between youth workplace cultures and union institutions. It is possible to imagine that the issues that move youth workplace cultures could be taken up by Local 7 as part of its union agenda; and that Local 7 interventions—whether educational, contractual, or mobilizing in nature—might support and develop youth workplace cultures. But in Box Hill, this doesn't happen. Few young workers, for example, ever file either formal or informal workplace grievances with their local to correct workplace injustices or to push through workplace improvements. Few young workers, as I noted earlier, ever go to union meetings to voice their workplace concerns. And few young workers ever attend union-run educational programs—for the simple reason that these largely do not exist.

For now, Box Hill presents an irony well encapsulated in the following comment by a young unionized deli clerk working in one of the supermarkets represented by Local 7. Committed to environmental issues and doing what she is able within her own department and among her own co-workers to reduce workplace pollution and waste, the deli clerk sighs as she expresses her sense that there is little she can do to affect her employer's overall environmental policies. "I could probably make a fuss," says the teenage grocery worker and member of a 12,000-worker-strong union local. "But it wouldn't do anything, because it takes a group to make a change."

THE UNION ADVANTAGE

> [A couple of years ago,] I had my first child. Two days after [he was born,] he was taken to Children's Hospital, for medical reasons, and after a while, it totalled $100,000 in doctor's bills. Without the union, I don't know if all that would have been paid, or if it was paid, the employer would have gotten whiny with me, may have done something against me just to stop it. [The union] just took care of everything that I could possibly want. . . .

> Until my son went into the hospital, the union had done nothing for me, as far as I could tell. Now that I see what they've done, I'll

gladly pay my thirty-dollar union dues, forty-, fifty-dollar union dues, whatever is needed. 'Cause I know what it takes. I tell everybody that says, "Well, what does the union do for me?" I tell everybody what it did for me.

—Box Hill grocery worker and Local 7 union member
in his early twenties

Talking about youths' union alienation is not the same as talking about anti-unionism among young workers. The point of focusing on the union's responsibility for such alienation in this chapter has been to highlight general problems that can exist in the interactions between youth and unions in North America. As I noted at the outset of this chapter, however, young grocery workers in Box Hill generally express at least a baseline appreciation for the value of unionism. Even when highly critical of their own union local, young workers in Box Hill often talk positively of the wages, benefits, or job security that come with a unionized grocery job but that they would be hard-pressed to find elsewhere in the youth labor market. I conclude this chapter by briefly considering the successes Local 7 has had in providing at least some of its young grocery members with a distinct union advantage.

The strongest expressions of support for Local 7 by young grocery workers come from those who have had to use the union's health-care benefits—as in the earlier quote from the young Box Hill produce clerk. Although many young workers in Box Hill are ineligible for Local 7 health benefits, many others have been able to join the union health plan. Part-time grocery workers working fifteen hours a week or more have access to full health-care coverage for themselves, and those working twenty hours a week or more have access to health coverage for their dependents. Full employer-provided health benefits are almost unheard of in the low-end service sector in the United States. In this area, at least, unionism can make a dramatic difference in the lives of young stopgap workers.

Many young workers in Box Hill also appreciate the sense of job security provided by unionization. Although few young workers have ever seen Local 7 actively intervene in the workplace to protect or assist themselves or their co-workers, the simple fact of having a union contract constrains—at least, to a degree—the possible range and nature of grocery employers' disciplinary actions toward employees. Union rules substitute "just cause" requirements for employee discipline and dismissal for the arbitrary "at will" contracts that govern the majority of U.S. workplaces. Except in cases of theft or drug abuse—offenses that can lead to immediate dismissal—union rules require employers to go through a system of progressive discipline (including verbal and written warnings) before terminating an employee for mistakes or problems they have had at work. A young produce clerk explained the significance of this union-provided protection:

> If you wanna keep your job security, if you wanna be able to come to work today and maybe be wearing tennis shoes, 'cause you forgot your shoes, if you wanna not get fired for that, that's what you need the union for. You need the union to protect you from just the stupid little prejudice they may have against you—you're walking slow today. I mean, you can get fired for anything at another company, where here you can't get fired unless you do something really wrong. There's a certain procedure that has to be gone through.

As another young grocery worker put it more directly: "The union makes it so I can't get fired unless I really fuck up. That's nice."

Some young grocery workers in Box Hill simply like the security of having a contract booklet available that spells out in exact terms the rules that govern their workplace. "When you're young," says a teenage bakery clerk, "you think your manager will tell you the right thing. Well, they won't always tell you the right thing, so it's nice to go by the rules." When the clerk feels that her manager is telling her something she doesn't believe is right, she is able to pull out her contract booklet and show her manager exactly what she should be doing at work.

In the handful of Box Hill supermarkets with shop stewards, some young grocery workers find they have an important friend and ally in their store's shop steward. "Janet rocks!" one young deli clerk says about her store's steward, from whom she regularly seeks advice about workplace issues. "I always talk to Janet." A bakery clerk in the same store says that she was having a hard time paying her union initiation fees and told Janet, her steward, that she wished she could pay in installments: "Janet's like, 'Well, you can, can't you? No? Well, that's not right, I'm going to call them up.' She gets right on the phone and everything!"

For those few young grocery workers who attend union meetings and other activities at the Local 7 hall, the union can be a site of interest, excitement, and learning. Bureaucratic protocols and staff monologues can be deathly boring, say young workers who have attended

Local 7's meetings. But meetings are not all boring all the time. A teenage bakery clerk recalls a memorable experience at a Local 7 meeting at which a discussion arose regarding the possibility of a new state law's being passed that would allow grocery employers to require employees to pay for their own uniforms:

> You learn a lot [at the union meetings]; every time you go there, you learn more and more—stuff you don't even think about, about dress codes, how they can change them right under you and not even know it. . . . One time I was very shocked that the secretary-treasurer, he started crying at a meeting because of the dress codes, and I thought, "He's very committed." That just really shocked me, how somebody could be so dedicated to this, and I think that's great.

Hearing union staff and members talk critically about issues affecting the grocery workforce can be a new and invigorating experience for young grocery workers. At some general membership meetings, emotions rise as debate and discussion from the membership floor flies during the closing minutes dedicated to new and unfinished business.

Finally, there is the matter of wages. Baggers' wages are clearly low in Box Hill. Wages for stockers and side-department workers (deli, bakery, floral) are a mixed bag. Workers in these departments are poorly paid compared with checkers and grocery and produce clerks in Box Hill supermarkets, especially when one considers that they do much the same work as those in the higher-paid classifications. But wages in these mid-level departments are still generally better than the wages that young stopgap workers can find in other low-end service and retail jobs in town. For the minority of young workers who manage to get themselves on a checker, produce clerk, or grocery clerk wage scale, and who stay with these positions for the equivalent of two years of full-time work (the time it takes to reach the top of these scales), unionized grocery work in Box Hill can offer what are, by most any reckoning, high wages for a young stopgap worker. For these young workers, grocery work is no longer seen as any old stopgap job that is as good or bad as the next one. Instead, unionization, for these workers, helps transform a stopgap job into a more lucrative and valuable stepping-stone job that can help support individual trajectories up into future adult identities and career occupations elsewhere.

7   The Youth Union

THE PRESIDENT of fast-food Local C in Glenwood likes to tell the story of a fifteen-year-old Fry House worker, who, a number of years ago, joined the local's health and safety committee—a committee that meets monthly with company representatives to address outstanding health and safety issues in the Glenwood Fry Houses. After only a brief time on the committee, the teenager, somewhat to the president's disappointment, quit his job at Fry House and dropped out of contact with the union local. The president did not know what had happened to the young worker until recently, when she received a letter from him. The young man was writing because he wanted the local's president to know that he had become an occupational health and safety officer working for the government.

The Local C president's story offers a striking example of the advantage unionism can bring to young stopgap service-sector workers. In this chapter, I take an approach opposite from that of the preceding chapter and focus on the connections that are made in Glenwood between Local C and its young Fry House members. By highlighting the local's successes in working with its youth membership, I seek to provide a portrait of the kinds of possibilities that unionism may have to offer for improving conditions in the youth labor market elsewhere in North America. As the local president's story suggests, the advantages unionism can bring to young stopgap workers can be described not just in terms of immediate gains in wages, benefits, and job security—although these, of course, are extremely important—but also in terms of farther-reaching, longer-term educational gains.

Local C is the "youth union." In recent years, the local has earned a reputation in Canada as a standout among unions for its work with young stopgap service-sector workers. This reputation is built largely on the local's recent string of organizing successes in Glenwood's youth labor market. But the reputation also rides on the fifty-odd Fry House outlets that Local C has represented for almost thirty years—a bargaining unit that constitutes one of North America's largest and longest-lived groups of unionized fast-food workers. Youths are central to Local C's very identity. Whereas staff in other unions often talk about youth as a problem to be addressed—in the collecting of dues or the communicating of the value of unionism—Local C's staff are more likely to talk about youth in terms of opportunity for social change, union growth, learning, and empowerment.

ALL-AGES UNIONISM

"I would not degrade myself by working at Mickey D's," a young Fry House supervisor says, point-blank. The supervisor articulates a sentiment, widespread among Glenwood Fry House workers, that unionization has made Fry House work far superior to work in other multinational fast-food chains, such as McDonald's:

> [McDonald's] is pretty brutal, the pay . . . because they don't have a union or anything to back them up. . . . I have a friend that I met there [at McDonald's]; she works there. . . . She'll just tell me of the problems she has. . . . The owners are like, whatever, we don't care, this is what you get paid, if you don't like it—. Talking about raises, she's been working there three years, the only raise she got was when the minimum wage went up. . . . I'm telling her to come over to Fry House. I mean not only do we start . . . above the minimum wage, you go up to [one-and-one-third times the minimum wage] after 500 hours or seven months.

Higher starting wages, guaranteed raises, employer-provided benefits, and just-cause job protection from arbitrary discipline and termination constitute the basic union advantage for young Glenwood Fry House workers.

Unionization in the Glenwood Fry Houses has had a marked impact on how young workers there evaluate the social status of their fast-food employment. Unionization (and union wages) help young workers feel that much of the stigma that is widely associated with working in a "dead-end" fast-food job is removed:

> When people ask me where I work, and I say Fry House, I sort of think they're laughing—like, ha-ha, loser place. But then they ask me how much I get paid, and I tell them; they'll be like astonished. They give me more respect.

"A lot of people look down on fast food," says another young Fry House worker. "But if you ever say you're union in a Fry House, people nearly drop."

This basic union advantage of wages, benefits, job security, and job status that Local C confers on its Fry House membership in Glenwood is similar to that conferred by Local 7 on its grocery membership in Box Hill. But whereas the value of unionism for workers in Box Hill varies dramatically according to whether one is young or old, temporary or long term, part time or full time in the workforce, such distinctions are much less salient in Local C's Fry House bargaining unit. Local C, unlike Local 7, practices an "all-ages" form of unionism—a unionism that is committed to protecting and representing the interests of youth as well as adult workers. Unlike with young grocery workers in Box Hill, one rarely hears young Fry House workers complain that their union provides more advantage in terms of lower dues, higher wages, or greater benefits to older members than it does to younger members.

Local C practices its "all-ages" unionism first by keeping the costs of unionism low for its part-time and temporary workers—workers who, in the Glenwood Fry Houses, are more likely to be youth than adult workers:

- *Youth and adult (part-time and full-time) fast-food workers in Glenwood all pay the same union-dues rates.* Dues rates are tagged to the number of hours members work each month, so part-timers and full-timers pay roughly the same proportion of their monthly earnings in union dues.
- *Youth and adult (temporary and long-term) fast-food workers in Glenwood all pay the same low union-initiation fees.* High initiation fees make unionism unappealing to workers who expect to work only temporarily within an industry. Initiation fees in Glenwood, while not tagged to length of member tenure, are kept low for all members: Initiation fees cost approximately 1.5 times a Fry House worker's starting wage. In Box Hill, by contrast, union initiation fees cost from nine to sixteen times a grocery worker's starting wage (depending on the department in which a worker enters the industry).

Local C further practices all-ages unionism by making sure that the value of unionism is quickly apparent to all of its members—not just to its adult, long-term, or full-time members:

- *All Fry House workers in Glenwood, young and old, enjoy equally the advantage of union-negotiated wages.* Unlike Local 7 in Box Hill, there are no separate, higher- and lower-paying "adult" and "youth" job classifications. Adult and youth Fry House workers in Glenwood all earn the same wages.
- *All Fry House workers in Glenwood, young and old, are on wage scales.* Everyone working in the Glenwood Fry Houses is guaranteed a series of tenure-based raises. (In Box Hill, by contrast, grocery baggers and stockers are excluded from wage scales.)
- *All Fry House workers in Glenwood, young and old, have seniority rights to job promotion.* New workers in the Glenwood Fry Houses do not have to be stuck in lower-paid cook and cashier positions indefinitely; they can move up into the slightly higher-paid supervisor and in-charge classifications. (In Box Hill, workers have no seniority rights to job promotion; baggers and stockers thus have no guarantee that they ever will move out of their entry-level "youth" jobs.)
- *Health and pension benefits, while not available to all Fry House workers, are nevertheless more accessible to young, temporary, and part-time workers in Glenwood than is the case in Box Hill grocery.* There is no minimum hours requirement for workers to be eligible for Local C's health-care plan. (In Box Hill, eligibility cuts off at fifteen hours per week.) Young Fry House workers are eligible to enroll in their health-care plan after one month of employment (as opposed to a three-month waiting period in Box Hill). Local C's pension plan has a three-year vesting period, after which time workers are entitled to all monies paid into the plan in their name. (Local 7's vesting period, by contrast, is five years.)[1]

These contrasts in the benefits of unionism for young stopgap workers in Box Hill and Glenwood are not accidental. Local C has made an explicit commitment to minimizing differences between junior and senior and younger and older workers in the Fry House bargaining unit. Wage differentials in the unit in particular have been kept narrow deliberately by the local. In place of stretching out wage scales so that senior employees can earn high wages while junior employees earn only low wages, or of creating separate job classifications so that certain (older) workers can earn high while other (younger) workers earn low—two strategies that Local 7 in Box Hill has used—Local C has sought over the years to push up all wages together in the Fry House bargaining unit. Local C has not been as successful as Local 7 has been in the Box Hill grocery industry in pushing up the top wages in the Glenwood Fry Houses. But it has been much more successful than Local 7 in securing a basic union advantage for its entire membership that minimizes contractual age discrimination between the old and the young.[2]

UNION INTERVENTIONS IN THE WORKPLACE

Local C intervenes regularly and assertively in the Fry House workplace in defense of its young (and old) members. In every Fry House outlet I visited in Glenwood, young workers could tell stories about having been helped out by their union in resolving formal or informal workplace grievances. Some of these grievances involved protracted conflicts between union and employer and had been taken through multiple steps of formal procedures, while many others had been resolved simply, quickly, and casually.

Young Fry House workers in Glenwood have been protected by their union from wrongful discipline and termination. In one Fry House outlet, for example, a cashier was fired when one hundred dollars went missing from her till. According to official company policy, cashiers are individually responsible for their registers, which only they are supposed to have access to during shifts. In practice, however, cashiers, supervisors and managers regularly use one another's registers to make service more efficient during customer rushes. In this case, the union challenged Fry House to produce concrete evidence that the cashier had taken the missing money. When no such evidence could be produced, the union was able to get the cashier her job back. It was later discovered that another worker at the store had been stealing money regularly from the company, and this worker was subsequently dismissed.

Local C has protected young Fry House workers from having shifts and hours taken away from them unfairly; it has helped young workers secure promotions and raises to which they are entitled; and it has protected young workers from management abuse. One cashier recalls a particularly bad store manager who verbally abused his young Fry House staff: "He would swear at us, he would tell us that we were all losers, that we were incompetent, that he was the only one who could do anything [right]." The manager would throw employees' personal belongings away if they had been left in the back of the store—although previous managers had long allowed workers to leave work shoes and other items overnight in the restaurant. The manager also tried to cut corners on cleaning and pay workers under the table to make his store budget look better. When workers complained to the Fry House corporation about the manager, their complaints were roundly ignored. So workers called the union. Under union pressure, the company quickly took action and decided to fire the manager.

Local C's workplace interventionism is motivated by a number of factors. Its union culture is oriented toward the aggressive pursuit of social justice both in its own bargaining units and in society and the workplace at large. Strong contract language in the local's Fry House collective-bargaining agreement supports Local C's desire to pursue aggressively members' formal and informal grievances. Perhaps most critical to Local C's workplace activism, though, is the local's commitment to developing and using a strong and pivotal shop-steward system that is run by its union membership. Shop stewards in Glenwood are (in theory, at least) elected by their co-workers in each Fry House restaurant, and—unlike stewards in Box Hill's Local 7—are expected to be workplace activists. Stewards are responsible in Local C (again, in theory) for handling the initial stages of the formal grievance process and for dealing informally with workplace problems that never come to formal grievance.

Shop stewards in the Glenwood Fry Houses play (in practice, not just theory) a central role in Local C's workplace interventionism. Many of Local C's interventions are carried out not by union staff but by shop stewards. As one young Fry House cook puts it, "I've never had to call [the union] because [the shop steward] has been there. She's really good." In the best circumstances, the steward's presence in the Fry House workplace provides young workers with both access to information about and immediate support from their union:

> Anything that we don't understand about the union, any rights that we
> don't know about, as soon as anything goes down in the store, it does-
> n't matter how little or big it is, he [the steward] is in there. And he
> knows what he's doing, so he knows what rights we have; he knows
> what we can say, what we can't say, what we can do, what we can't do.
> He's right in there to back us right away, so it works good. It works
> really good.

The shop steward's presence helps to put a familiar face on the union and to increase young workers' comfort levels in contacting their local. "Natasha's our shop steward," says a teenage Fry House cashier, "and she knows everything that happens to me—at work, anyway. So it's not like I need to go talk to somebody I don't even know [when there's a problem at work], that I'm not even close to." Even when stewards are not directly involved in union workplace interventions, they are often instrumental in encouraging co-workers to get in contact with their local in the first place so that such interventions can continue forward.

The union's workplace interventionism brings immediate and concrete material benefits to young stopgap workers. But interventionism has other, less direct effects, as well. Participation in a union grievance can be an important educational experience for a young worker. Grievance procedures not only allow young workers to see how their union works—or, in the case of grievances that progress to a labor-board hearing, to see how the provincial labor board works—they also allow young workers to recognize the limits of their store managers' authority, as senior company representatives and union staff challenge and overrule in-store managers' decisions. Union grievances, in fact, are a major site in Local C for young Fry House workers' deciding to become more involved in their union: Many of today's shop stewards in the local first came into contact with union staff via a workplace grievance.

Union interventionism creates an interplay between Local C's union culture and the youth workplace cultures of the Fry House restaurants. The union's workplace interventions help youth workplace cultures survive times of crisis that are created by managerial turnover. Young Fry House workers are sometimes able to protect their jobs and local workplace practices, when these are threatened by the arrival of a new store manager, by calling for union assistance to get rid of the new manager or shape up the new manager's workplace behavior. In these instances, workers often work in conjunction with union leadership to document managerial abuses against them (in support of formal union grievances), and in parallel with union leadership as they pursue their own in-store strategies to put pressure on the disruptive manager.

Finally, interventionism helps young Fry House workers defend their union-negotiated rights and privileges by themselves on an ongoing and regular basis. With the credible threat of union intervention behind them, and with their rights and privileges laid out clearly in a union contract, some young Fry House workers are able to negotiate effectively with store and area managers without ever involving shop stewards or union staff:

> The little green [union contract] book.... I love that book! Everytime I'd read it—: "Ben [the store manager], you gotta pay me more, 'cause it doesn't matter. If I work six days a week, on my sixth shift I'm supposed to get double time." ... He'd try and get away with it and say, "Time and a half." I'd say, "No, Ben." I'd say, "Open it, read it." And then he'd pay me.... I've never had reason to call the union; like, Ben's never put his foot down and said no to me about anything. He always backs down.... If I had a big problem [and the store manager didn't back down] ... , before I would go to the union, I would go to our area manager.... I wouldn't want Ben to lose his job or something, 'cause he's already had dealings with the union before.... I'd call the area manager; I'd say, "Ben and I are not getting along; we're not seeing eye to eye. Could you come down here, 'cause I'd rather go to you than go to the union."

Particularly in stores that have had a history of union intervention, young Fry House workers often find that the mere threat of calling the union is enough to spur company management into action. Indeed, most young Fry House workers express a preference for solving store problems at the store level. "If it's something big, we go to the union," says a Fry House shift supervisor, "but most of the time we try to fix things ourselves, because we know what's going on."

YOUTH SHOP STEWARDS

"I try to find out as much as I can before the meeting." A young Fry House cashier and shop steward with several years' work and union experience is explaining how she prepares for a grievance meeting with her store manager. In the grievance meeting, the steward says, "I always think of myself as being there for the employee, arguing for his or her case against management." But to support her co-workers effectively, the steward first has to be well informed of the details of the case. As a full-time college student who works part time for Fry House, the steward does not always have firsthand knowledge of the events behind a co-worker's complaints:

I try to find out as much as I can before the meeting—first off, number one, by talking to the employee. Then if the employee names other names, like other employees involved, I'll try to talk to them, find out what happened, as much as I can. A couple of times, I would try to have a quick talk with the manager about what's going on. Then I plan out what we should do, which approach here. Then when the time comes, I would say my bit in defense of the employee, see if that works.

Some grievance meetings, the steward says, are cut-and-dried: "Sometimes managers come and go, they don't really know much about the contract agreement, they don't know the rules and procedures. So it's just basically sitting down and showing it [the contract] to them." Other meetings are more complicated: "things that were arbitrary, they can go either way, it's one person's word against another person's word." In a couple of grievances the steward has worked on, she has been unable to come to a resolution with the store manager, and the grievance has had to go on to step two of Local C's formal grievance procedure. At this point, the steward and store manager step aside, and the grievance is debated between a Local C union representative and a Fry House area manager.

One of the most remarkable aspects of Local C's work with young Fry House workers is that it allows them to play such important roles in their union and workplace. Unlike Local 7 in Box Hill, Local C offers at least a handful of its young members opportunities to participate actively in union affairs. Teenagers and youths in their early twenties (along with older, adult co-workers) have become shop stewards, attended labor educational programs and conferences, worked as union organizers, and joined bargaining and health and safety committees in Local C. Such union positions provide young workers with leadership roles, social responsibilities, and learning opportunities that vastly exceeds those that are typically available in the low-end service-sector workplace. While young Glenwood Fry House workers are trained by their employer in how to act to best please their customers and increase their employer's profit margins, young Fry House shop stewards and union activists are given an opportunity by their union to learn how to act in support of their fellow co-workers against unfair managerial and company practices, and how to push for the broader accomplishment of social justice in the workplace.

Only a tiny minority of young Fry House workers in Glenwood are ever able to take on activist roles in their union. Nevertheless, the experiences of this small group of youth stewards and activists are important, because they help shed light on the broad educational significance that unionization could have for young stopgap service-sector workers elsewhere in North America. Youth stewardship in the Glenwood Fry Houses demonstrates the remarkable educational opportunities that union activism can have for young workers. However, it also highlights some of the educational limitations that union activism can have—at least, when the activism is practiced the way it is in Glenwood.

Local C's training of young workers as shop stewards rests on its commitment to all-ages unionism. In encouraging young workers to get involved with their union, Local C's staff reject popular and prejudicial stereotypes of youths' apathy and disengagement from stopgap work. When given the opportunity by institutions such as Local C, union staff argue, stopgap youths are quick and eager to take on temporary leadership positions in the union and workplace, as elsewhere. When the local has bad experiences working with young stewards and activists, they generally do not invoke prejudicial stereotypes of youths' immaturity and irresponsibility, as is so often done; instead, they point to the many positive experiences they have had in working with youths and attribute individual difficulties to factors of individual character and context.

In training young workers to be stewards and activists, Local C has had to look beyond the bounds of its own institutional structures. Most young Fry House workers are stopgap workers who leave their fast-food jobs after relatively brief periods of time. Local C is neither wealthy nor large, and it costs the local a considerable amount of time and money to train and retrain youth workers to be stewards and activists as they continually enter and leave the Fry House bargaining unit. In some ways, it would be cheaper for the local to reserve steward and activist positions for adult Fry House workers, who are generally more likely to stay with the company for longer periods of time. But the local is commited to training young stewards and activists, and accepts, as part of this commitment, that these young stewards and activists occasionally will have very short Fry House tenures. The local justifies its extra expenses by citing the hope and belief that the experience these youths have with Local C in the short run will benefit both these youths as individuals and Canadian society as a whole in the long run.

To train its stewards, Local C runs a weekend-long shop-steward course at least twice a year; stewards who attend the course are compensated by the local for lost work time. The training course, which brings together new stewards from different bargaining units in Local C and neighboring locals, makes extensive use of role playing, buzz groups, and team problem solving to help new stewards flesh out the complexities and subtleties that complicate their workplace strategy and action. Stewards are trained in how to read collective-bargaining agreements closely; how to distinguish grievable offenses from "violations" of workers' rights and interests that are not protected by union contract; how to investigate, write up, and fight different kinds of workplace grievances; and how to act as a steward in a fair and just manner that will maintain the respect of both managers and co-workers. Stewards are also introduced to provincial labor codes and human-rights legislation; to ways to recognize and confront harassment in the workplace; and to the union's broader political and educational programs. Not all of the Fry House stewards I met in Glenwood had taken Local C's steward-training class, but all had been invited to attend, and those who hadn't taken it already expected to do so in the near future.

Young Fry House shop stewards perform a number of important roles in their own workplaces in addition to handling formal grievances. Stewards provide accessible and non-threatening sources of union and workplace information and advice for other young workers. "People come to me before they go to the manager," a teenage steward says, "mainly because I'm their age and we can talk. They won't be afraid their head will be bitten off. The manager wouldn't do that, but they can speak more freely with me."

Stewards also are frequently able to interact informally with store managers on behalf of their co-workers: Corrections in shift scheduling and proper payment, for example, usually can be handled without a formal grievance meeting. One steward explains how he was able to persuade his manager, simply through casual conversation, not to suspend a recently hired co-worker for repeated lateness. The co-worker had been late to shift several times, but, the steward pointed out, the restaurant had a couple of long-term workers who had been chronically late for years, and nothing had been said to them. The manager agreed that the fairest thing to do would be to wipe everyone's prior records clean and announce a new store policy of disciplining any and all workers for multiple late arrivals to shift.

Being a steward in the Glenwood Fry Houses is not always easy. The best courses of action to take in the workplace are not always clear, as some problems seem to defy easy solution. Fry House stewards must sometimes struggle with deciding how to handle difficult or ambiguous workplace situations, and they often end up making mistakes. Understanding the kinds of problems young stewards in Glenwood face, along with the kinds of errors or "misfires" they make in performing their steward work, is a critical part of understanding these workers' on-the-job learning. It is also a critical part of recognizing some of the limitations that Local C's practices and structure create for these stewards' learning processes. To provide a sense of the nature of "on-the-job" learning among young Fry House shop stewards, I will describe three fairly typical struggles and "misfires" that stewards have made in the course of everyday union workplace activism.

Dan, a shop steward in his early twenties, talks about his struggles to balance being an activist in the workplace with being too aggressive with his managers and co-workers. He knows, and his co-workers confirm, that although he is sometimes successful in his work-site interventions, at other times, he ends up making everyone unhappy. A recently hired cook at the Fry House where Dan works describes her ambivalence about a time that Dan tried to come to her assistance:

> I was cleaning the fryers, and I have to change the oil. I have to empty it into a bucket, take it outside, around, up, dump it in the pit. I was like, "Oh my god, I don't want to do this." I was just freaking out. I was new. . . . "Oh my gosh, it's hot, grease, ow, ooh, I don't want to do it." Dan realized I really didn't want to do it. I was just scared—hot grease, I wasn't used to handling it in the first place. It was only the second time I'd put it in the fryers. . . .
> But I guess there's proper lids you're supposed to have on top [of the buckets]. We don't have those. [Dan] said to the manager, "I'm not going to let her do that." Him and [the manager] had just had a confrontation, so I was, "Oh god, no—I can take it. I'll take it out; don't worry about it." . . . Dan's like, "No, she's a trainee; there's not proper lids for these

things. I'm not letting her take it out. If she gets burned with these, it's your head. She's not taking it out." So [the manager] ended up taking them [the buckets of hot grease] out.

"At times, [Dan] does look out for everyone else," the young cook says, "but sometimes I think he's doing it [speaking out] just to piss off the manager."

"Dan's really good at what he does," says another young cashier, who has worked at the restaurant for a couple of years, "which I guess is why he's so nosy. 'Cause he kinda has to be. But he's gotta learn; that's why people shut him out: 'You're too nosy, shut up, butt out.'" Dan took Local C's training course when he first became a steward a little more than a year before I interviewed him. But since that time, he has had no extended interaction with anyone from the union—and he has never met any of the other Fry House stewards to hear about or compare their workplace experiences. Dan attempts to judge how he is doing as shop steward from the varying positive and negative reactions he receives from his co-workers.

Another young Fry House steward, nineteen-year-old Lucia, talks about her struggle to figure how best to handle employee theft of company money—a problem that is endemic in her Fry House restaurant:

> OK, you're at work, you know somebody's stealing money. . . . I have to protect this person if they're saying—. I might know it, but I can't really say, look, this person's stealing. I did that once, and I feel bad about it. I got that person fired. This was before I was shop steward. If I do it now, I don't know what would happen to my shop-steward status. So I just say, "Hey, if you steal, whatever you do, don't come to me. I won't protect you." . . . It's hard, though. . . . [If a co-worker who has been stealing does ask for help], even if I know it, then I have to protect this person. And then I think in my own head, OK, this person's probably doing the wrong thing, but I've gotta do my job. That's what I'm here for. So in that case, that's where I don't like the union. People use it to their advantage.

In Local C's shop-steward classes, union instructors emphasize that, although it is the union's duty to represent fairly all of its members, stewards need to be wary of appearing to support wrongful actions on the part of their co-workers, as this can undermine their credibility in the workplace. However, Lucia knows from personal experience that Local C staff have protected workers in her store *who really were stealing money* from losing their jobs by demanding that the employer produce evidence of these workers' theft—evidence that the employer did not have. Assuming that her union is in the habit of protecting bad workers, Lucia has not tried to talk with union staff about her misgivings.

A third Fry House steward, Peter, who is in his mid-twenties, recounts an early mistake in which he actually ended up getting a co-worker fired. This co-worker had started raising a fuss in Peter's restaurant about other workers' habit of giving discounts on company food and drinks to Fry House delivery drivers when the drivers were off shift. Although official company policy states that delivery drivers (unlike in-store employees) are entitled to discounts only during their shifts, workers at the restaurant felt that the company was treating the drivers like second-class citizens and that they should be given the same discounts as everybody else in the store.[3]

The worker refused to let the matter drop. The worker herself, however, was also breaking the company's official food policy by taking a free drink home with her every night after her shift was over:

> She just has a big time giving that thing [complaining about the delivery drivers]. Then every night before she leaves, she gets a cup, fills it with ice, fills it with pop, and walks out of the store. I said, "What do you call that?" I said, "That's a theft. Though it's just a small thing, it's a theft." So I wrote a letter as a shop steward. I brought it to the manager, saying this is what happened and could you please take appropriate action, according to the food policy and the collective agreement.... She totally denies she's not doing it, and the [security] camera is right there. So they pull out the [videotape evidence from the] camera.

"I wrote the letter just wanting her to get disciplined," says Peter. "I didn't know it was gonna be all the way, that she was gonna be out of the company." Peter had felt that, to keep things fair at work, the self-righteous worker should be held to her own high standards. Peter has not had a chance to talk to union staff or other stewards about how he understood and handled the situation. He now treats the incident as a personal learning experience and as something his conscience will just have to live with. "Sometimes you look bad," Peter says ruefully, "just because you try to do the right thing."

What is striking in listening to these young Fry House shop stewards talk about the difficulties of their work is their isolation from one another and from union staff. Stewards simply do not have any regular opportunity to talk with and learn from other union activists about their experiences, strategies, successes and failures in conducting steward work. They frequently have to struggle alone through the decisions they make as stewards. Most Fry House stewards have been to one of Local C's stewardship classes, but once they are finished with this weekend class, the union provides no institutional structure for ongoing feedback and dialogue between union and steward. Stewards can and do call the Local C office for assistance on specific problems or questions, of course, but these calls do not tend to provide occasions for general reflection on overall experiences in performing steward work.

Local C used to run a regular localwide steward meeting at its union hall, but it canceled this meeting some years ago due to lack of attendance. It is thus not entirely clear what kind of institutional structure Local C could create that would be effective in bringing young Fry House stewards into regular contact with their union and with one another. It does seem clear, though, that workplace isolation creates an unsupported learning environment for these young union activists that can, at times, constitute a serious obstacle to their ability to perform the union work that Local C relies upon them to handle.

The individual isolation of young Fry House shop stewards is largely passive and shaped by a lack of collective and interactive practices and structures in Local C. But Fry House stewards are also sometimes actively (if unintentionally) isolated by the practices of Local C staff. Some stewards complain that union staff perform union work for which stewards are supposedly responsible. Although the shop steward is, in theory, the union's front line in handling workplace problems, some stewards complain that co-workers tend to call the union office directly for help—and that the union office readily receives and responds to these workers' calls. "I guess they don't know that I am the union," one young steward says about his co-workers. "They figure they gotta phone [the union office]. I gotta get it through that I am the union: 'Don't worry. I might not know 100 percent what I'm doing all the time, but I'm learning.'"

Stewards in the Glenwood Fry Houses point to two problems that can arise when union staff take over the initial handling of workers' questions and problems. First, the shop steward's credibility risks being undermined. When stewards are cut out of the union member–union staff loop, the union work that Local C supposedly expects them to perform can be made more difficult, as they may lose stature in the eyes of their co-workers and managers.

The second problem, some stewards say, is that union staff are outsiders to their workplaces and thus often don't have a feel for the overall dynamics of a particular restaurant, which inevitably stand behind each and every grievance:

> If they tell [the union staff] something, [the union staff] is gonna get half the message. If I'm there, and sometimes maybe I'm present right when the thing happened. I can talk to another person, another [cashier] or another cook, if I'm not there. I'll be able to have a better picture, and I know this person better than any of the union staff [do]. . . . It's not, like, just whatever happened in that very moment. You got to look back and forth, what was happening, how this thing—. Because when a problem creates, it just doesn't create by the moment, these things get built up. . . . If the manager's not happy, or he's not happy with the manager, everybody starts giving attitude to each other. Before the union just jumps onto it, they should work with the shop steward.

When union staff intervene to resolve an individual grievance without knowing the full work-site picture, other Fry House workers may come to feel disgruntled with the union's meddling. In some instances, the course that outside union intervention takes might actually be misguided—as is arguably the case, for example, with the union's defense of thieving workers in Lucia's store.

Local C staff are in a difficult position in terms of knowing when and whether it is best to redirect members' calls to shop stewards. In light of the miscues that stewards can be expected to make as they attempt to learn their roles in isolated workplace settings, union staff may feel that directly handling workers' grievances and problems themselves offers the best form of assistance to their membership. As workplace insiders, on the other hand, stewards may often be better placed to intervene at their work sites than are union staff. Further, over the long term, direct interventions by union staff may undermine the very institutional structures that the union has created to foster and support workplace activism in the Fry House restaurants. For union staff intervention feeds back into the problem of unsupported steward learning environments:

The more union staff take over the handling of workers' questions and grievances, the less pressure there is on the local to take seriously and begin addressing the problems caused by the workplace isolation of individual Fry House shop stewards.

YOUTH UNION ALIENATION

Local C's interactions with its young Fry House members are, of course, marked by other limitations and failures. Shop stewards' isolation is symptomatic of a much broader isolation in Glenwood of young workers from their union. "We never see them, ever," a young Fry House cashier says angrily about Local C staff:

> It would be nice if the union would call to see how things are going, check-ins, is everything all right.... It just seems they take our money and don't even care. They say they care so much in their newsletter, but.... It seems they don't care how we're doing. Not that it's that big of a deal, but it would be nice to have a phone call.... The only time I've heard from the union in the last two years is when [the local president] called about [being interviewed for this research project].... Workers in our store joke, "Is the union still alive? We haven't heard anything." They never come out to the store. A phone call, a letter to acknowledge you're still alive, that we still exist, something.

New Fry House workers especially often know next to nothing about who or what the union is. As a three-year veteran Fry House cashier, who had filed a couple of grievances with the union, explains: "The new people [working in our store], they don't even really know what's going on in the union. They sign a form saying they'll be in the union, and that's it. That's as far as they know."

The causes of youths' alienation from Local C are, in many ways, much the same as were seen for Local 7 in Box Hill in the preceding chapter. For despite its interventionism, Local C often fails to maintain a strong workplace presence in all of its stores, or even to make minimal connections with all of its young members. The organization of the fast-food industry obviously does not help foster union–member interactions: Fry House workers are isolated at small work sites spread out over hundreds of square miles around Glenwood. But Local C's union structures and practices must also share some of the blame. The local has no outreach program to introduce new members to the union. Many young, starting Fry House workers say, in fact, that they have never even received a copy of their union contract, so they are unable to see for themselves their union-negotiated rights and privileges.[4]

Local C staff do not regularly visit Fry House restaurants. Instead, the local predicates its ability to interact with its membership and introduce new members to the union on having an active shop-steward system. But this strategy, in practice, has several flaws—not the least of which is that as many as a third of the Glenwood Fry Houses have no shop stewards. As I noted earlier, in the high-turnover fast-food industry, it is hard for Local C to hang on to its stewards. But in some Fry House restaurants, crews have been without stewards for such long periods that the very concept is alien to them. As the local has come to rely on the union staff's handling of workplace grievances, it has occasionally been lax about replacing and training stewards at all of its work sites.

In Fry House outlets where there are shop stewards, meanwhile, union–member relations are made problematic by the fact that the union's in-store presence is typically limited to a single shop steward. For young Fry House workers who are not shop stewards, there are really few opportunities to participate in any meaningful way in the life of their union. Positions on union bargaining, health and safety, human rights, education, and organizing committees and programs are limited—and they tend, in any event, to be given to and taken up by Fry House stewards. Local C has general membership meetings that are held bimonthly at the Local C union hall, but these meetings are essentially a burlesque, run by union staff on the apparently nonsensical (though correct) assumption that the general membership will not show up. Local C's national parent union runs one of the strongest labor-education programs of any union in North America. The local's union literature claims that these programs are available to any group of fifteen or more workers who desire a particular course. But few young Fry House workers have participated in these courses—in fact, the vast majority are unaware of their very existence.

The fact that the shop steward in each Glenwood Fry House outlet tends to be the only active, in-store link between Local C and its members has several effects on union–youth interactions. First, young Fry House workers tend to see the shop steward as the only worker in their store who really needs to be concerned about union affairs. In other words, they see the union as being individualized in the person of the shop steward; they certainly don't see themselves as being involved with or constituting "the union." Second, stewards' individual isolation in the Glenwood Fry Houses is increased, because stewards often don't have anyone else in their own workplaces to work with on union issues. Third, if young workers are dissatisfied with their steward, they are as likely to turn their backs on the union as a whole as they are to call for a new steward in their store.

According to Local C's bylaws, the election of shop stewards should be "held and/or reviewed annually" within each Fry House restaurant. But in practice, the local has no regular structure in place for communicating with or keeping tabs on its Fry House stewards, or for soliciting members' opinions about their stewards. Some young workers complain that their shop stewards are inactive, that they know little about the union contract and do little to assist their co-workers in the store. Other young workers feel alienated from their stewards because of personality conflicts or differences in race, gender, and age. Because the steward is generally the worker most closely linked with the union in each Fry House restaurant, however, workers who are dissatisfied with a steward are often unlikely to initiate calls to their union to ask for a new steward election. They are more likely simply to resign themselves to the fact of having an inactive union presence in their workplace— or even, as one Fry House cashier put it, to the conviction that "the union just doesn't work for me."

The only contact between Local C's union staff and young Fry House workers who are not shop stewards tends to come through in-store workplace grievances. Non-steward Fry House workers consequently tend to know their union, at best, as an entity that comes into their workplaces sporadically to help workers bring grievances about outstanding workplace problems. Other possible contexts for union–member interactions are essentially unknown. A broad and major implication of this narrow "union-equals-grievance" identification for union–member relations in the Glenwood Fry Houses is that many young workers come to see their union, paradoxically, as an essentially individualist and individualizing institution.

By individualist, I mean to say that the union is typically seen by young Fry House workers as a body that can help workers with individual workplace problems that can be resolved fairly simply via a one-time union intervention—getting a worker his or her shifts back, for example, or even getting rid of an abusive manager. The union, however, is not seen by Fry House workers as being much help in dealing with structural workplace problems—with situations whose resolution would require an ongoing and collective program of education, strategizing, and coordination of effort at levels inside and outside the workplace.

I analyze one such structural workplace problem—that of handling speed-ups and off-the-clock work—in the next chapter. Other examples in the Glenwood Fry Houses include work processes and environments that put workers' health and safety at risk; work relations with abusive customers; and workers' dissatisfaction at not having extended control over shaping and improving the quality of their stores, products, and service. Such structural workplace problems simply are not easily addressed via an individual grievance filed by a union with limited work-site presence. "As soon as the union gets involved," a young Fry House cashier says about dealing with violations of health and safety procedures in her restaurant, "they're [the managers are] kinda like, 'Oh OK; you guys have to do this now.' But that only lasts about a week." "I used to call the union," a cook sighs about chronic understaffing in his store: "But nothing ever changes, you're wasting your time. It's impossible to change. You're back at wherever you were."

Many young Fry House workers also see Local C as an individualizing institution. Not only do union interventions in the Fry House workplace frequently focus on an individual's problems at work, they also often pit individual Fry House workers against one another. One of the classic interventions that Local C makes over and over, for example, involves returning shifts and hours to senior employees that have been taken away unfairly and given to more junior employees. Apart from its triennial contract negotiations, Local C provides its Fry House membership with few if any opportunities to work or participate collectively as a group in a defined union project (a project, for example, that one could imagine might involve workers coming together to redress one of the structural workplace problems mentioned earlier).

The president of Local C often rolls her eyes when she hears about young workers enthusiastically competing in one of Fry House's multitude of incentive programs: She sees such programs as being divisive, as pitting worker against worker within the Fry House chain, and as being contrary to the union spirit of worker solidarity. But for many young Fry House workers (as was discussed in Chapter Three), company incentive competitions are taken up precisely as an opportunity to work together as a team in a defined project. For many young Fry House workers in Glenwood, it is their employer that gives them opportunities—that they can seize selectively and strategically if and when they desire—to work as a collectivity. And it is their union that, by failing to provide them with opportunities for collectivity—whether these be in the context of labor education or union activism—frequently isolates them as individuals in the workplace.

UNION CONTRACT NEGOTIATIONS: THE IMPORTANCE OF YOUTH INVOLVEMENT

Problems of union individualism and members' isolation in Local C can be traced in part to the Fry House bargaining unit's history of contract negotiation—a history in which most young Fry House workers have only ever been marginally involved. Two facts about Local C's past are important to recognize: First, the union that was originally formed in the Glenwood Fry Houses was a company union; and second, until recently, the Fry House bargaining unit was the junior twin of a second and larger bargaining unit based in a popular Glenwood chain of family-style dinner houses called "The Old Ballpark" restaurants. Until the late 1980s, the Glenwood Fry Houses and The Old Ballpark restaurants were under common and local ownership.

The Glenwood Fry House and The Old Ballpark restaurant chains were first "unionized" during the 1960s. At that time, a considerable amount of union organizing was going on in Glenwood. When rumors started surfacing of union activity among staff at The Old Ballpark restaurants, the chain's owner acted pre-emptively and voluntarily signed a labor agreement recognizing what was essentially a company union (later described in one report by the labor-relations board as having "less than an 'arm's length' relationship with the employer"). This original union was called The Old Ballpark Restaurant Employees Association (OBREA). A few years later, the owner signed the Glenwood Fry House chain into this employees' association, as well.

Through the 1970s and 1980s, the employees' association that had started out as OBREA started to gain independence and slowly began to negotiate stronger contracts. (The association also went through a series of name changes and mergers to become today's Local C.) Restaurant workers walked out on strike at The Old Ballpark restaurants in the mid-1970s and again, for more than ten weeks, in the late 1980s. No strikes—no strike votes, even—were ever called at the Fry House restaurants, as employees there had a "piggyback" contract based on what The Old Ballpark restaurant workers were able to negotiate for themselves.

This early history of the Fry House bargaining unit most likely had an impact in shaping the unit's current problems with union individualism and members' isolation. For at no time during this period in its history did Local C (or its predecessor unions) ever need to launch a large-scale mobilization of the Fry House membership. The original union organization was top-down and employer-driven. Subsequent contract negotiations were based upon the mobilization of The Old Ballpark restaurant membership, not the Fry House workforce. Thanks to the activism of The Old Ballpark restaurant workers and the common ownership of The Old Ballpark and Glenwood Fry House restaurant chains, Local C could afford to have a largely inactive and uninvolved Fry House membership and still be able to negotiate relatively good bargaining agreements for the unit.

Since the late 1980s, two significant changes have swept through the Fry House bargaining unit and altered how its contract negotiations are conducted. First, the Glenwood Fry House chain was reacquired by its international parent company in the early 1990s. For the first time in Local C's history, The Old Ballpark restaurants and the Glenwood Fry Houses had separate owners. Contracts in the two units had to be negotiated independently.

Local C felt the impact of this change in ownership in its 1995 Fry House contract negotiations, when the new Fry House owners and the Local C bargaining committee reached an impasse. Rejecting the employer's "final contract offer" as inadequate, Local C initiated the Fry House bargaining unit's first-ever strike-authorization vote. The vote won the majority support of the Glenwood Fry House membership. However, the new Fry House owners took advantage of a provincial law that allowed them to bypass the bargaining committee and force a direct membership vote on the proposal that the committee had already rejected. Sweetening their proposed deal with signing bonuses of five hundred dollars for full-time employees and three hundred dollars for part-timers, the Fry House owners were able to get a majority of their Glenwood workforce to vote in favor of their offer, against the recommendation of the Local C bargaining committee.

During my fieldwork, Local C's union staff (along with many Fry House workers) explained the outcome of the previous round of contract negotiations by pointing to the pivotal role of the youngest and newest stopgap workers in the Glenwood Fry Houses—those workers with fewer than three years' job tenure. This sizable group of workers generally had minimal interaction with their union and, consequently, were not fully aware of the union's arguments for rejecting their employer's "final offer." Moreover, as stopgap workers who did not expect to stay long in their Fry House jobs, this group of workers also tended to believe that an up-front signing bonus measuring in the hundreds of dollars would be worth much more to them than the few extra cents that Local C wanted to tack onto their hourly wage. Going into the 1998 contract negotiations, therefore, union staff at Local C were particularly concerned—in a way they had never had to be before—about reaching out to the mass of young stopgap Fry House workers.

A second set of changes that took place during the 1990s reinforced the attention that union staff paid to young Fry House workers in the lead-up to the 1998 contract negotiations. It was during the 1990s that, thanks to its high-profile organizing in Glenwood's youth-dominated service sector, Local C began to acquire its reputation as the "youth union." Whereas it had long played second fiddle to The Old Ballpark restaurant unit within Local C, the Fry House unit, with its youth-dominated membership, started to gain increasing prominence. With outside labor and media interest growing in Local C's work with youth workers, local staff could point to their Fry House unit as a site in which they had been working with young stopgap service workers for decades. As the "youth question" came to frame Local C's external image, the union's staff became increasingly oriented toward thinking in general terms about how unionism could work best for young stopgap service workers, and in more specific terms about how the local could reach out and centrally involve young Fry House workers in the 1998 contract process.[5]

As a result of these two sets of changes, Local C, in preparation for the 1998 Fry House contract negotiations, worked to mobilize the 750 member Fry House workforce in a way it had never fully attempted to do before. The local began by calling all of its Fry House stewards and union activists together for a general "pre-contract negotiation" meeting. The purpose of this meeting was both for union staff to learn from rank-and-file activists what current conditions were like in the Fry House restaurants, and for workplace activists to learn from union staff the larger company, union, and industry contexts in which the upcoming negotiations would be taking place.

The local then asked Fry House stewards and activists to return to their stores and hold "workshops" with their co-workers that would replicate in miniature what had been done at the unit-wide pre-negotiation meeting—in this case, with stewards explaining to their co-workers the "bigger picture," and co-workers talking to stewards about the workplace issues that were of most concern to them. To help the stewards structure their workshops, the local prepared a survey form with a series of open-ended questions that asked members to write in their own most pressing workplace concerns as well as to discuss the relevance to themselves of a series of workplace issues that union staff thought might be problematic throughout the unit (members being pressured to work off the clock, race- and gender-based harassment, health and safety concerns, inadequate training).

In the months following the initial pre-negotiation meeting, Local C called two more preparation meetings. The purpose of these meetings was for Fry House stewards to discuss their experiences in running their in-store workshops and read the survey forms that had been filled out by and collected from the Fry House membership at large. At the second of these meetings (the "steering committee meeting"), Local C staff asked the Fry House stewards to develop an initial set of contract demands—based on the information they had gathered from the workshops and survey sheets—and to elect a bargaining committee to be made up of four of their peers. From this point on, the contract-negotiation process proper began, and the bargaining committee took over primary responsibility for representing the general Fry House membership. The committee, however, continued to use the informal steward-based, in-store workshop system that the local had created as a way to maintain two-way communication with other Fry House workers.

Local C's early efforts to mobilize its membership paid off handsomely throughout the 1998 contract-negotiation process. Once again, the local was pushed by employer intransigence to take a strike-authorization vote—and the local again received overwhelming support from Fry House workers to call a strike should the need arise. Once again, the Fry House owners attempted to bypass the local's bargaining committee by forcing a direct membership vote on an offer that the bargaining committee had already rejected. This time, the Fry House owners offered their Glenwood employees an eight-hundred-dollar signing bonus if they accepted its contract proposal. Unlike in 1995, however, Glenwood Fry House workers in 1998 rejected their employer's supposed "final contract offer" and signing-bonus bribe. The Fry House contract negotiations then went into provincial labor-board mediation, and the membership ended up voting to accept a contract recommended by the mediator (and bargaining committee) that contained none of the forty-odd concessions their employer had initially demanded and that had kept many of the union's original demands (albeit at reduced levels) that had first been formulated at the local's Fry House steering committee meeting several months earlier.

Local C's mobilization of its Fry House activists and members was a clear success within the context of its 1998 contract negotiations. Not only did the negotiation process lead to the securing of a strong three-year bargaining agreement—an agreement that Local C union staff say is, for the first time ever, stronger than the agreement in place in The Old Ballpark restaurant chain—but the process itself offered young Fry House activists and members potentially powerful learning experiences. The bargaining committee's members (one of whom was twenty-one years old) were active and present at every step in the negotiation process. Young Fry House stewards and activists, too, were centrally involved both in the local's preparations for negotiations and in mobilizing and educating their co-workers during the negotiations.

As for young Fry House workers as a whole, they were asked to participate in steward-run workshops, to fill in open-ended union surveys, and to cast their votes on three separate occasions during the negotiations (on strike authorization, on the employer's contract offer, and on the final contract suggested by the labor-board mediator). As Local C staff pointed out, the larger significance of this voting experience is that

Fry House workers were able to see that their employer's "final contract offer" was not necessarily the final contract that they could get their employer to offer them, and that they could approve a strike vote, reject a "final contract offer," and secure a preferred contract without actually having to go on strike.

Local C's mobilization of Fry House stewards, activists, and members during its 1998 contract negotiations may help lead to improvements in reducing union individualism and members' workplace isolation in the Glenwood Fry Houses. At the very least, it seems likely that the unit's first real mass member mobilization will have increased young Glenwood Fry House workers' familiarity with their union (in particular) and with unionism (in general). In the broader context of a concern over the role unions might be able to play in improving work environments for young stopgap workers in North America, the particular contract history of the Glenwood Fry Houses tells a clear story of the importance of, and the potential for, involving young stopgap workers centrally and collectively in negotiating the terms of their own working conditions.

8   Handling Time

July 4th is a time for picnics and family—but not for retailers, who
are not so privileged. . . . DO NOT ASK FOR CRITICAL TIME OFF DURING
THE JULY 4TH WEEKEND. THE NEEDS OF THE STORE COME FIRST.

—Notice posted in staff room of a Box Hill supermarket

There's no respect there. . . . [Good Grocers] always comes first,
everything else is secondary. They make people come in [to work]
even when they're really sick. . . . They don't respect the family
lives or the needs of their workers.

—Twenty-four-year-old produce clerk, Box Hill

IT IS an old saw in North America that paid work in the formal
economy instills in the young worker an appreciation of and respect for
time. "Work," as the sociologist William Julius Wilson (1996: 73) writes
grandly,

> is not simply a way to make a living. . . . It also constitutes a framework
> for daily behavior and patterns of interaction because it imposes disci-
> plines and regularities. . . . Regular employment provides the anchor for
> the spatial and temporal aspects of daily life. . . . In the absence of regu-
> lar employment, life . . . becomes less coherent.

Working during one's adolescence in low-level food-service and retail
jobs, many commentators argue, can help youths "learn those skills that
we [employed adults] take for granted. You learn what it means to work,
to get up in the morning, to be on time, to plan your day and plan your
activities" (Willis, as quoted in Widalvsky 1989: 37). Although work in
the McDonald's of this world may be poorly paid and even demeaning
at times, commentators say, this work experience can be instrumental
in reinforcing a strong work ethic and sense of time discipline in the
young worker.

Such conventional notions of the significance of time in youths' work
experience represent, at best, a highly apolitical and unidimensional
portrayal of the nature of time management in the youth workplace. For

time in the fast-food restaurant and grocery store is not simply given a (normative) order and regularity by employers that is then passively learned by young workers. Rather, in these and other such workplaces time is more often a battleground, a site of constant struggle between workers and employers as each group seeks to pursue what are sometimes overlapping, but more often conflicting, sets of interests. Time in the service and retail workplace is valued as both resource and reward, and employers and workers alike continually seek to gain control over how time is to be used as a resource at work and how it may be dispensed as reward for work.

Indeed, for young service and retail workers, the handling of time is one of the most critical workplace issues. Hours, scheduling, breaks, sick time, holiday time, vacation time, involuntary part-time work, forced overtime work, and off-the-clock work (working for free for one's employer) are at the heart of some of the most pressing concerns and complaints of young (and old) workers in grocery and fast food in Box Hill and Glenwood, as elsewhere. Time in the service and retail workplace, when subjected to the unconstrained whims of employers, is far from "regular" or "disciplined." Hours, schedules, breaks, and overtime in such industries continually threaten to fluctuate wildly and to introduce disorder and instability into workers' lives. It may well be true that work experience helps young workers learn to respect time—their employers' time, especially. But it is also all too often the case that work experience in the formal economy teaches young workers that their employers can and regularly will fail to respect employees' time—that is, their personal, family, work, and (in the case of working students) school time.

In this chapter, I continue my discussion of how unionization shapes the work experiences of young workers in Box Hill and Glenwood by focusing on the impact (or lack thereof) that unionization has had on two of the most important time-related workplace issues in these two sites: scheduling and off-the-clock work. My purpose in discussing these issues is threefold. First, I seek to show that time management in the contemporary youth workplace is a site of conflict and concern for young stopgap workers; it is not simply a "skill" taught to young workers by their employers. Second, I highlight the importance to young stopgap workers of differences in union strategies for improving how time is managed in the workplace. And third, in addressing the phenomenon of off-the-clock work, I present an example of the kinds of problems that arise when union institutions fail to connect with and support youth workplace cultures.

SCHEDULING

> Scheduling ... is the number one issue in service sector hospitality [collective-bargaining] agreements. That's the key for service workers: the ability to manage their lives, the hours they're scheduled. ... Knowing that a schedule is posted and that shifts won't change without your agreement; none of this stuff where you arrive at work and are told that they've canceled your shift tonight because they're a bit slow.
>
> —Staff leader of a Canadian service-sector union

In her ethnography of a McDonald's restaurant, Leidner (1993: 62–64) describes the kinds of scheduling insecurities that nonunionized foodservice and retail workers regularly confront. Workers at the restaurant could not count on having a regular number of work hours from week to week. Instead, managers retained full control over the weekly dispensation of work hours so that they could enjoy complete flexibility in scheduling, to the optimum convenience of their business, and they could have added leverage over their employees in granting and taking away weekly work hours. Workers were expected to compete with one another for labor hours and prove themselves worthy (in their managers' eyes) of the work hours they desired "through conscientious job performance" (ibid.: 62). Managers regularly cut back workers' hours to show their displeasure with performance and attitudes and often got rid of disliked workers by decreasing their scheduled hours "until they got the message" (ibid.).

Weekly shifts as well as hours were often unpredictable. Although hourly employees in the fast-food (and grocery) industry in general are typically classified as part-timers, managers widely expect them to have full-time work availability—again, so the managers can enjoy maximum scheduling flexibility (see also Reiter 1991; Hughes 1999). Leidner points out that in the McDonald's restaurant she studied, even workers who placed restrictions on their work availability were not guaranteed scheduling stability. Managers frequently scheduled workers at times they had said they would be unavailable. "Once on the schedule," writes Leidner (1993: 64), workers "were held responsible for finding a replacement."

Business in food service and retail tends to come in waves and lulls. Although some of these are fairly predictable, others are not. Managers thus often try to use scheduling practices that make employees bear much of the cost of such uncertainty. Leidner's description of scheduling practices at McDonald's is not unusual:

> On the work schedule . . . a line for each crew person showed the hours she or he was scheduled to work. A solid line indicated hours the employee could count on working, and a zigzag line marked an additional hour or so. If the store was busy when a worker's guaranteed hours were finished, she or he would be required to work that extra time; if it was not busy, she or he would be asked to leave. In addition, it was quite common at unexpectedly quiet times for managers to tell workers they could leave before their scheduled hours were completed or even to pressure them to leave when they would rather have kept on working. I heard one manager say, "Come on, can't I make a profit today?" when a crew member resisted being sent home fifteen minutes early. Conversely, when the store was busy, managers were reluctant to let workers go when their scheduled hours, including the optional time, were done. (Ibid.: 63)

As Leidner notes, the uncertain schedules that followed from such time-management practices made it difficult for McDonald's workers to plan around their work time: "Arrangements for transportation, social activities, child care, and so on could be disrupted by unexpected changes in the schedule" (ibid.: 64). Inconsistent work schedules that were posted at the last minute made it difficult, in the first place, for workers to plan other activities with more than a few days' notice. With uncertain hours, workers could not easily predict how much money they would earn each week, making it difficult to plan budgets.

In Box Hill, unionization has brought grocery workers limited protection against the kinds of scheduling insecurity, such as those described by Leidner, that nonunionized food-service and retail workers typically face. Work schedules, by contract, must be posted on Thursday for the workweek starting the following Sunday; once posted, schedules can be changed by managers only when employees are given forty-eight hours' notice. (In Leidner's McDonald's, managers could post and change work schedules whenever they wanted.) Unscheduled loss of time and overtime is also protected against: Workers can neither be forced to go home early on slow days nor to work last-minute overtime on busy days. Practices such as putting "zigzag lines" on posted schedules are prohibited. If workers do voluntarily agree to come in early or stay late on the day of their shifts, they are entitled to an unscheduled overtime "bonus"—a wage premium on top of their regular pay.

Most important, grocery workers in Box Hill have seniority rights to labor hours. Unlike in Leidner's McDonald's, grocery managers in Box Hill cannot (in theory, at least) easily play favorites with their employees or get rid of employees they dislike through their weekly dispensation of work hours. Workers in Box Hill supermarkets are not guaranteed a specific number of weekly labor hours. But they are assured that, to the degree that they wish to maximize their weekly hours, their managers cannot arbitrarily reduce their work time by giving more hours to junior than to senior employees within any given job classification. The longer a grocery worker in Box Hill stays at his or her job, the more secure his or her claims become, all else being equal, on having the maximum number of work hours—up to the full-time work load of a forty-hour week—that he or she desires.

But despite these and many other scheduling protections in Local 7's grocery contract, scheduling instability remains an issue of great concern to young grocery workers in Box Hill. Why? Because there are two fundamental flaws in Local 7's collective-bargaining agreement. First, grocery workers in Box Hill have no seniority rights whatsoever to working specific shifts or on specific days. Managers may schedule workers for any day of the week and any time of day they wish. Young workers in Box Hill thus complain that their schedules are "all over the place"—that the shifts they work from one week to the next can change completely. Because managers do not have to post schedules until Thursday for the workweek that starts on the following Sunday (a lead time of just two full days), workers have little advance notice of the hours they are scheduled to work each week. As with Leidner's MacDonald's workers, Box Hill grocery workers complain that such scheduling vagaries make planning the rest of their lives around their work time difficult.

Grocery workers in Box Hill can gain some control over the shifts they may be asked to work each week by placing restrictions on their availability. High-school and college students must, of course, block time from work for the periods during which they need to be in classes.

But restricting one's work availability in Box Hill is not without problems. Workers are required to state their work availability before they are hired. If they place too many restrictions on their availability, they may not be offered a job; whereas if they place too few, they may be offered a job but end up having to work hours that are disruptive to their non-work lives.

In any event, as with Leidner's MacDonald's workers, some young grocery workers in Box Hill find that their employers often schedule them for hours outside their stated work availability. One bakery clerk and community-college student I interviewed ended up quitting her grocery job over this very issue:

> I was like, you know what, I can see that they are not going to give me any help with dealing with homework and school and stuff. . . . The week before last, they gave me a shift from 2 to 9 on a schoolday. Well, my last class lets out at 2. OK, I would have had to skip my class in order to get to work on time. . . . They knew that and they didn't care. I missed [came in late to] work that day. I'm sorry, I do not—. If you give in once and skip class and go to work, they'll do it again, and they'll do it again, and they'll do it again. You cannot give in to that.

Because Local 7's grocery contract provides no punitive measures for employers who schedule workers outside their stated availability, there is really little disincentive from the union for employers not to try pushing their employees' scheduling limits.

The real problem with restricting one's work availability in Box Hill, however, is created by the second fundamental flaw in Local 7's contract: According to the contract, grocery workers in Box Hill have seniority rights to weekly work hours, *provided that* they are available to work the shifts their employers ask them to work. Some employers take this "availability clause" to mean that, if an employee has any restrictions on his or her work availability, then he or she forfeits all seniority rights to work time—even if it would be perfectly feasible to schedule that employee for maximum hours within the constraints of his or her limited availability, given the various scheduling needs, demands, and rights of that employee's other departmental co-workers.[1]

Grocery workers in Box Hill thus find themselves facing a Catch-22. Although they may desire more stability in their schedules, many workers deliberately do not block any of their work availability for fear of losing seniority rights to labor hours. Meanwhile, grocery workers who have to place restrictions on their work availability (e.g., student workers) may effectively be denied their seniority rights to weekly work hours. Thus, even though they have a union contract with an array of ostensible scheduling protections, some young Box Hill grocery workers find that they are little better off—in terms of their scheduling stability, at least—than workers in nonunionized establishments.

The weaknesses in the Local 7 contract's scheduling language do much more than affect the stability of grocery workers' schedules in Box Hill. They also shape social and political relations between workers and managers. Many workers in Box Hill say that they hesitate to challenge their managers or to call their union for assistance with workplace problems, because they fear that managers will "use the schedule" to punish them. The Local 7 contract's language prevents Box Hill grocery managers from arbitrarily reducing the hours of workers who have some seniority in their departments (although, as seen earlier, this is often contingent on workers' not having restrictions on their work availability). But managers in Box Hill do have the discretion arbitrarily to assign disliked employees "bad shifts" (what counts as a bad shift, of course, varies to some degree by employee).

This free discretion to schedule shifts, in fact, allows Box Hill grocery managers—like their counterparts in Leidner's McDonald's restaurant—to play favorites regularly by rewarding preferred employees with optimal weekly shifts and schedules. Managerial freedom in shift scheduling frequently leads to situations in which grocery workers find themselves having to compete with one another to get the shifts they desire. "You have to suck up to the manager to avoid getting stuck with crappy hours," a young bagger in Box Hill explains matter-of-factly. Over the long run, such scheduling insecurities and the resulting worker-on-worker competition can be draining. "I'm sick of the politics of the schedule," a young checker with six years' work experience complains as she explains one of the primary reasons she would never consider a career in the grocery industry. "I just can't stand having to be 'Angel of the Week' all the time so you can get rewarded with the best schedule."[2]

Thus, scheduling security in the unionized Box Hill supermarkets and Leidner's (nonunionized) McDonald's restaurant contrast by only a matter of degrees. Scheduling in the unionized Glenwood Fry Houses, however, has been lifted into another realm altogether. For the most part, workers in Glenwood simply do not speak of scheduling as one of their major workplace problems. Unionization has brought young stopgap workers in Glenwood a measure of scheduling stability that it has not managed to secure in Box Hill. The critical difference between the Local 7 contract and Local C contract in terms of scheduling protection is that Local C has secured constraints on managerial discretion in the weekly scheduling of shifts for its Fry House members.

As with grocery workers in Box Hill, Fry House workers in Glenwood have seniority rights to the number of weekly hours they are allotted. But they also have seniority rights to be assigned their preferred work shifts each week. (They typically choose between day and evening shifts.) Not only is there no "availability" loophole in the Local C contract's language, but Fry House workers can often stabilize their weekly work schedules without having to place special restrictions on their availability—thanks to their seniority rights to shifts. Local C's contract, moreover, goes beyond simply establishing the principle of shift preference by seniority. It also provides senior Fry House workers with "set shifts." When a worker has been working a specific shift—for example, the Tuesday night closing cashier shift—for a period of six consecutive months, that shift becomes a contractually protected "set shift" that cannot be taken away arbitrarily by Fry House managers.

The workplace consequences of the Local C contract's strong scheduling language are dramatic: The "politics of the schedule" that dominate workplace social environments in some Box Hill supermarkets are largely absent in Glenwood. Unlike in Box Hill, one rarely hears young workers in Glenwood complain of scheduling "favoritism" or of managers "using the schedule" to punish workers they dislike. Fry House workers with a year or more seniority tend to have fairly regular schedules— with only their particular days off each week changing around. Workers with two years or more seniority have mostly set schedules, in which they generally work the same shifts and same days from week to week. Unlike grocery workers in Box Hill with comparable levels of seniority, one rarely hears these more senior Fry House workers complain about scheduling instability or about the attendant problems—so commonly experienced by North American food-service and retail workers—of not being able to plan the rest of their lives around their work time.

Scheduling insecurities have not disappeared completely from the lives of young Fry House workers. Because Local C uses worker seniority as its guiding principle in achieving scheduling security, the most junior Fry House workers in Glenwood often find themselves unable to work the number of hours they would like each week and unable to count on a stable weekly schedule. Workers who have only recently started working for Fry House can find themselves working on an "on-call" basis, in which they are assigned whichever shifts happen to be left over once more senior workers have been given the shifts to which they are entitled (the type and number of "leftover" shifts vary each week according to predicted business demand and whether senior workers have asked for extra time off).

As with Leidner's McDonald's workers, junior Fry House workers sometimes confront scheduling insecurities that can make planning and budgeting for their non-work lives difficult. As one young cashier with two and a half months' work tenure complains:

> Everybody else [working in the restaurant] gets five days [of work each week]. With me, I'm just below Allie [in seniority], and she gets all her hours, and everybody above her gets all their hours, and I get whatever I get. . . . It's really hard. . . . I gotta get another job, cause I can't—. I can't just go into work and find out I only got three shifts [this week]. And then somehow I gotta figure out how I'm going to pay my rent, where I'm going to get the money from.

Several of the most junior Fry House workers I interviewed in Glenwood said that they had considered looking for a different job or a second job because they were unable to count on being able to support themselves on their irregular Fry House work schedules.

Seniority is, of course, an imperfect system for securing workplace justice. Because seniority correlates with age, seniority-based systems can often serve to institutionalize age-based discrimination in the workplace. There are, however, two points to keep in mind when evaluating the use of seniority in scheduling at sites such as the Glenwood Fry Houses. First, there are many different ways to use seniority in worker scheduling. Local C uses a straight scheduling-by-seniority system. Because worker turnover is high in Glenwood, new workers generally are able to benefit fairly quickly under this system. It may be, however, that Local C could do a better job by its newest members and should consider adapting its scheduling system so it is fairer to all of its members. Possible adaptations could include rotating best and worst shifts among workers of comparable seniority; establishing an absolute length of tenure by which a worker can count on increased scheduling stability; or even taking into account workers' different need for shifts. A single mother in her early twenties with young children, for example, might be said to have greater need to work a regular weekday schedule than does an older woman in her fifties whose children have already grown up and left home, even though that older woman's seniority might give her first rights to premium weekday shifts.

Second, it is important to remember that, despite its problems, shift scheduling by seniority in Glenwood has made a dramatic difference in the lives of young Fry House workers. When discussion can center on dealing with the subtleties and complexities of achieving maximum fairness in worker scheduling instead of on the unfairness of scheduling in general, then we know that we have come miles from the wildly insecure temporal world that characterized Leidner's nonunionized McDonald's restaurant. Local C's accomplishment is extraordinary. Scheduling insecurity in Glenwood is no longer a fast-food worker's problem, or even a young fast-food worker's problem—as it is virtually everywhere else in Canada and the United States. It remains only as the newly hired fast-food worker's problem. In this light, it is perhaps not surprising that many new Fry House workers in Glenwood support Local C's scheduling-by-seniority system, even though they do not yet directly benefit from it. "I'd like to work a little more, of course," says one young cashier with two month's job tenure. "But when it comes to that, I totally have respect for the people [who have] been working there longer than me. I figure, I'll keep working, and I'll make my fair share eventually."

Off-the-Clock Work

> *Question 8:* Do you ever start your shift early or work past your scheduled time without getting paid for it?
>
> *Answer:* Yes. . . .
>
> *Question 10:* If the answer to question 8 is yes, do you ever stop to think how much money you are owed if you added it up over a week, a month, or a year?
>
> *Answer:* No, nor do I want to. I might smack myself in the head.
>
> —Local C Fry House pre-contract negotiation survey
> with one member's response

Breaks, hours, these things are already protected in the contract. . . .
You have an absolute right to breaks. . . . Why is there hesitation
to enforce what we already have? This is important to address,
because we can have the best contract in the world, but if we don't
get what's in there. . . .

—Local C President speaking to Fry House workers at a
pre-contract negotiation meeting in which off-the-clock work
had emerged as one of the largest issues in the bargaining unit

Off-the-clock work—which refers to workers' missing breaks, starting
work early, or working late without receiving extra overtime pay—
is one of the most common complaints employees make against their
employers in North America today. U.S. Department of Labor records
show that, in the United States, the two biggest industry offenders in
off-the-clock and other wage and hour violations of the law are restaurants—especially fast-food restaurants—and supermarkets (Tumulty
1997). Over the past decade, major lawsuits have been filed over off-the-
clock work by employees of Taco Bell; Walmart; Motel 6; Food Lion and
Albertson's (both grocery companies); Mervyn's and Nordstrom's (both
department stores); and the Krystal Company hamburger chain (Faludi
1990; Liddle 1997; Neuborne 1997; Reckard 1997; Tumulty 1997).

In Box Hill and Glenwood, Local 7 and Local C are strongly opposed
to the illegal practice of off-the-clock work and have included contract
measures and launched initiatives that address the issue specifically.
But despite such measures and actions, off-the-clock work has been,
and continues to be, widespread in the Glenwood Fry Houses as well
as in many of the Box Hill supermarkets. In Glenwood, in fact, off-the-
clock work is endemic. A pre-contract negotiation survey of the Fry
House membership conducted by Local C in early 1998 found that
48 percent (104 of 215) of workers who responded were not always
getting their contractually guaranteed work breaks, and 46 percent (100
of 215) had started work shifts early or worked late after the end of their
shifts without pay. In some cases, missed breaks and unpaid overtime
were fairly sporadic, but in other instances, off-the-clock work was a
daily fact of Fry House work life. During my fieldwork, I found Fry
House restaurants in Glenwood in which no worker ever took a contractually guaranteed fifteen-minute work break and in which the
entire staff routinely started work fifteen or so minutes before their
scheduled shifts began.

For union officials in Box Hill and Glenwood, the prevalence of off-the-clock work in their bargaining units is somewhat puzzling. It is understandable that workers in nonunionized establishments might work off-the-clock under employer pressure: These workers often have little immediate institutional protection at hand to support any resistance they might make to their employers' demands. But surely, wouldn't union workers be able to turn to their union before having to start skipping breaks or working unpaid overtime?

Union officials in Box Hill and Glenwood explain the phenomenon of off-the-clock work in their stores by pointing to workers' shortsightedness: Workers see off-the-clock work as the simplest way to ease stressful workplace situations and don't recognize that their actions provide only a Band-Aid solution that can actually worsen their situations, as employers come regularly to expect the provision of free labor. Union staff in Box Hill also point to workers' greed and selfishness: Workers work off the clock in the (often mistaken) hope that they will garner their managers' good favor and earn promotions. In the process, they "steal" paid hours of labor from their co-workers (and themselves) by freely performing work that their employers would otherwise have to pay somebody to do.

Short-sightedness and self-interest, indeed, do play some role in the Box Hill and Glenwood workers' choosing to work off the clock. As the quotation at the beginning of this section suggests, many young workers agree to work an extra ten minutes here and an extra fifteen minutes there without pay in part because it seems petty to them to demand payment for such short periods of time. These workers don't always give much thought to how such small increments of time can add up when they become a regular part of their work lives. Relief of workplace stress, too, is a major factor behind off-the-clock work. But off-the-clock work in Box Hill and Glenwood is a more complex phenomenon than is suggested by these kinds of casual explanations. Off-the-clock work in Box Hill and Glenwood results from the interaction of three forces: workplace conditions that put great temporal pressure on workers; unions that have limited workplace presence and restricted ability to confront structural problems from within the workplace; and youth workplace cultures that diverge from preferred union strategies for handling time at work.

Before entering into a discussion of these three factors that motivate behind off-the-clock work, it may be useful to identify the basic forms

that off-the-clock work takes in Box Hill and Glenwood. For this purpose, we can think of off-the-clock work in these sites as being of three
basic types:

- *Missed breaks.* Local 7 and Local C contracts provide for both paid rest
  breaks (fifteen minutes every four hours) and unpaid meal periods
  (a half-hour in shifts longer than five hours). Two problems can arise
  over breaks: first, a worker regularly being denied his or her breaks;
  and second, a worker being pushed to work through a break without
  receiving extra compensation.
- *Working late and starting early.* Workers in Glenwood and Box Hill can
  work an hour or more of unpaid overtime before or after their shifts.
  More commonly, though, workers work unpaid overtime for shorter
  periods of ten, fifteen, or twenty minutes at a time.
- *Off-site errands and work on days off.* Particularly in the Glenwood Fry
  Houses, workers are often asked to run errands for their employers—
  to go to the bank or pick up needed supplies—on their own time.
  Workers also sometimes come in to work to help out in a crunch on
  their days off, without clocking in. Several Fry Houses have held
  "pizza cleaning parties" in which workers are asked to come in on
  their days off to clean the store in return for pizza but no wages.

The work-site conditions that foster these types of off-the-clock work
are created by the incessant efforts of Box Hill and Glenwood grocery
and fast-food employers to maximize their profits by eliminating every
last possible minute of "excess" labor from their production budgets.
Employers in both Box Hill and Glenwood use computerized scheduling programs that map their business flows over the course of each day,
week, and month—often in increments as small as fifteen minutes—and
that schedule labor hours precisely according to predicted changes in
service demands. These programs spit out weekly labor budgets that
set the maximum number of hours a store or department is permitted
to have.

Workers in Box Hill and Glenwood often know exactly what the labor
budget is for their store or department, and they know that, as far as
management is concerned, these budgets are considered to be set in
stone. "That's one of Fry House's majors," says a young supervisor
who, like many supervisors in Glenwood, is responsible for drawing up
her store's weekly schedule. "Do not go over labor budget; death

becomes you. If I don't hit labor budget [for the week], I get in trouble." At the same time, workers know that their managers will hold them to task to make sure that they complete all of the work for which they are responsible before they leave at the end of their shifts.

Workers in Box Hill and Glenwood point out numerous problems with tight and rigid labor budgets. Actual schedules are generally set with one shift fewer than the number calculated by the computer-generated labor budgets. This is done to accommodate the possibility of employee illness or absenteeism: If a worker misses a shift that then has to be covered by someone else at an overtime rate of pay (e.g., at time and a half), this can push an initially maximized schedule over the allowed labor budget. Another problem is caused by "office managers." Labor budgets typically assume that managers will work a certain number of hours on the floor each week. But some managers "hide out" in their offices and thus leave these work hours unaccounted for.

More fundamentally, workers in Box Hill and Glenwood criticize their employers' efforts to predict sales "scientifically" and match sales to labor hours. Customer flow frequently runs counter to expectations—and tight labor budgets leave workers little extra capacity to handle unexpected customer rushes. In any event, workers say, labor hours cannot be tied as closely to sales figures as employers' scheduling formulas try to make them. As a Box Hill deli clerk explains, for example, even on a slow sales day, particular patterns in customer flow or service demand can create a need for overtime work:

> [Food City has] me on such a tight schedule, especially at night, that if one customer comes up, they can throw me completely off schedule. Then I feel like I'm being rude to that person because they're making me upset. Especially if they want something special [such as freshly sliced deli meat]. If I've just cleaned the slicer, one person can set me back twenty minutes.... Ninety percent of the time, I'm late off because of customers. Every once in a while, we'll be slow all day, then when I get alone [on the evening shift], I get a string of people. I notice that when people come in at night, they want to take their time.... They think we have all the time in the world to wait on them. The manager never closes, so he doesn't know, ... no matter how hard you try to explain it to him, that it can be one customer that sets you behind.... You'd think that as long as you were taking care of a customer, with [Food City's] emphasis on customer service—. I think he [the manager] thinks we just stand around at night and talk. I wish I got to stand even for two

seconds at night. Running here, running there, I get so worn out [that] when I get out, I just sit down. I don't want to do anything.

Workers in Box Hill and Glenwood complain that their employers often don't schedule extra hours (or enough extra hours) so they can take care of basic prep and cleaning work, train new hires, or perform the new tasks or make the new products that are constantly being added to their regular work loads.

Employers in Box Hill and Glenwood use a variety of techniques to turn back their employees' claims that they need extra (paid) work time to finish the tasks for which they are responsible. Managers insist that labor budgets are sacrosanct and frown heavily on requests for overtime. Managers secure extra unpaid work from their employees by "forgetting" to send them for their breaks or by acting irritated and expressing uncertainty when employees ask them when they will be able to take a break. Managers define certain tasks—for example, counting out cash-register floats at the beginning and end of one's shift—as "pre-work" and "post-work" tasks that employees are expected to do before they clock in and after they clock out. Overtime in Box Hill and Glenwood is generally paid only when it has been officially approved by a manager. Managers, however, don't always make themselves available at the end of a worker's shift to approve overtime—and if they are available, they generally kick up a fuss about having to go over the labor budget. Because many of the companies in these two sites tie managers' bonuses to their ability to keep their stores' labor hours on or under budget, many managers have strong incentive to turn back employees' demands for compensation for extra work time.

There are other, less direct methods for resisting requests for added paid work time. In his classic essay on the development of time-consciousness in early industrial society, E. P. Thompson (1967) writes that in the nineteenth century, before watches were widely available, employers manipulated factory clocks to extract extra labor from their employees. Circumstances, it seems, have changed only slightly over the past century. Managers in Box Hill and Glenwood frequently "edit" workers' time cards. If a manager sees that a worker has punched or written in for overtime that was not officially approved and that the manager believes was not necessary, he or she will "edit out" that overtime claim. Employers argue that editing is required to prevent

employees from padding their weekly labor hours by willfully showing up early and staying late without cause. Employees, on the other
hand, see the practice as cheating them of pay for work they have performed for their employer's benefit. As a Fry House cook explains:

> We didn't have to punch in or out before; now we have to punch in
> when we get there. But then they go back and edit it. Say you started at
> twenty to or quarter to [for a shift that begins at five on the hour]. They
> go back and edit it; you didn't start until five o'clock. I'm off at ten after
> or twenty after [nine], I go back and punch it out. . . . They go back and
> edit it: You were off at nine, you weren't off at nine twenty. So there's
> forty minutes. You think you're getting paid for the extra half-hour;
> you don't get paid for it.

Even when employers officially approve overtime, they can subsequently "forget" to add the extra pay to an employee's paycheck. Securing proper pay for missed breaks or unscheduled overtime, workers say,
requires constant vigilance and pressure on their employers. Payroll
"mistakes" can be particularly effective in limiting labor expenses for
employers with high-school-age workers—who, in the excitement of
having their first paychecks, say that they sometimes forget to check
carefully the precise accounting details that go into producing their
biweekly wages.

These, then, are some of the basic or root workplace conditions that
foster off-the-clock work in Box Hill and Glenwood. Workers speak of
the intense temporal pressures that are created at work by their employers as placing them in a Catch-22. Managers kick up a fuss if workers
don't finish their assigned tasks by the end of their shifts. Managers kick
up a fuss if workers ask to work overtime to finish their assigned tasks.
And, well, managers say that workers shouldn't be working off the
clock, but they don't actually seem to mind when a worker skips a break
(without asking for extra compensation) or stays late (without asking
for extra pay) to finish his or her work.

Both Local 7 and Local C have attempted to protect their members
against such pressure to work off the clock. In the new members meeting that it runs in Box Hill, Local 7 tries to educate workers about off-
the-clock work. Union staff use a chart to show new members how an
extra free fifteen minutes of work each day can add up over the weeks,
months, and years to cost individual employees large amounts of
money—and to cost the union jobs that could have been made available

to other workers. Local 7 staff urge new hires to resist workplace pressure to work off the clock, to insist on punching in for every single minute that they work, and to contact the union when they have problems resulting from their refusal to work for free.

In the year before I began my fieldwork, Local 7's parent union actually launched a class-action lawsuit against one of the chain supermarkets in Box Hill because of off-the-clock work. The lawsuit charged that the company had knowingly, deliberately, and systematically pressured its employees into violating union contract and labor law by working off the clock. The parent union produced a video documenting both the problem and the lawsuit and mailed it to all of the chain's employees in Box Hill. Workers who had been pressured to work off the clock were urged to fill in a back-pay-claim form and join the lawsuit.

Despite such aggressive measures, however, the message Local 7 sends to its young (and old) members about off-the-clock work is a mixed one. Local 7 is not involved in any way in its parent union's class-action lawsuit. The reason? In the early 1990s, Local 7 signed a letter of understanding with Box Hill grocery employers promising never to become involved with class-action litigation or corporate campaigns against any of the signatory employers. Young workers at this grocery chain are thus being approached about off-the-clock work through the mail by an institution that is even farther removed from them than their already distant union local. Local 7 union representatives—whose faces, at least, are somewhat familiar to young workers in this chain—can say nothing to these workers about participating in the parent union's lawsuit. Several young workers I spoke to in this chain said that they vaguely remembered receiving a video about a union lawsuit, but that, although they had worked off the clock, they didn't know enough about the lawsuit to be moved to fill out the necessary paperwork to put in a back-pay claim.

Outside of the class-action lawsuit, Local 7's approach to protecting its youngest members against off-the-clock work becomes even more murky. Some union staff feel that off-the-clock work isn't much of an issue in other grocery chains in Box Hill. When staff do continue to see off-the-clock work as a live issue, they often feel that it primarily affects older, more senior grocery workers in Box Hill—department heads, in particular—and do not worry much about monitoring possible abuses of younger, more junior workers. Most problematically, however, Local

7 has included a clause in its collective-bargaining agreement that holds individual employees responsible for off-the-clock-work violations, that positions the union as a policeman of such violations, and that threatens employees guilty of such violations with losing their jobs. Local 7 staff occasionally try to run "stings" to catch members suspected of working off the clock in the act. In such circumstances, it is perhaps not surprising that grocery workers in Box Hill who may have been pressured in the past into working off the clock do not go running to their union local for assistance.

Local C's approach to off-the-clock work in Glenwood is also something of a mixed bag. In an attempt to remove ambiguity over how and whether "extra" work time in its Fry House bargaining unit should be compensated, Local C has negotiated into its collective-bargaining agreement a painstaking array of time-based language. All minutes of overtime worked should be accumulated over the workweek, then rounded up to the nearest quarter-hour, and then added to employees' time sheets. A half-hour lunch break that is interrupted when an employee is called back to the shop floor to help his or her co-workers should be recommenced after the point of interruption and continue for a full and uninterrupted half-hour rest. Paid rest breaks and unpaid lunch periods that are missed—as the union recognizes will inevitably happen from time to time in the unpredictable food-service business— must be paid for by the employer. Indeed, Local C's contract provides a chart detailing exactly how extra pay for different combinations of missed breaks on shifts of various lengths should be calculated.

On the down side, though, Local C has no general education program to teach its new (and old) Fry House members about the problem of off-the-clock work, and, with limited day-to-day contact between union staff and workers, it is not always able to monitor whether its members are being pressured to work off the clock. Indeed, it was largely via my research presence in Glenwood that Local C staff first became aware of off-the-clock work as a major problem. They subsequently sent mailings to all of the Fry House restaurants urging workers to claim compensation for unpaid work time; they included questions on the topic in their 1998 pre-contract negotiation survey to gauge the extent of the problem; and in pre-contract negotiation meetings, they talked with Fry House stewards about how and why workers were agreeing to forgo breaks and overtime pay. "Why," the local president (as quoted in the second epigraph to this chapter section) asked the gathered stewards, "is there hesitation to enforce what we already have [secured in our current contract]?"

Why, indeed, do young workers agree to work off the clock? Off-the-clock work in Box Hill and Glenwood is not solely the effect of employers' pressure and unions' absence from the workplace. It is also mediated by workplace cultures in which young workers are active and creative participants. One must recognize two factors to understand the practice of off-the-clock work in youth fast-food and grocery communities. First, off-the-clock work varies from worker to worker and situation to situation. Despite its roots in employer-created temporal pressure, off-the-clock work is not always and everywhere the same. Workers vary in their awareness of working off the clock (some work off the clock without fully realizing it, while others know exactly when they are working off the clock) as well as in their emotional response to, and sense of voluntarism about, working off the clock (some feel distraught over being forced to work off the clock, while others see it largely as a free choice that they make).

Second, youth fast-food and grocery communities themselves generate temporal values and practices that blur rigid distinctions between work time and rest time, employer time and personal time, paid time and free time in the workplace (see also Marshall 1986). These values and practices do not result solely from workplace time pressures. But in the context of tight and rigid labor budgets, these values and practices can make it difficult for young workers to know when they are working off the clock because they want to and when they are doing so because they are forced to. These values and practices also work against the strategies that Local 7 and Local C have adopted for protecting their members from off-the-clock work. For neither union local really attempts to work in conjunction with its young members to confront and change the root conditions that foster off-the-clock work. Instead, both locals rely on strategies that call for workers to respond to these conditions by measuring and accounting for every single minute of their work time precisely and rigidly. The problem with such strategies is that the central orientations of youth workplace cultures in Box Hill and Glenwood tend to veer away from such highly bureaucratic forms of time-consciousness.

One cultural practice that leads young workers in Box Hill and Glenwood into off-the-clock work is workplace socializing. It is not uncommon for workers to show up at their work sites early to see co-workers who are working the earlier shift. Young workers sometimes go to their work sites on their days off to check in on their friends at work. And young workers may stick around after the end of their shifts—possibly to wait for a friend who doesn't get off work until a half-hour or an hour later. In each of these situations, it is easy for the visiting off-the-clock worker to pitch in a little, to do a little work: Helping their on-the-clock friends can, of course, garner a few extra minutes of chat time. However, it is also easy in these situations for the visiting off-the-clock worker to start taking on work tasks that are not so much casually helping out co-workers as they are consistently helping out the employer. A Fry House cashier articulates just this sense of ambiguity:

> I start early 'cause it's voluntary, I don't mind. I mean, you know, the company might be getting work from me. Whatever; I don't care. It might be like ten minutes. . . . I'll just go stand in the packing area and just like gab to everybody. [I go in early] just to be social, but I don't usually do any work, I might pack a small fries or something. . . . [I go in to] see how busy it was, catch up on the latest gossip, I guess, see what [the manager's] done that day, what she hasn't done. . . .
>
> Like, I'm on at four o'clock. I'll go in today at three thirty and just sit in the office and read [the company's daily e-mail messages], and just gab to everybody. . . . I usually set the [store] safe early, 'cause I have to get out to the bank [to deposit the day's earnings]. I guess that's an issue; I shouldn't be starting the safe until four o'clock. . . . But sometimes I don't have time to do it [open the safe and go to the bank at the start of my shift], 'cause we get real busy at four o'clock, and then I have to stay.

The cashier begins by emphasizing personal reasons for starting work early and highlighting the contingent nature of any work tasks he performs off the clock. But it then emerges that the cashier also regularly has to come in early to take care of off-the-shop-floor tasks that are not easily done when his shift officially starts and the customer rush hits. It is, in fact, common in both Glenwood and Box Hill for employers to expect employees to take care of "pre-work tasks"—which often involve paperwork of one kind or another—before they clock in for their official shifts.

Workplace socializing is also a contributing reason for some young workers' working through or cutting short their breaks at work. In the sociological literature, breaks are often regarded as an important time for worker socializing (Linder and Nygaard 1998). But at small work sites such as the Glenwood Fry Houses, the reverse can actually be true. At these work sites, breaks are generally taken one worker at a time. Workers can thus find breaks isolating and boring; the social action in their workplace is centered on the shop floor. The incentive can be strong, then, to stay on the shop floor during one's break. And when one stays on the shop floor during a break, one quickly finds that co-workers will have more time to chat and socialize if one helps them take care of customers. But, finally, if the employer starts to squeeze the restaurant's labor budget, one may find that working through or shortening one's breaks becomes a necessity rather than a luxury, and that the pace of work, even with such "extra" help, doesn't ever seem to let up much.

Closely overlapping with workplace socializing as a factor in off-the-clock work is the strong commitment many young workers in Box Hill and Glenwood have to helping co-workers. When Local C surveyed its Fry House membership on the topic of off-the-clock work, helping co-workers out was the number-one reason that workers gave for missing breaks and working unpaid overtime. One Fry House supervisor I interviewed spent hours doing paperwork for her restaurant (inventory, ordering, scheduling) on her own time at home. Although she wasn't particularly happy about having to do this, she couldn't bring herself to sit in the office doing paperwork while she was on the clock when she saw what she felt was an understaffed crew struggling to handle massive customer flow. Instead, she regularly joined her co-workers on the floor to help out with cooking and service tasks.

Workers who work off the clock to help co-workers may seem to be responding directly to workplace time pressures. But this practice is culturally mediated in that workers, in the face of time pressure, actively prioritize helping co-workers out over the alternative practices of getting all their breaks or receiving pay for all the overtime they work. This practice also shows itself to be culturally mediated in that workers sometimes shorten their breaks at work to help one another out, even when it is not absolutely necessary. As a Fry House supervisor, who works in a restaurant where workers constantly fail to get their breaks, observes:

> Missed breaks is a big big big big thing at our store.... We need to start giving ... breaks. I mean, when I'm working I should say, "OK, go sit down for half an hour." But a lot of them won't. One customer comes in

the door, and they're up, they're helping me. And I appreciate it. I think it's great: It's good to know that they have that appreciation or respect for me; too, that they want to help me. But we have to start enforcing it [breaks]. But it's . . . hard to say you have to go sit down for half an hour and forcing the issue. Sometimes they just won't.

Saying that workers sometimes interrupt breaks to help co-workers when they don't really need to is not, the supervisor emphasizes, to say that off-the-clock work is entirely a voluntary matter that employers can do little about. The supervisor lays the original blame for off-the-clock work in her restaurant on the understaffing that follows from overly tight labor budgets and tells stories of co-workers' having to work seven and eight hours straight without a chance even to go to the bathroom because they had nobody else to cover while they were off the floor.

A third motivation young workers in Box Hill and Glenwood point to for working off the clock is their investment in the quality of their work, customer service, products, and stores. Some young workers buy into the labor budgets their employers give them and feel proud when they are able both to do a good job at work and come in under or at the labor budget. Many workers, when push comes to shove, prioritize being able to do a good job over being able to secure all of their breaks and overtime pay. Those Fry House workers in Glenwood who show up for "pizza cleaning parties" do so out of the pleasure of workplace socializing, the desire to help their co-workers, and their investment in the quality of their stores' appearance.

In some instances, workers' willingness to work off the clock to improve or maintain quality in their stores comes under extreme duress. Workers in one Fry House restaurant that I visited regularly worked off the clock, partly out of the fear that their restaurant (which had been losing sales in recent years) might be disciplined, franchised out, or even closed:

> [Fry House] only gives us [X number] of [weekly] hours. Even then it's really short-staffed sometimes. The union says we're supposed to get a half-hour break. Ha-ha, never, ever. . . . So there's, actually—, if you look at most of our schedules, they say no breaks. Sometimes we're paid extra if we miss breaks; it depends, really. 'Cause we don't want to go over our hours, either. So sometimes if we're maxed out on hours that day, we'll say OK, no problem.
>
> *Stuart:* Why don't you just go over the hours?

Because then it goes against our store's food costs and against our store's labor. So it just makes our store look really, really bad. So if we already know, if we know we can kinda save face, then we will. It's like, no problem, we'll work through break. It's a lot of sacrifice. I go in there early all the time without getting paid; I stay late without getting paid; I go in on my day off.

Stuart: What would happen if you went over hours and the store looked worse?

I don't know if they'd close it or franchise it out. Or whatever—the store would get disciplined, anyways. They would either cut a person, say we can't have an extra person on Friday. It'd just make things worse.

In other cases, investment in the quality of their work drives workers to work off the clock voluntarily, even in circumstances in which it is not absolutely necessary. A young dairy clerk I spoke to in Box Hill was proud of his ability to keep the dairy case in his store—for which he was solely responsible—looking fully stocked throughout the day. The clerk explained that sometimes, when he walked past the dairy case on his way out after his shift, he would see that there had been a sudden run on the milk or the yogurt that had left a gaping hole in the neat rows of product. When this happened, he often would turn back and take an extra ten minutes or so to fill the hole—without bothering to clock back in. "That [dairy case] wall," the clerk explained cheerfully, "that's my reputation."

As union leaders in Local 7 and Local C recognize, workers in Box Hill and Glenwood also work off the clock to ease the stress of the rest of their working day. For the more time a worker has to complete his or her tasks, the more relaxed the pace of the work can be. A Fry House cashier thus explains that he regularly tries to start work early so that he can make work less "hell" and more "fun":

I come in an hour early all the time. If I'm half an hour early, then I'm late. . . . I come into a mess sometimes, a madhouse, because it's been so busy and they [the early shift] haven't had time to clean. . . . [I go in early] just to help out; I don't go in to have fun. . . . I don't go in to look for extra money. It'd be nice if one day they saw the effort I'm making and say, "Hey, we'll give you a prize." But I'm not in there for that. I just want to make sure I do the job as best I can, make sure my cash area is clean, stocked up, so when I get on shift, I don't have to do anything. I can just deal with customers. Then as my stock gets lower, I can run back when it's not busy. . . . Because otherwise, it's just hell, and you don't want that. You gotta enjoy what you do or else it's not gonna be fun.

With their employers' labor budgets tied ever more closely to customer sales, workers in both Box Hill and Glenwood find that, to avoid an exhaustingly fast-paced workday, they have to dip into their own personal time to take care of required preparation and cleaning tasks at work.

Once again, though, the decision to work off the clock to ease the pressure and slow the pace of work is a complicated one, and young workers do not automatically link this decision with actions their employers have taken to squeeze labor costs. The optimum pace of work varies from worker to worker. Some young workers—especially those who have just started and are still getting the hang of their jobs— feel hesitant to ask their employers to pay for missed breaks and overtime, because they blame themselves for being slow. Often such workers are likely to try to hide the fact that they have to work extra to complete their tasks. Within a few months, many new workers find, after all, that jobs that once took them an extra half-hour of overtime to complete can now be wrapped up in no time at all. Some workers, on the other hand, actively decide that they prefer to work more slowly, to have time during the workday to relax on the shop floor, to chat with customers and co-workers, perhaps even to play around and have a water fight or two. The cost of being able to shape the preferred pace and mix of activities in their workday is having to start a little early, work a little late, miss a break here and there.

Workers who see themselves as fast or good workers commonly will blame other workers for being slow or lazy and for requiring them to work off the clock. In both Box Hill and Glenwood, day-shift and nightshift workers get into sparring matches as they blame each other for leaving their work stations filthy and unstocked at the end of their shifts. In many cases, such hostilities are clearly misplaced: prep and cleaning work are often left incomplete because the day shift or night shift was understaffed and simply overwhelmed by customer rushes—rushes that workers on the alternate shifts aren't around to see. But it is also true that some workers are slower than others, that some workers do like to chat or play around at work more than others, and thus that some workers are more likely to complete all of their prep and cleaning tasks by the end of their shifts than are others.

Union leaders in Local 7 and Local C give lip service to the importance of respecting the fact that people inevitably work at different paces.
But there is nothing in these locals' collective-bargaining agreements—
and there is no active discussion between these locals and their memberships—that addresses the right of workers to work at different paces,
or the right of workers to have a say in the preferred pace of their workday. There is, in other words, no real attempt to address the root conditions of off-the-clock work that would help workers gain more control
over the length and texture of their working days. Without such a dialogue, it becomes difficult for young workers to know what they can consider acceptable paces and pressures at work, and what is unacceptable.

Lack of dialogue between union staff and membership over what
should be considered ideal or preferred temporal work pacing and texture also affects the impact of one final cultural value or practice that
leads young workers in Box Hill and Glenwood into off-the-clock work.
In addition to the motivations discussed earlier that move young workers into blurring lines in the workplace between on- and off-the-clock
time, workers also blur temporal lines at work because such blurring is
itself a cultural value. Many workers I interviewed in Box Hill and Glenwood spoke of their preference for having some temporal "give and
take" in their work lives—they didn't like the idea of having to account
minutely for every moment of time that passed at work. In their ideal
cultural model, workers get a little extra time here, employers get a little extra time there, and it all balances out in the end.[3]

Although the Local 7 and Local C contracts specify precisely the
length, timing, and number of rest breaks at work, many young workers opt not to take set breaks. In part, this decision has to do with their
desire to socialize at work. But this decision is also guided by a "give
and take" temporal logic—as can be seen in the following discussion of
breaks by a young Fry House cashier:

> We've all come to an agreement [in my restaurant]: We don't take our
> half-hour, fifteen, whatever. . . . We kinda work it out that we take stag-
> gered breaks, 'cause the majority of us smoke. So we'll go back and eat,
> smoke, sit there, 'cause we got a monitor in the office [that shows the
> front of the restaurant]. We can just watch the monitor, eat and smoke
> and gab. Sometimes it works we get more [break time], sometimes it
> works we get quite a long time, I would say! I'd say some days we'll
> sit there for like two hours, it'll be so dead. . . . And then some days
> we don't get a half-hour break, not even a fifteen.

"Give and take" functions within a single shift so that workers work during their play and rest periods in order to be able to play and rest more during their work periods. But it also functions across shifts so that on slow days workers take extra breaks, while on busy days they take fewer (if any) breaks.

Blurring of rigid break rules makes a lot of sense from a worker's point of view. As Marc Linder and Ingrid Nygaard (1998: 42) write of typical break rules in North America:

> The military precision and discipline with which workers have historically been required to comply with rest-period rules . . . seem almost designed to subject them to further anxiety and nervousness rather than to relax them.

Blurring of break rules helps workers restore restfulness to their rest periods. "I like not having scheduled breaks," a Fry House cook says, because "that way you're not making sure you take an exact half-hour break."

But blurring of rigid break rules also puts young workers in Box Hill and Glenwood at greater risk of temporal exploitation by their employers. Workers' sense of temporal give and take across slow and busy days helps their employers transfer the cost of waves and lulls in business to their employees. This sense of give and take across slow and fast days reflects an understanding among young workers that they are being paid for specific tasks that they actively perform at work. When workers have fewer such tasks to perform on slow business days, they feel that they are "taking" time from their employers. Fast-food restaurants and supermarkets, however, are two paradigmatic examples of businesses that trade on their public image of being open all the time: Competitive pressures drive employers in these two industries to stay open even during slow and unprofitable days and hours (Fine 1990; Tilly 1996). Thus, fast-food and grocery workers more than many other categories of workers are paid for their time simply to be ready at their work sites to meet the demands of possible walk-in customers. Because neither Local C nor Local 7 engages in dialogue with its membership about the nature of work pacing across shifts, many of these unions' members are voluntarily, and perhaps unnecessarily, giving up union-won rest periods on busy days and shifts because their employers happen, from time to time, to suffer unexpectedly slow days and shifts.

Blurring of rigid temporal lines in the workplace more generally puts young workers at risk of temporal exploitation because their employers' accounting of temporal "give and take" tends to be highly one-sided. As many young workers start to realize after a few months or years on the job, there is rarely a "two-way street" in the workplace when it comes to temporal accounting: All too often, employers take, take, take, and workers give, give, give. Employers can be very casual when workers choose to come in early or leave late, but reverse the terms—attempt to arrive late or leave early—and employers can suddenly become minute counters with the best of them. As long as Local C and Local 7 rely on precise temporal accounting to protect their members' time in the workplace, young workers' decisions to abandon such things as set breaks make it difficult for these workers to enlist the union's assistance when their employers start to renege on informal (and ostensible) "give and take" understandings. For when young workers' temporal practices diverge from preferred union time-handling strategies, union grievance procedures can often have little to go on.

Off-the-clock work in Box Hill and Glenwood is a product not just of employer time pressures and union absences but also of youth workplace cultures—and of employers' ability to hook into and profit from these cultures, combined with Local C's and Local 7's inability to work with, as opposed to against, the time values and practices of their young (and old) members. Foregrounding the agency of youth workplace cultures in fostering off-the-clock work, as I have done, may create the impression that employers are less responsible for off-the-clock work than, say, unions would have them be. This impression would be misguided. As I have emphasized, the root conditions for off-the-clock work in Box Hill and Glenwood are created by employers' cutting labor budgets in the service of maximizing profits.

In discussing the nature of time practices and values within youth workplace cultures, it is critical to differentiate young workers' acceptance of (and even preference for) less rigid boundaries between on- and off-the-clock time at work from the acceptance of less paid work time made available to perform work tasks in the fast-food restaurant and grocery store. Although young workers often accept or prefer blurred time at work, these workers also complain widely about their employers' insistence on slashing labor budgets and understaffing stores.

I close this chapter on handling time in the workplace, therefore, with a typical complaint about lost work time that was made by a nineteen-year-old Fry House supervisor. This supervisor was deeply invested in the quality of her store and in the social relationships she had with her co-workers, and she had voluntarily logged many hours of off-the-clock work—including missed breaks, early starts, and "pizza cleaning parties" on her days off. I asked this supervisor about the changes she would most like to see in her workplace. This was her response:

> If I could have what I wanted at work? Probably just the hours. If I could just have that many more hours, it would make my life so much easier. I could afford to sit in my office [and do paperwork while on the clock]. My staff could afford to put the apron on and the gloves up to here and the stupid goggles [i.e., they could follow the proper safety procedures that they currently skip over]. And everything else, but we don't have the time, so we don't do it ever. That's where a lot of it comes from. The stressing out comes from it. The negligence [the mistakes workers make at work] comes from it.

Conclusion

People say, "Get a real job" or "Why don't you just leave and work somewhere else?" But that's not the point. The same thing will happen somewhere else.

> —Bryan Drapp, nineteen-year-old McDonald's worker and strike leader, Macedonia, Ohio (quoted in Samuel 1998)

I've been working a long time at Starbucks. It seems sad, but you know, everyone I know has a job just like mine, and we're all living paycheck to paycheck, doing grunt work, the same damn thing over and over again, just digging ourselves into our own little rut, it's just not fair, it's just not damn fair.... This is not what you studied, this is never how you imagined your life would be when you were eight years old. What the hell am I doing here? And you know, you can't just quit and pick up and go somewhere else, cause you're gonna have the same job with a different manager and a different group of people, it's still gonna be the same job.

> —Twenty-four-year-old Starbucks barista and union organizer, Vancouver, Canada (personal interview, 1997)

Somebody's got to work at Starbucks. Why the hell shouldn't it be me? And why the hell shouldn't I have a livable wage to do it?

> —Liz Carr, twenty-nine-year-old Starbucks barista and union organizer, Vancouver, Canada (quoted in Bailey 1997)

IN THE SPRING of 1998, nineteen-year-old Bryan Drapp became an overnight media celebrity when he led fifteen of his co-workers out on strike against the Macedonia, Ohio, McDonald's where he worked. Drapp was spurred to take action after he witnessed a sixty-six-year-old co-worker being reprimanded so harshly by a McDonald's manager (for leaving a stack of clean garbage bags next to a trash can) that she burst into tears. Fed up with management harassment—managers regularly screamed and swore at workers, calling them "jerks" and "morons" and telling them they were "stupid"—and rebuffed in his request for a meeting with the store's owner–operator to air general

211

grievances, Drapp persuaded co-workers to join him on a picket line outside the restaurant.

Holding signs that read, "Overworked and Underpaid," "Honk for Compassion," and "Did Somebody Say Unqualified Management?" (playing off of the "Did Somebody Say McDonald's?" advertising campaign), the mostly teenage strikers drew the attention not only of store management and local passers-by, but also of the national media. CNN, *Good Morning America,* most of the country's major daily newspapers, and even *People* magazine covered the story, while the "McStrike" became favorite fodder for Howard Stern's and Jay Leno's comedy routines. A Teamster local offered its support and advice, signing up a number of the strikers as non-dues-paying members, and Teamster drivers delivering supplies to the store refused to cross the picket line. After five days off the job, the striking employees met with the franchise owner and secured his consent to most of their demands: raising the base pay; making sure experienced workers were paid more than new hires; providing one week's paid vacation for full-time employees after a year on the job; posting work schedules four days in advance; holding four crew meetings a year; providing written performance reviews, anniversary pins, and other forms of employee recognition; sponsoring summer outings for employees; and requiring managers to attend "people skills" workshops (Colton 1998; Fields-Meyer and Sweeney 1998; Samuel 1998).[1]

Although the news media made much of the novelty of the teenagers' walkout in Macedonia, the McDonald's strike was not a completely isolated event in North America. The United States has recently seen a scattering of youth labor organizing in the low-end service and retail sectors. In 1997 and 1998, young workers at Noah's Bagels outlets in Berkeley and San Francisco voted to unionize with the United Food and Commercial Workers union (Irvine 1997). Also in 1998, in an action similar to that of Drapp in Macedonia, seventeen-year-old Josh Whitman led a strike at the suburban Washington, D.C., McDonald's where he worked: After six days off the job, strikers secured promises from management of better staffing, regular wage reviews, and advance notice of work scheduling (*Labor Notes* 1998). During the mid-1990s, young workers (mostly in their twenties) were engaged in union drives at Borders Books and Music stores across the country (Slaughter 1997). And in the late 1990s, bicycle messengers (again, many in their twenties) launched an effort in San Francisco to unionize the city's courier industry with the support of the International Longshore and Warehouse Union (Lazarus 2000; Thompson 2000).

In Canada, there has been a small wave of youth labor organizing in the service and retail sectors through the course of the 1990s. In a story similar to that of Drapp in Ohio, seventeen-year-old Sarah Inglis attracted international media attention in 1993 when she led a unionization drive at the McDonald's where she worked in Orangeville, Ontario. Motivated by her frustration at management harassment and favoritism, and at sudden and arbitrary changes and reductions in working hours for staff, Inglis managed to get sixty-seven of the 102 employees at her store to sign union authorization cards—enough for automatic union certification under Ontario labor law at the time. But employees' complaints (of uncertain merit) about deception and intimidation by Inglis and other organizers during the card-signing drive led to a lengthy labor-board hearing and a management-sponsored anti-union campaign—in which workers were provided with "Just Say No" buttons, "Just Say No" paid time crew meetings, and a pep rally that had employees lying in the snow outside the store to spell "No." The result was the eventual defeat of Inglis's initiative in a seventy-seven to nineteen vote against unionization (Inglis 1994; Lorinc 1994).

In the same year that Inglis was working to improve conditions at the Orangeville McDonald's, nineteen-year-old David Coburn was leading a union drive at a Harvey's hamburger restaurant in Toronto. Coburn and his co-workers were fed up with management harassment and outraged to find that some of them were being paid below minimum wage. Since then, workers in their teens and twenties have spearheaded union drives at mall fashion outlets in the metropolitan Toronto region (at Levi's 1850, Limité, Suzy Shier); at Walmart and at the casinos in Windsor, Ontario; and at several Starbucks outlets and at a Chapters bookstore in Vancouver, British Columbia—to name only some of the more prominent examples (see Cross 1995; Hartviksen 1996; Klein 1996, 1994; Lorinc 1994; and McArthur 1997).

As has been the case in the United States, some of these recent efforts in Canada have ended in failure—with store closings, broken managerial promises, and legal defeats—while others (notably at Walmart and Starbucks) have gone on to win union recognition and negotiate first contracts. The issues motivating these workers have been similar everywhere: wages, hours, scheduling, and management harassment and favoritism. The most recent in this string of efforts to organize youth labor to gain international attention was the extended but ultimately unsuccessful unionization campaign in a Squamish, British Columbia, McDonald's outlet that was led by two young workers, seventeen-year-old Jennifer Wiebe and sixteen-year-old Tessa Lowinger (Featherstone 1999, 1998; Gray 1998; Keating 1998).

Youth labor organizing in the low-end service and retail sectors, it is important to recognize, is not a new phenomenon in either Canada or the United States. In Canada, for example, there were union-organizing drives at McDonald's, Ponderosa, and Winco Steak n' Burger outlets in London, Ontario, during the 1970s, and for a brief time at the end of that decade, workers at a Shawnigan, Quebec, McDonald's outlet enjoyed certification as members of the Confederation of National Trade Unions (Reiter 1991: 159). National Labor Relations Board records in the United States show scattered union elections (almost all of which were unsuccessful) being held at Burger King, Kentucky Fried Chicken, McDonald's, and Taco Bell outlets across the country from the late 1960s onward. In the early 1980s, in Detroit, the community-activist organization ACORN launched an independent union that focused on organizing among young fast-food workers in the area; the union briefly won certification at a Detroit-area Burger King in 1983 (ibid.: 159–60; Luxemberg 1985: 162–63).

Indeed, in his history of the McDonald's corporation, John Love reports that in the late 1960s and early 1970s, McDonald's had a "'flying squad' of experienced . . . store managers who were dispatched to a restaurant the same day that word came of an attempt to organize it" (1995: 394). During this period, the company successfully fought off some *four hundred* separate attempts to unionize McDonald's outlets around the United States (ibid.; see also Boas and Chain 1976: 81–97). Although the identities of the individuals involved in these organizing attempts are largely lost to the annals of history, it is likely, given the predominantly youth-based workforce at McDonald's, that at least some of these would-be organizers were in their teens and twenties. As Stan Luxemberg wryly observes, "While the [fast-food] companies spend little on paychecks, they have made substantial investments to prevent workers from rebelling against unsatisfying jobs" (1985: 163).

BEYOND MONDAY MORNING

Previous studies of youth and work, after documenting the problems that youth workers confront in contemporary society, typically have looked everywhere but at the youth workplace itself for solutions to improve the conditions of youth work. Most of the time, these studies conclude by suggesting that changes be made in the school classroom or educational system that will raise youths' chances of success in the world of work. This is what might be called the "Monday morning" paradigm. As Willis writes at the end of his classic ethnography of youth and work, *Learning to Labor* (1977: 186), for example, "practitioners [meaning teachers and other educational staff and officials] have the problem of 'Monday morning' "—that is, of what to do in the classroom when the school week starts up again. "If we have nothing to say about what to do on Monday morning," Willis says, then "everything is yielded to a purist structuralist immobilising reductionist tautology: nothing can be done until the basic structures of society are changed but the structures of society prevent us making any changes" (ibid.)

This book has attempted to move beyond Monday morning. Without denying that there are, indeed, many important efforts and changes that could and should be made in classrooms, schools, and educational systems in both the United States and Canada to help youths in their work and non-work lives, this study has investigated another set of institutions that could also play a significant role in improving youth work conditions. This set of institutions, of course, constitutes the U.S. and Canadian labor movements. I have argued that unionism—as exemplified, in particular, by the practices of Local C in Glenwood, but also by Local 7 in Box Hill—can make an important difference in the work lives of young stopgap service-sector workers. Unionism can help to improve wages, benefits, scheduling, and job security for young stopgap workers; it can also play a critical role in educating young workers and providing them with an opportunity to have a voice in shaping their own stopgap working conditions.

Educators, researchers, and policymakers who have considered the problems affecting young workers in the United States and Canada have almost completely ignored the role that unionization might play in improving the work lives of young stopgap workers. In past years, perhaps, educators, researchers, and policymakers could legitimately defend their failure to consider unionization as a solution to youth workplace disempowerment by arguing that unionization in the youth labor market was not practical or feasible. Such arguments, however, are increasingly weak.

The recent examples of youth labor organizing in the United States and Canada that I have described suggest that young service and retail workers, at certain times and places, have both the interest and ability to turn to collective workplace action and unionization in order to press their demands for improved working conditions. Youth labor organizing, moreover, is just one of an increasing number of sites of interaction between youths and unions across North America. Youth labor organizing has been predominantly youth-driven rather than labor-driven, as young workers have often met with reluctance on the part of unions to become involved with their issues. Sarah Inglis, for example, had to contact four different unions before finding one that would take on her case. But unions, too, have launched their own efforts to reach out to youths.

The highest-profile investment that the labor movement in either the United States or Canada has recently made to reaching out to a younger generation of students, workers, and activists is probably the "Union Summer" program run by the AFL-CIO (the American Federation of Labor–Congress of Industrial Organizations, the umbrella organization of trade unions in the United States). Union Summer, which has been run yearly since it was launched in 1996, recruits students on college campuses to participate in paid summer union internships that are held in cities around the country. In these internships, students are given a general educational overview of the history and structure of the U.S. labor movement and the opportunity to work hands-on in ongoing union-organizing campaigns. The overall goal of Union Summer, according to its directors, is to "inject a large dose of class consciousness into the politics of the next generation (Moberg 1996: 26; see also Cooper 1996; Goldin 1996; Levin 1996; Lewis 1996).

Union Summer has not been without its difficulties. As one former participant put it, "a lack of sober second thought prevents Union Summer from sufficiently addressing the inherent cultural/generational conflicts that exist between the young activist participants and the union itself" (Noorani 1998). Some Union Summer interns have found themselves stranded with unions that have little idea how to use or engage with their interests, energies, and talents, while others have rebelled when they have felt that they were being used as pawns in union publicity stunts or when they have come up against traditional top-down and directive union staff members who have little time or interest in critical input and thinking from young interns. Nevertheless, in getting people both inside and outside the labor movement to start thinking seriously about the notion that there could be a productive relationship between youth and unions, Union Summer has had an enormous impact.

Beyond Union Summer, there are numerous other sites throughout North America in which relationships between youths and unions are being tentatively forged. At its 1995 annual convention, the Canadian Labour Congress (CLC)—Canada's equivalent to the AFL-CIO—created a "Youth Caucus" to focus specifically on youth issues in the labor movement. Under the threat of walkout by the handful of youth activists present, the CLC even agreed to define "youth" as age twenty-five or younger (as opposed to, say, age forty or younger), and to make an extra effort to bring more of the severely under-represented youth delegates to the conference. Large unions in both Canada and the United States are now likely to sponsor regular workshops and discussion papers at their national and regional conventions that focus on the topic of "youth and unions." And the AFL-CIO's Organizing Institute has recently stepped up its recruiting activities on campuses across the United States in support of its drive to develop a new generation of highly committed and talented union organizers (Chaplin 1998).

Unions have increased their interest in educating as well as organizing youths in North America. The 1994 School to Work Act in the United States provided a spur for unions across the country to develop or get involved with a host of work-oriented educational initiatives at the elementary-school, high-school, and community-college levels. These initiatives have included "Labor in the Schools" curriculum packages, union internships, pre-apprenticeship programs, school-to-career bridging programs, skills-enhancement programs, job-shadowing programs, counseling and mentoring programs, and so forth. Many of these initiatives were heavily dominated by the employers who were also involved in their development, and critical engagement with workplace social-justice issues in School to Work educational programs has frequently been sorely underdeveloped, all too often limited to brief and unintegrated discussions of what is called (in the act's jargon) "All Aspects of Industry." However, at their best, these programs represent an effort to rescue labor education from its absurd current status in the United States as a marginal segment of adult education, and to make labor education instead a central part of the general education of youths in this country.

College campuses in the 1990s have constituted a major site for youth labor activism in both Canada and the United States. Graduate students from the University of California, Los Angeles, to Yale University, to New York University are currently organizing in large numbers to form unions (Nelson 1997; Cooper 1999). The issues confronting graduate students are not, in fact, unrelated to the issues confronting the young fast-food and grocery workers who have been the focus of this book. For graduate labor activism is motivated in large part by the fears many students have that the teaching work they do while in graduate school has become more a stopgap form of employment that benefits primarily their employers' (the universities') bottom lines, and less a form of stepping stone, apprenticeship-type employment for futures in tenure-track academia that such teaching work traditionally has been assumed to be.

Meanwhile, undergraduate students at colleges across Canada and the United States have launched a powerful and well-publicized anti-sweatshop campaign (Cooper 1999; Greenhouse 1999; Klein 1999a; Krupa 1999). Students are demanding that the companies that produce college clothing lines not use overseas sweatshops, and they have used sit-ins, rallies, and teach-ins to spread their message and press their demands. Significantly, it has widely been reported that a number of the leaders in the student anti-sweatshop movement in the United States are former interns from the AFL-CIO's Union Summer program.

Finally, in the 1990s some unions in North America have started once again to support the interests of youth workers in their collective-bargaining activities and to resist employers' attempts to divide older and younger workers against each other. To date, this tentative shift has been symbolized most powerfully by the Teamsters' extraordinarily popular UPS strike in the summer of 1997. As was widely reported, the UPS strike focused on improving the work conditions of part-time workers in what was a tiered workforce split between full- and part-timers: In 1997, full-time workers at UPS earned almost twice what part-time workers earned per hour (Greenhouse 1997). Less widely reported was that the strike was also about supporting the interests of youth workers: The part-time workforce is considerably younger than the full-time workforce at UPS and is composed of large numbers of college students.

The tiered wage scales at UPS had, in fact, been agreed to by the Teamsters themselves in the early 1980s. As in most unions, young, part-time UPS workers—who also were frequently temporary, stopgap workers—played little role in internal Teamster affairs at that time. The full-time and permanent adult workers who dominated the union's affairs were thus able to protect their own interests at the bargaining table by sacrificing the interests of a younger generation of workers. By 1997, however, this situation had changed. Older Teamsters rejected their employer's arguments that part-timers didn't deserve a hefty wage increase because they were "just" college students working their way through school. And for their part, because their interests were for once being promoted front and center at the bargaining table, younger Teamsters made a strong and decisive commitment to the strike effort.

In light of this current context, unionization therefore warrants consideration as a potential force for improving the working conditions of young stopgap workers in Canada and the United States. Labor laws— in the United States, in particular—may continue to make union organizing in the youth labor market extremely difficult. But now is as good a time as any for educators, researchers, and policymakers to pay serious attention to the ways in which unionization and other forms of collective workplace activism can help young stopgap workers improve their working conditions. After all, as has been documented in this book, some unions are already working in the youth labor market—sometimes with considerable success—and can provide models for what youth unionization could and should look like.

AGE DISCRIMINATION AND PREJUDICE IN THE LABOR MOVEMENT

Over the past few decades, both the U.S. and Canadian labor movements have moved increasingly to address and confront the ugly reality of racism and sexism in their past and present histories. Labor activists have focused on attacking both the blatant and more subtle forms of race and sex discrimination in their unions and on changing those everyday practices of traditional unionism (styles of discourse, for example, or the timing and location of union meetings) that have worked, effectively if indirectly, to marginalize and exclude women and minorities. However, at the same time that this consciousness-raising over racism and sexism in the labor movement has been developing, there has been by comparison a deafening silence over the history and practice of ageism—of the marginalization of youths—in the North American labor movement. Indeed, not only has there been a striking absence of discussion of ageism in union circles, but since the late 1970s, many unions have engaged in one the most blatant forms of age and generational discrimination that can be found in the labor movement: the negotiation of two-tiered wage and benefit contracts.

This book lends support to increasing the amount of attention paid to the possibilities of unionization in the youth labor market; however, it also warns against easy optimism about the positive impact that unions can have on the lives of young stopgap workers. The history of ageism and anti-youth discrimination in the North American labor movement is long and recent—and largely unacknowledged. Despite the recent renewal of interest in youth among labor leaders and activists across the continent, there has yet to be a serious and sustained discussion of this discriminatory and ageist history in the way that there has been of labor-movement racism and sexism. Until such a discussion occurs, I argue, the success that unionization can have in the youth labor market will remain limited. As I have shown in my analysis of Local 7 in Box Hill, many are the ways in which unions in North America continue, deliberately and unintentionally, to fail to protect the interests or welcome and enable the full participation of their younger members.

Even for unions that are actively committed to representing the interests, and welcoming the participation, of young workers, the youth workplace can be a challenging site to provide collective, supportive, and structured environments for workplace learning, activism and change. Young service-sector workers are stopgap workers with high rates of turnover, and they work predominantly at small work sites scattered throughout all sectors of our communities. As I suggest in my analysis of Local C in Glenwood, unless unions can find consistent ways to mobilize young workers in their workplaces over extended periods of time, their ability to resolve structural problems in the youth workplace—problems that revolve around the fundamental question of who has control over basic working conditions in the workplace—is likely to remain limited, and the potential for dramatic educational impact is not likely to be fully realized.

If unions are ever to play a significant role in improving overall work conditions throughout the youth labor market, they—along with educators, researchers, policymakers, and other workplace activists—will need to move beyond old and familiar stereotypes of youths as workers. As I have shown in this study, these stereotypes fail to represent adequately the complex and shifting experiences, interests, and agencies of young stopgap service-sector workers. Unions that ignore young stopgap workers because they assume such workers are apathetic and disengaged from the world of work ignore these workers in error. Likewise, unions that assume young stopgap workers have a purely materialist interest in their work, and that they care only about having higher wages and benefits, are more likely than not to be in the wrong.

The president of Local C in Glenwood tells with considerable amusement the story of a young Fry House worker who once called the union office irate because a new store manager was insisting that workers put only nine to eleven fries in a small order of fries, when they had always put in eleven to fourteen pieces. The size of fry orders is simply not something in which Local C tends to involve itself; the issue can seem trivial in comparison with the local's daily efforts to stop companies from abusing its membership. Young stopgap workers, however, often develop a strong sense of local investment in their work and work sites and of solidarity with co-workers as well as with customers. Unions in North America have often failed to demand a central role in deciding how work should and should not be done at their work sites, but to reach out to young stopgap service-sector workers—workers who tend to have strong local, work-site-based senses of solidarity—unions may find that they will have to foreground precisely such kinds of interests in shaping basic work processes.

On the other hand, as stopgap workers, young service sector workers are not career workers. In fact, they often tend to be fundamentally anti-careerist in their orientations toward their low-end service-sector jobs. Unions who enter the youth labor market assuming that the majority of youths there want to turn their low-end service jobs into career jobs are likely to be disappointed. All of the young labor organizers who were described at the beginning of this chapter—the Bryan Drapps and the Sarah Inglises of the world—considered themselves, at the time of their labor activism, to be stopgap workers. They tried to organize the workplaces in which they worked so that these workplaces would be better places for themselves and for future generations of young stopgap workers to work in *during the short term.*

Instead of trying to help young workers only as future career workers, unions in North America need to think about how they can help young workers as stopgap workers. If unions do work seriously at attempting a radical transformation of the jobs that today are relegated largely to the continent's young (along with other marginalized groups), then there may indeed come a day when today's youth jobs become tomorrow's highly sought-after career jobs. But to get to that point, unions need first—in their organizing strategies, their contract demands, and their day-to-day work with their own members—to approach young service-sector workers in North America as being quintessential stopgap workers.

YOUTH AND WORK IN THE SERVICE SOCIETY

Regardless of whether unionization will ever take hold as a significant force in the lives of young service-sector workers in the United States and Canada, this book raises issues of more general concern to those interested in understanding and improving the lives of youths and workers in contemporary society—whether in the context of community development, education, government policy, or socially responsible business endeavors. Some of the issues raised in this book extend beyond youth stopgap workers to hold relevance for other groups of workers, as well. For we live today in a service society: More than 70 percent of all workers in North America work in the service sector, many in jobs not altogether dissimilar to the fast-food and grocery jobs of Glenwood and Box Hill (Macdonald and Sirianni 1996).

In this book, I have held out a vague and somewhat idealized notion of what actually comes after the period of stopgap work in the lives of individual workers in Canada and the United States. I have referred to this post-stopgap period variously as involving "career," "serious," "adult," more stable, higher-wage, and higher-status forms of employment. Although it is true that most individuals do see some such shift in working identities and conditions between their youth and adult working years, it is also the case that many adults work in the low-end service sector—and, indeed, in the fast-food and grocery industries themselves. Much of what I have written about working conditions for stopgap youth workers therefore also holds relevance for many adult workers.

Researchers, activists, and policymakers concerned with improving conditions in the low-end service sector have often pointed out that North America's retail, food, hospitality, entertainment, and business-service industries have tended to take a "low-road," "low-skill," low-wage approach to work organization, as opposed to a "high-road," "high-skill," high-wage approach (e.g., Bailey and Bernhardt 1997; Herzenberg, Alic, and Wial 1998). These observers have expressed interest in bringing variants of the "high-performance" model to the low-end service sector in the hope of improving productivity and skill requirements and, consequently, wage levels, job status, and work conditions. This study warns against any easy embrace of the high-performance model and urges researchers and activists, first and foremost, to look carefully at the power dynamics that stand behind such managerial reforms. But this study also shares the concerns of those who want to bring a "high-road" approach to the low-end service sector. I have pointed out that fast-food and grocery workers *already* develop considerable local expertise in performing their work—expertise that needs to be recognized, valued, and appropriately recompensed. At the same time, I have noted ways in which the current organization of fast-food and grocery work blocks worker expertise and performance, and I have suggested the need to rethink and reorganize the fast-food and grocery work process to give workers greater control over the work that they do.

Time is a further example of an issue that is of general concern to service workers of all ages. In recent years, we have seen a proliferation of research on time in the workplace—on part-time work, overtime work, balancing work and family time, and so forth (e.g., Epstein et al. 1999; Hochschild 1997, 1989; Schor 1992; Tilly 1996). In a service society, such growth in concern with work and time is not surprising, for service work tends to be broadly characterized by part-time work, shift work, and irregular and often unpredictable hours and schedules. Low-end service employers, moreover, have deliberately sought to hire workers who have prior claims on their personal time: students who must balance work with school and women who traditionally have been responsible for balancing work with family. This study seeks to contribute to the burgeoning literature on work and time, and the concerns raised here about just-in-time labor systems, irregular scheduling, and off-the-clock work are relevant for many adult as well as youth service-sector workers.

However, alongside these and other such universalist implications, this book also points to the need for greater particularism in the way we think about work and workers in the contemporary service society. Over the past decade, considerable attention has been paid in the United States and Canada to the spread of temporary and contingent forms of labor (e.g., Herzenberg, Alic, and Wial 1998; Osterman 1999; Sennett 1998). All too often, researchers and policymakers have overlooked age and life stage as key variables in the conditions and experiences of temporary and contingent work. Indeed, youth stopgap workers often are not even included in discussions of the problems inherent in the proliferating forms of temporary and contingent work.

This study suggests that age and life stage must be held central to any understanding of temporary and contingent work. (See Doeringer 1990 and Jorgensen 1999 for similar claims.) It argues, further, that stopgap youth workers constitute a distinct, life-stage-particular category of temporary worker. Adults can and increasingly do experience work in Canada and the United States as stopgap work. But because adolescence (or youth more generally) is ideologically and institutionally constituted as a stopgap life stage writ large in North America, stopgap work meshes with the institutions and ideologies of youth outside the workplace in a way that it does not mesh with non-work institutions and ideologies of adulthood.

The role of age in the workplace is particularly important to recognize in a service society. For personal identity, as Cameron Macdonald and Carmen Sirianni point out, is more relevant for service workers than for any other kind of worker:

> Service work differs most radically from manufacturing, construction or agricultural work in the relationship between worker characteristics and the job.... Service occupations are the only ones in which the producer in some sense equals the product. In no other area of wage labor are the personal characteristics of workers so strongly associated with the nature

of the work. Because at least part of the job in all service occupations is to "manufacture social relations" ... [worker] traits such as gender, race, age and sexuality serve a signalling function, indicating to the customer/employer important cues about the tone of the interaction. (1996: 14–15)

Significantly, Macdonald and Sirianni include age in their brief list of the key characteristics of service workers. Yet although researchers have explored at considerable length the significance of gender and race, and (to a lesser degree) sexuality, in the experience and performance of service work, it is age—and especially young age—that is almost continually overlooked as a central component of worker identity in our service society.

This study, finally, argues that age discrimination against the young and age stratification of youth and adult workers are critical phenomena in the labor market and workplace that have been sorely underacknowledged by researchers and policymakers. Age discrimination against the young intersects, of course, with the more widely recognized forces of gender, race, and class discrimination (Lucas 1997). Age discrimination against the young also has many parallels with the recognized forces of gender, race, and class discrimination—one can think, for example, of historical stereotypes of female workers as being workers who work only for "pin money," and who consequently do not "need" or "deserve" full wages and benefits in their places of employment. But age discrimination against the young is a powerful force in its own right. Age discrimination against youth workers within key labor-market institutions—employers, unions, and government bodies—plays a central role in shaping the very existence and conditions of youth stopgap work (see also Klein 1999b: 195–275). With the ongoing erosion of lifetime, career employment, it is likely that age and age discrimination will only increase in importance as key sites and forces in the stratification of the labor market.

Notes

INTRODUCTION

1. The 1967 Age Discrimination in Employment Act in the United States prohibits discrimination in the workplace against individuals older than forty, but it does not protect youths from workplace discrimination. As Howe and Strauss (1993: 112) quip: "From where [youth workers] sit, even federal discrimination laws are a stacked deck. They prohibit employers from firing someone over forty because he lacks energy (the natural advantage of youth), but say nothing about firing someone under forty because she lacks experience (the natural advantage of age)."

2. Defining "youth" as opposed to "adult" workers in terms of chronological age is inevitably going to be a somewhat arbitrary process. In this study, my focus has been on "youth" workers who are younger than twenty-five—the age cutoff conventionally used in many statistics and studies of youth workers in the United States. This age limit was not absolute in my fieldwork, however, as I ended up interviewing workers in their late twenties, as well. What I argue in this book is that, in the context of the workplace, it is stopgap-worker status itself that defines "youth" as opposed to "adult" workers. On the one hand, individual workers can position themselves and be positioned as stopgap workers well into their thirties, and on the other, some workers in their early twenties and even in their teens can position themselves as already being beyond the stage of stopgap work, and as being "adult" or "serious" or career-track workers.

3. Working youths in Canada and the United States do not, of course, all work in the low-end service and retail sectors. Youths—especially in their early twenties—work in virtually all sectors of the economy, and not just as hourly workers, but as interns, apprentices, enlisted servicemen and servicewomen, volunteers, salaried managers, small-business owners, and so forth. The conditions, experiences, and identities that I describe in this book for young stopgap workers in the low-end service and retail sectors will have relevance for some, but certainly not for all, youths who work in other capacities in other industries and settings.

4. Many significant differences exist in the labor laws, labor movements, union cultures, and social-welfare policies of the contemporary United States and Canada. In this book, I do not focus on these U.S.–Canadian differences. My assumption is that the organization of youth work in the low-end service and retail sectors in these two countries is highly similar—not least for the fact

that the same multinational companies frequently dominate these sectors in both countries. Although differences between Local 7 in Box Hill and Local C in Glenwood are clearly shaped by broader differences in these two locals' national labor contexts, my assumption is that there are (business-oriented, adult-centered) unions similar to Local 7 (U.S.) in Canada and, vice versa, that there are (social-movement, youth-inclusive) unions similar to Local C (Canada) in the United States.

5. My decision not to involve employers in my research was based on several factors. Two reasons stand out, however. First, I have been concerned about the extent to which the literature on youth and work has been either dominated outright by employer interests or else extremely reticent about questioning or challenging employers' prerogatives in the workplace. Such bias, I believe, has been directly shaped by employers' control over access to the workplace and their influence on the research process. I therefore wanted to establish as much distance and freedom as I could from employers' agendas and restrictions in my fieldwork. Because I was studying unionized workplaces, I had the opportunity to gain institutional access to workplaces in Box Hill and Glenwood without having to go through employer channels.

The second reason that I eschewed employer involvement was that I simply did not believe, ahead of time, that employers in Box Hill and (especially) Glenwood would want to participate actively in my research. The fast-food industry has a widespread reputation for being rabidly anti-union: I saw no reason that Fry House would want to publicize the fact that a number of its outlets in Canada have been successfully unionized. In retrospect, I continue to believe that my strategy of not involving employers in my research, though obviously limiting, was nevertheless well advised. In Glenwood, considerable tension has arisen between Local C and Fry House management. During their 1998 contract negotiations, Fry House actually sent out a gag order to all of its employees prohibiting them from speaking to outsiders about workplace conditions and the state of ongoing negotiations. (Local C immediately rejected this gag order as being a clear violation of its collective-bargaining agreement with Fry House.)

I should point out that my decision to conduct workplace research by securing only union, and not employer, consent is by no means unprecedented. Ely Chinoy used the same strategy for his classic *Automobile Workers and the American Dream* (1992 [1955]). Likewise, Ken Kusterer, in his study of the working knowledge of "unskilled" workers (1978), and Donald Roy, in his study of labor-organizing campaigns (1970), question the advisability and possibility of securing "dual entry" to workplaces by obtaining both unions' and employers' consent; both opted instead to obtain "single entry" by securing only union consent for their workplace research projects.

6. My interview sample reflects this workforce diversity. In Glenwood, I interviewed thirty-four young Fry House workers. Interviewees ranged in age from seventeen to twenty-eight, but most (three-fifths) were between eighteen and twenty-one. In terms of educational status and achievement, three of my thirty-four interviewees were high-school students; ten were high-school grad-

uates; three were high-school dropouts; five were dropouts who were working on a high-school-equivalency degree; seven were community-college students; two were university students; one had a community-college degree; and three were community-college dropouts. In terms of sex, nineteen of my thirty-four interviewees were female and fifteen were male. In terms of race and ethnicity, twenty-two of my thirty-four interviewees were white; four were East Indian; four were Hispanic; two were Chinese Canadian; one was Fijian; and one was Filipino.

In Box Hill, I interviewed sixty-one young grocery workers. Interviewees ranged in age from sixteen to twenty-eight, and most (two-thirds) were between seventeen and twenty-one. In terms of educational status and achievement, twelve of my sixty-one interviewees were high-school students; nineteen were high-school graduates; five were high-school dropouts; two were dropouts working on a high-school-equivalency degree; thirteen were community-college students; two were university students; one had a community-college degree; two had bachelor's degrees; three were community-college dropouts; and two were university dropouts. In terms of sex, thirty-one of my sixty-one interviewees were female and thirty were male. In terms of race and ethnicity, thirty-eight of my sixty-one interviewees were white; seven were African American; six were of Filipino background; four were Latino; three were of Southeast Asian background; two were of Samoan descent; and one was from India.

CHAPTER ONE

1. To keep the overview brief, I focus my discussion in this chapter on a single key text from each of these four bodies of literature. Each body, of course, incorporates a diversity of arguments and viewpoints that cannot be captured by referring to a single text. My intention here is not to provide a comprehensive survey of the youth, work, and education literature, however. Rather, it is to offer a simple roadmap of the dominant ways in which youth workers have been variously positioned in mainstream research, theory, and policy.

CHAPTER THREE

1. I should emphasize that although unionization may strengthen the development of store-level solidarities in the Glenwood Fry Houses, these solidarities are no more reducible to a union identity than they are to a company teamwork program. Union interventions in individual outlets are sporadic, at best. Young Fry House workers often distinguish their workplace communities from their union in much the same way that they differentiate such communities from company-sponsored models for work teams.

CHAPTER FOUR

1. Contrasts that young workers make between school and the workplace do not all favor the world of work. Many young grocery workers—especially

those who are no longer in school—miss the organized social events of school, as well as the sheer mass of people their own age. These workers wish that their stores would sponsor dances and other local staff events. Many young workers—again, especially those who are no longer attending school—also speak of missing the pleasures and challenges of being able to learn. For them, grocery work all too quickly becomes routine.

2. Box Hill supermarkets justify excluding high-school-age workers from checker positions by invoking state and federal laws that prohibit teenagers from selling tobacco and alcohol in their stores.

CHAPTER SEVEN

1. It should be noted that the dollar value of the union-negotiated health care plan in Local 7 in Box Hill is considerably greater than that of Local C. The Local C plan acts as a supplemental plan to the government-provided health care plan that covers all individuals in Glenwood's province. In Box Hill, as elsewhere in the United States, there are no government-provided, universal healthcare plans. The Local 7 plan thus provides for the entirety of a worker's healthcare coverage. My goal in comparing Local C and Local 7 here is to assess the relative advantages each union brings to its younger as opposed to older members, not to compare the unions' absolute advantages. It is the relative advantages for young and old members that reveal whether a union is practicing more of an adult-centered or all-ages model of unionism.

2. Local 7 in Box Hill controls more than a 90 percent share of the regional grocery market. The local thus enjoys considerable bargaining leverage and can effectively take wages out of competition in the Box Hill grocery industry. Indeed, grocery wages in Box Hill are among the highest in the industry anywhere in North America. By contrast, the Glenwood Fry Houses are the only unionized fast-food chain in Glenwood. Local C does not even represent all of the Fry House restaurants in Glenwood, let alone restaurants in other fast-food chains.

3. Delivery drivers in the Glenwood Fry Houses are contract workers and are not part of the Local C bargaining unit. Concern for delivery drivers is widespread among young Fry House workers in Glenwood. Many feel that drivers are underpaid and poorly treated by the company. It is thus common for young Fry House workers to disregard official company policy on delivery drivers— to invite them into their stores to use the offices while waiting for delivery calls, to give them free or discounted drinks and meals, and so forth.

4. Local C staff say that they send union contracts to each Fry House restaurant and that they have sent out many more contracts than there are Fry House workers in Glenwood. It is not clear exactly what happens to these contracts. Some workers tell of store managers regularly throwing into the garbage union materials that come into their stores. Others say that contracts and other union materials get shunted (deliberately or accidentally) to the back of locked cabinets in store offices—so that although there are contracts in the store, they are inaccessible to workers.

The issue of getting contracts to members highlights a broader problem in union–member communication in Local C: Union staff rely on sending written materials to Fry House restaurants to communicate information from the local and tend to assume that, once such materials have been sent, union–member communication has occurred. However, conversations with young Fry House workers reveal that this strategy frequently is ineffective, for a number of reasons: 1) written materials are lost or thrown out or never made accessible; 2) written materials may be posted on union bulletin boards, but young workers rarely look closely at them because they see these boards as blending into the background of the restaurant environment (similarly, contracts may be given to young workers, but these workers never read the contracts because they are seen as background forms that have official rather than practical use); 3) young workers may read written materials, but the style in which such materials are written—often a form of bureaucratic union-speak—makes these texts largely impenetrable and foreign.

5. My own presence in Local C during the lead-up to the 1998 Fry House contract negotiations was part of the general change that had put the "youth question" in the foreground for local staffers. My research position in Local C was a collaborative or participatory one. I regularly discussed my research with local staff (and with young Fry House workers). The local's decision to run store-based workshops in preparation for its 1998 negotiations (a decision I describe later) was motivated in part by concerns I was raising at the time about the workplace isolation of young Fry House workers.

CHAPTER EIGHT

1. According to the Local 7 Grievance Department, Box Hill grocery employers are within their rights to interpret the contract's seniority language this way. The problem with the scheduling language, union staff say, is that the contract was originally written when most Box Hill supermarkets were still only open six days a week, from 9 A.M. to 6 P.M. each day. In that era, demanding open work availability in return for seniority rights to hours still left employees with considerable quantities of protected time. Today, many Box Hill supermarkets are open twenty-four hours a day, seven days a week, so this is no longer the case. Not all Box Hill grocery employers take this extreme reading of the Local 7 contract's "availability clause." Many schedule workers according to seniority unless these workers have extensive restrictions on their availability that make it infeasible to grant them the hours they desire.

2. I should point out that there are grocery workers in Box Hill who have steady, regular schedules week in and week out; who always get the time off they need; and who never have problems with being scheduled outside their availability. Many grocery managers in Box Hill are conscientious and careful schedule planners who go out of their way to make their employees' work lives predictable and unstressful. My point in this chapter, however, has been to describe the impact that unionization has had on improving scheduling security

for young workers in Box Hill. There are, of course, excellent scheduling managers in many nonunionized food-service and retail establishments—including McDonald's—just as there are in unionized grocery stores. Newman (1999), for example, describes what is apparently a group of unusually high-minded fast-food-restaurant owners in Harlem who consistently prioritize the scheduling needs of their young workers. The issue being addressed here is the extent to which young unionized workers no longer have to count on good luck in getting a caring and supportive (paternalistic?) manager—which is always a risky way to hedge one's scheduling bets in industries with such high managerial turnover—but can rely instead on the steady protection of (worker-negotiated) union-contract scheduling language.

3. This is not true of all young workers in Box Hill and Glenwood. Some workers are rigid accountants with their work and personal time and adamantly refuse to work off the clock under any circumstances. My discussion here focuses on the large group of young workers in these two sites who do— at least occasionally—work off the clock. I noted earlier that off-the-clock work varies from worker to worker and situation to situation. The same can be said for workers' decisions to work only on the clock.

CONCLUSION

1. The strikers may have been less successful than was originally reported. A little more than a month after the strike, Drapp and his co-workers launched a unionization drive with the Teamsters, after finding that the store's owner was reneging on his strike-settlement promises. Pay discrepancies among employees remained, as the owner insisted that adjustments be made case by case, based on ability, availability, and seniority; the starting minimum wage at the store was lowered; employees were asked to sign a new employee handbook that reminded them of their at-will employment status and barred them from talking to the union or to journalists; former strikers reported experiencing retaliation from managers; and four strikers quit under management pressure.

In mid-June, Drapp and a co-worker were fired and banned from the store, allegedly for threatening a manager and blocking an exit after showing up for work with "Union" and "Go Union" painted in glitter on their faces. Shortly thereafter, the Teamsters dropped their unionization bid at the store, citing insufficient employee support. However, the local reported being contacted by employees at a dozen other fast-food restaurants (McDonald's, Taco Bell, Burger King) in northeastern Ohio who were interested in unionizing. Whether the local, which represents workers at an aerosol-can factory and an electronics company, will have any success organizing in the fast-food sector remains to be seen. (For follow-up stories, see Robb 1998a, 1998b; Payne 1998.)

References

Allahar, Anton, and James Côté. 1994. *Generation on Hold: Coming of Age in the Late Twentieth Century.* Toronto: Stoddart Publishing Company.

America's Choice: High Skills or Low Wages. 1990. Rochester, N.Y.: National Center on Education and the Economy, Commission on the Skills of the American Workforce.

Apple, Michael. 1980. "The Other Side of the Hidden Curriculum: Correspondence Theories and the Labor Process." *Interchange* 11, no. 3: 5–22.

Associated Press. 1998. " 'Service with a Smile' Not So Popular with Some Safeway Employees." September 2, 1–2.

Babcock, Charles. 1997. "Rising Tuitions Fill Loan Firm Coffers; Constellation of Businesses Grows Around Education Financing." *Washington Post,* October 27, A1.

Bailey, Ian. 1997. "Coffee Workers Try to Brew First Union Contract; Many Eyes on Starbucks' Only Organized Shop." *Toronto Star,* March 29, E5.

Bailey, Thomas, and Annette Bernhardt. 1997. "In Search of the High Road in a Low-Wage Industry." *Politics and Society* 25, no. 2: 179–201.

Barker, James. 1993. "Tightening the Iron Cage: Concertive Control in Self-Managing Teams." *Administrative Science Quarterly* 38: 408–37.

Bernhardt, Annette, Martina Morris, Mark Handcock, and Mark Scott. 1998. *Work and Opportunity in the Post-Industrial Labor Market.* Brief No. 19. New York: Institute on Education and the Economy.

Boas, Max, and Steve Chain. 1976. *Big Mac: The Unauthorized Story of McDonald's.* New York: Mentor.

Borman, Kathryn. 1991. *The First "Real" Job: A Study of Young Workers.* Albany: State University of New York Press.

Burawoy, Michael. 1979. *Manufacturing Consent: Changes in the Labor Process under Monopoly Capitalism.* Chicago: University of Chicago Press.

Chaplin, Heather. 1998. "Kids in the Hall." *San Francisco Bay Guardian,* June 3, 19–22.

Charner, Ivan, and Bryna Fraser. 1988. *Youth and Work: What We Know, What We Don't Know, What We Need to Know.* Washington, D.C.: William T. Grant Foundation Commission on Work, Family and Citizenship.

Chinoy, Ely. 1992 [1955]. *Automobile Workers and the American Dream.* 2nd ed. Urbana: University of Illinois Press.

Colton, Michael. 1998. "Big Mac Attack: Did Somebody Say Strike? The Kids Who Took on McDonald's—and Won." *Washington Post,* April 26, F1.

Cooper, Marc. 1999. "No Sweat: Uniting Workers and Students, a New Movement Is Born." *The Nation*, June 7, 11–15.

———. 1996. "The Boys and Girls of Union Summer." *The Nation*, August 12, 18.

Cross, Victoria. 1995. "People Like Us: Diary of a Casino Strike." *Our Times* (July), 36–40.

Doeringer, Peter, ed. 1990. *Bridges to Retirement: Older Workers in a Changing Labor Market*. Ithaca, N.Y.: ILR Press.

Duffy, Andrew. 1996. "Future Job Seekers May Face Test of Emotions as well as Employment Skills." *Ottawa Citizen*, October 19, E6.

Du Gay, Paul. 1996. *Consumption and Identity at Work*. London: Sage.

Epstein, Cynthia, Carroll Seron, Bonnie Oglensky, and Robert Saute. 1999. *The Part-Time Paradox: Time Norms, Professional Life, Family and Gender*. New York: Routledge.

Faludi, Susan. 1990. "At Nordstrom Stores, Service Comes First—But at a Big Price." *Wall Street Journal*, February 20, p. A1.

Featherstone, Liza. 1999. "The Burger International Revisited." *Left Business Observer*, no. 91 (August).

———. 1998. "The Burger International." *Left Business Observer*, no. 86 (November).

Fields-Meyer, Thomas, and Shari Sweeney. 1998. "McHoffa." *People*, May 18, 137–38.

Fine, Gary Alan. 1990. "Organizational Time: Temporal Demands and the Experience of Work in Restaurant Kitchens." *Social Forces* 69, no. 1: 95–114.

Flint, Troy. 1998. "First a Diploma, Then Loan Repayments; Concerns over Debt Hampering College Students Even after School." *Houston Chronicle*, November 30, B3.

The Forgotten Half: Non-College Youth in America. 1988a. Washington, D.C.: William T. Grant Foundation Commission on Work, Family and Citizenship.

The Forgotten Half: Pathways to Success for America's Youth and Young Families. 1988b. Washington, D.C.: William T. Grant Foundation Commission on Work, Family and Citizenship.

Freeman, Richard, and David Wise, ed. 1982. *The Youth Labor Market Problem: Its Nature, Causes, and Consequences*. Chicago: University of Chicago Press.

Gabriel, Yiannis. 1988. *Working Lives in Catering*. London: Routledge.

Gaskell, Jane, and Marvin Lazerson. 1981. "Between School and Work: Perspectives of Working Class Youth." *Interchange* 11, no. 3: 80–96.

Goldin, Greg. 1996. "Class Struggle 101: The AFL-CIO's Union Summer Enrolled Students in the Hardest Course Around: Helping Workers Win Their Rights." *LA Weekly*, September 20, 30.

Gray, John. 1998. "Is Labour's Mac Attack a Losing Battle?" *Globe and Mail*, September 9, A1.

Greenberger, Ellen, and Laurence Steinberg. 1986. *When Teenagers Work: The Psychological and Social Costs of Adolescent Employment*. New York: Basic Books.

Greenhouse, Steven. 1999. "Activism Surges at Campuses Nationwide, and Labor Is at Issue." *New York Times,* March 29, A14.

———. 1997. "Parcel-Workers' Strike Shows Labor's Focus on Low-Wage Workers." *Seattle Times,* August 10, A6.

Griffin, Christine. 1993. *Representations of Youth: The Study of Youth and Adolescence in Britain and America.* Cambridge: Polity Press.

Grimsley, Kirsten. 1998. "Service with a Forced Smile: Safeway's Courtesy Campaign also Elicits Some Frowns." *Washington Post,* October 18, A1.

Hartviksen, Wynne. 1996. "Wynne's World: Bringing the Union to the Mall." *Our Times,* (September), 20–23.

Hays, Constance. 1997. "Trying to Get a Job? Check Yes or No." *New York Times,* November 28, B1.

Herzenberg, Stephen, John Alic, and Howard Wial. 1998. *New Rules for a New Economy: Employment and Opportunity in Postindustrial America.* Ithaca, N.Y.: ILR Press.

Hochner, Arthur, Cherlyn Granrose, Judith Goode, Elaine Simon, and Eileen Appelbaum. 1988. *Job-Saving Strategies: Worker Buyouts and QWL.* Kalamazoo, Mich.: W. E. Upjohn Institute for Employment Research.

Hochschild, Arlie. 1997. *The Time Bind: When Work Becomes Home and Home Becomes Work.* New York: Metropolitan Books.

———. 1989. *The Second Shift.* New York: Avon.

———. 1983. *The Managed Heart: Commercialization of Human Feeling.* Berkeley: University of California Press.

Howe, Neil, and Bill Strauss. 1993. *13th Gen: Abort, Retry, Ignore, Fail?* New York: Vintage Books.

Hughes, Katherine. 1999. *Supermarket Employment: Good Jobs at Good Wages?* Working Paper No. 11. New York: Institute on Education and the Economy.

Inglis, Sarah. 1994. "McDonald's Union Drive-Thru: Sarah Inglis Tells Her Story." *Our Times* (June), 19–28.

Irvine, Martha. 1997. "Rising Number of Young Employees See Unions as Way to Go in Workplace." *Seattle Post-Intelligencer,* August 18, B4.

Jacobs, Jerry. 1993. "Careers in the US Service Economy." Pp. 195–224 in *Changing Classes: Stratification and Mobility in Post-Industrial Societies,* ed. Gosta Esping-Anderson. London: Sage.

Jorgensen, Helene. 1999. *When Good Jobs Go Bad: Young Adults and Temporary Work in the New Economy.* Washington, D.C.: 2030 Center.

Kantor, Harvey. 1994. "Managing the Transition from School to Work: The False Promise of Youth Apprenticeship." *Teachers College Record,* vol. 95, no. 1, 442–61.

Keating, Jack. 1998. "Small Fries Win Big Mac Attack." *The Province,* August 20, 1.

Kelley, Robin. 1994. *Race Rebels: Culture, Politics, and the Black Working Class.* New York: Free Press.

Klein, Naomi. 1999a. "Anti-Sweatshop Crusade Gathers Steam." *Toronto Star,* February 26, 1.

———. 1999b. *No Logo: Taking Aim at the Brand Bullies.* New York: Picador.

———. 1996. "Can a McJob Provide a Living Wage?" *Ms* (May), 32–38.

———. 1994. "Salesgirl Solidarity." *This Magazine* (February), 12–19.

Krahn, Harvey, and Julian Tanner. 1996. "Coming to Terms with Marginal Work: Dropouts in a Polarized Labor Market." Pp. 65–83 in *Debating Dropouts: Critical Policy and Research Perspectives on School Leaving,* ed. Deirdre Kelly and Jane Gaskell. New York: Teachers College Press.

Krupa, Gregg. 1999. "The Battle Cry Against Sweatshops Resounds Across College Campuses." *Boston Globe,* April 18, F1.

Kusterer, Ken. 1978. *Know-how on the Job: The Important Working Knowledge of "Unskilled" Workers.* Boulder, Colo.: Westview Press.

Labor Notes. 1998. "NewsWatch" (December), 4.

Laz, Cheryl. 1998. "Act Your Age." *Sociological Forum* 13, no. 1: 85–113.

Lazarus, David. 2000. "Road Warriors: Bike Messengers Risk All to Deliver the Goods, but Unionizing Is New Terrain." *San Francisco Chronicle,* January 28.

Leidner, Robin. 1993. *Fast Food, Fast Talk: Service Work and the Routinization of Everyday Life.* Berkeley: University of California Press.

Levin, Andy. 1996. "Race, Class and Union Summer." *Poverty and Race* 5, no. 6: 3–9.

Lewis, Diane. 1996. "Labor '96: Unions Look to the Young." *Boston Globe,* September 2, A1.

Lewis, Theodore, James Stone, Wayne Shipley, and Svjetlana Madzar. 1998. "The Transition from School to Work: An Examination of the Literature." *Youth and Society* 29, no. 3: 259–92.

Liddle, Alan. 1997. "Jury Finds Taco Bell Guilty in Wages Suit: Chain to Appeal Case's Class Action Status." *Nation's Restaurant News,* April 21, 1.

Linder, Marc, and Ingrid Nygaard. 1998. *Void Where Prohibited: Rest Breaks and the Right to Urinate on Company Time.* Ithaca, N.Y.: ILR Press.

Lindsay, David. 1998. "True Lies." *This Magazine* (January), 4.

Lorinc, John. 1994. "Fast Food, Slow Bargaining." *This Magazine* (June), 25–30.

Love, John. 1995. *McDonald's: Behind the Arches.* Rev. ed. New York: Bantam Books.

Lucas, Rosemary. 1997. "Youth, Gender and Part-Time Work—Students in the Labour Process." *Work, Employment and Society* 11, no. 4: 595–614.

Luxemberg, Stan. 1985. *Roadside Empires: How the Chains Franchised America.* New York: Viking.

Macdonald, Cameron, and Carmen Sirianni. 1996. "The Service Society and the Changing Experience of Work." Pp. 1–26 in *Working in the Service Society,* ed. Cameron MacDonald and Carmen Sirianni. Philadelphia: Temple University Press.

Males, Mike. 1999. *Framing Youth: Ten Myths about the Next Generation.* Monroe, Maine: Common Courage Press.

———. 1996. *The Scapegoat Generation: America's War on Adolescents.* Monroe, Maine: Common Courage Press.

Marshall, Gordon. 1986. "The Workplace Culture of a Licensed Restaurant." *Theory, Culture and Society* 3, no. 1: 33–47.

McArthur, Jane. 1997. "Walmart: A New Face in the Union." *Canadian Dimension* (May), 44–45.

McNichol, Tom. 1998. "My Supermarket, My Friend: Is That Forced Safeway Smile a Customer Service or an Annoying Attempt to Control?" *San Francisco Weekly*, November 11–17, 22–26.

Miller, Joanne. 1988. "Jobs and Work." Pp. 327–59 in *Handbook of Sociology*, ed. Neil Smelser. Newbury Park, Calif.: Sage.

Mishel, Lawrence, Jared Bernstein, and Edith Rasell. 1995. *Who Wins with a Higher Minimum Wage*. Washington, D.C.: Economic Policy Institute.

Moberg, David. 1996. "The Young and the Restless." *In These Times*, November 25, 26.

Molstad, Clark. 1986. "Choosing and Coping with Boring Work." *Urban Life* 15, no. 2: 215–36.

Moody, Kim. 1997. *Workers in a Lean World: Unions in the International Economy*. New York: Verso.

———. 1988. *An Injury to All: The Decline of American Unionism*. New York: Verso.

Mortimer, Jeylan, and Michael Finch. 1986. "The Effects of Part-Time Work on Adolescent Self-Concept and Achievement." Pp. 66–89 in *Becoming a Worker*, ed. Kathryn Borman and Jane Reisman. Norwood, N.J.: Ablex.

Myles, John, Garnett Picot, and Ted Wannell. 1993. "Does Post-Industrialism Matter? The Canadian Experience." Pp. 171–94 in *Changing Classes: Stratification and Mobility in Post-Industrial Societies*, ed. Gosta Esping-Anderson. London: Sage.

A Nation at Risk: The Imperative for Educational Reform. 1983. Washington, D.C.: National Commission on Excellence in Education.

Nelson, Cary, ed. 1997. *Will Teach for Food: Academic Labor in Crisis*. Minneapolis: University of Minnesota Press.

Neuborne, Ellen. 1997. "'Off-the-Clock' Time: More Work for No Pay." *USA Today*, April 24, B1.

Newman, Katherine. 1999. *No Shame in My Game: The Working Poor in the Inner City*. New York: Alfred Knopf.

Noorani, Arif. 1998. "How to Talk to Your Kids about Unions." *This Magazine* (January), 26–27.

Oppenheimer, Valerie, and Matthijs Kalmijn. 1995. "Life Cycle Jobs." *Research in Social Stratification and Mobility* 14: 1–38.

Osterman, Paul. 1999. *Securing Prosperity: The American Labor Market: How It Has Changed and What to Do about It*. Princeton, N.J. Princeton University Press.

———. 1980. *Getting Started: The Youth Labor Market*. Cambridge, Mass.: MIT Press.

Parker, Jennifer. 1996. "Labor, Culture, and Capital in Corporate Fast Food Restaurant Franchises: Global and Local Interactions Among an Immigrant Workforce in New York City," Ph.D. diss., City University of New York.

Parker, Mike, and Martha Gruelle. 1999. *Democracy Is Power: Rebuilding Unions from the Bottom Up.* Detroit: Labor Notes.

Parker, Mike, and Jane Slaughter. 1994. *Working Smart: A Union Guide to Participation Programs and Re-Engineering.* Detroit: Labor Notes.

———. 1988. *Choosing Sides: Unions and the Team Concept.* Boston: South End Press.

Payne, Melanie. 1998. "Union Fever Hits Ohio Fastfood Eateries: Teamsters Get Inquiries in 12 Locations." *The Record,* June 29, H12.

Pollert, Anna. 1981. *Girls, Wives, Factory Lives.* London: Macmillan.

Progressive Grocer. 1996. "Special Report: The Front End" (May).

Rafaeli, Anat. 1989. "When Cashiers Meet Customers: An Analysis of the Role of Supermarket Cashiers." *Academy of Management Journal* 32, no. 2: 245–73.

Reckard, E. Scott. 1997. "Working Longer—For Less?" *Los Angeles Times,* June 11, A1.

Rehnby, Nadene, and Stephen McBride. 1997. *Help Wanted: Economic Security for Youth.* Ottawa: Canadian Center for Policy Alternatives.

Reiter, Esther. 1991. *Making Fast Food: From the Frying Pan into the Fryer.* Montreal: McGill-Queen's University Press.

Rinehart, James. 1978. "Contradictions of Work-Related Attitudes and Behaviour: An Interpretation." *Canadian Review of Sociology and Anthropology* 15, no. 1: 1–15.

Ritzer, George. 1996. *The McDonaldization of Society: An Investigation into the Changing Character of Contemporary Social Life.* Rev. ed. Thousand Oaks, Calif.: Pine Forge Press.

Robb, Donna. 1998a. "NLRB Gets Union Cards from Macedonia McDonald's Workers." *Plain Dealer* (Cleveland), June 2, B1.

———. 1998b. "Two at McDonald's Dismissed." *Plain Dealer,* June 12, B1.

Ronai, Carol Rambo. 1992. "Managing Aging in Young Adulthood: The 'Aging' Table Dancer." *Journal of Aging Studies* 6, no. 4: 307–17.

Rosenthal, Patrice, Stephen Hill, and Riccardo Peccei. 1997. "Checking Out Service: Evaluating Excellence, HRM and TQM in Retailing." *Work, Employment and Society* 6, no. 4:. 307–17.

Roy, Donald. 1970. "The Study of Southern Labor Organizing Campaigns." Pp. 216–44 in *Pathways to Data,* ed. Robert Habenstein. Chicago: Aldine.

Ryan, Paul. 1987. "Trade Unions and the Pay of Young Workers." In *From School to Unemployment?,* ed. P. N. Junankar. London: Macmillan.

Samuel, Leah. 1998. "'McTeamsters' Win Concessions at Fast Food Giant." *Labor Notes* (June), 1.

Schor, Juliet. 1992. *The Overworked American: The Unexpected Decline of Leisure.* New York: Basic Books.

Sennett, Richard. 1998. *The Corrosion of Character: The Personal Consequences of Work in the New Capitalism.* New York: W. W. Norton & Company.

Slaughter, Jane. 1997. "Can Selling Books Ever Be a 'Good Job'?" *Labor Notes* (November), 3.

Stanback, Thomas. 1990. "The Changing Face of Retailing." Pp. 80–121 in *Skills, Wages and Productivity in the Service Sector*, ed. Thierry Noyelle. Boulder, Colo.: Westview Press.

Statistics Canada. 1989. "Labour Force Survey."

Staples, Brent. 1998. "Going Bankrupt to Get a College Education." *New York Times*, April 20, A18.

Stern, David, Martin McMillion, Charles Hopkins, and James Stone. 1990a. "Work Experience for Students in High School and College." *Youth and Society* 21, no. 3: 355–89.

———. 1990b. "Quality of Students' Work Experience and Orientation Toward Work." *Youth and Society* 22, no. 2: 263–82.

Thompson, A. Clay. 2000. "Bikes on Strike." *San Francisco Bay Guardian*, January 19, 16.

Thompson, E. P. 1967. "Time, Work-Discipline, and Industrial Capitalism." *Past and Present* 38: 56–97.

Tilly, Chris. 1996. *Half a Job: Bad and Good Part-Time Jobs in a Changing Labor Market*. Philadelphia: Temple University Press.

Tucker, James. 1993. "Everyday Forms of Employee Resistance." *Sociological Forum* 8, no. 1: 25–45.

Tumulty, Brian. 1997. "Many Low-Wage Workers Being Short-Changed on the Job." Gannett News Service, December 15.

U.S. Bureau of Labor Statistics. 1996. *Employed Persons by Detailed Industry, Sex, and Age, Annual Average 1996*.

Walsh, John. 1993. *Supermarkets Transformed: Understanding Organizational and Technological Innovations*. New Brunswick, N.J.: Rutgers University Press.

Weis, Lois. 1990. *Working Class Without Work: High School Students in a De-Industrializing Economy*. New York: Routledge.

Wexler, Philip. 1983. "Movement, Class and Education." Pp. 17–39 in *Race, Class and Education*, ed. Len Barton and Stephen Walker. London: Croon Helm.

Widalvsky, Ben. 1989. "McJobs: Inside America's Largest Youth Training Program." *Policy Review* (Summer), 30–37.

Willis, Paul. 1977. *Learning to Labor: How Working Class Kids Get Working Class Jobs*. New York: Columbia University Press.

Willis, Susan. 1998. "Teens at Work: Negotiating the Jobless Future." Pp. 347–57 in *Generations of Youth*, ed. Joe Austin and Michael Willard. New York: New York University Press.

Wilson, D. Mark. 1998. "Increasing the Mandated Minimum Wage: Who Pays the Price?" *Heritage Foundation Backgrounder*, March 5, 1–11.

Wilson, William Julius. 1996. *When Work Disappears: The World of the New Urban Poor*. New York: Vintage Books.

Workforce 2000: Work and Workers for the Twenty-First Century. 1987. Indianapolis: Hudson Institute.

Zernicke, Kate. 1998. "College Costs Take Biggest Bite from Neediest Families, Survey Finds." *Globe* (Boston), October 8, A5.

Index